CHASING LOVE

A Story of Self-Sabotage

Parrell ♡
thank you xo

SASHA PARRELL

Manufactured in the United States of America

ISBN: 978-1-7363853-5-7

Library of Congress Control Number: 2022900440

Follow Sasha Parrell

Social Media Outlets:

Facebook: @Sasha.lynn.129

Instagram: @the_breakthrough_guru

Email: chasinglovebysashaparrell@gmail.com

CONTENTS

Dedication

This book is dedicated to anyone who is trapped in pain. That is – who has ever experienced something so painful, that it took something from their soul and changed them forever, leaving them in a relentless pursuit of trying to fill some kind of void.

For so many years, I lived my life on autopilot – my only motive to numb the pain that consumed me. I was a victim to my circumstances, hiding behind the walls I built and allowing life to keep happening TO me.

This is the story of my old self. The person I was before I discovered the power I truly possess.

I must warn you, that the contents of this book are very raw and disturbing. I feel that it is so important for me to share my story in full transparency so that other people who have experienced similar traumas can relate and find healing in my message.

I spent so much of my life feeling alone and misunderstood, wanting nothing more than love and connection. When I finally began to open myself up and share my story, I realized that so many people – of all ages, from all walks of life – have endured many of the same experiences I was still suffering through. Writing this book is my attempt to impact more lives and create more awareness around the roles we play in our own lives – even when we have been victimized.

It has taken me four years to write this book. I repressed so many memories that my brain did not want to remember, and it took a lot of work to bring them back up to the surface.

I spent many nights crying in pain, causing myself to relive some torturous experiences to bring you this memoir. It has been confronting, scary, and very emotional. But it has also been transformational. To reflect back on the mentality that I once had as a fearful, naïve, and vulnerable young woman, to recognize my role in how my life unfolded, and to witness the growth that has occurred along the way, has provided me with an incredible insight that allows me to connect with others along every part of their healing journeys.

Acknowledgements

While there have been so many magnificent people who have impacted my life and supported me along this crazy ride, this book is dedicated to the four people who have been most influential to my self discovery and self-acceptance.

Jayda Lynn – My beautiful daughter, this book is inspired by you. When I became your mother, I finally found my purpose – to break the cycle of generational trauma in our family and become the role model that you deserve. There is no way that you will ever suffer the ways that I did, or ever feel the sense of unworthiness, emptiness and insecurity I endured. I vow to continue growing into my best self and to set you up for the most fulfilling and abundant life I possibly can.

Josh – You have always held me to my highest and challenged me to aim beyond what I ever thought possible for myself – even if it meant me hating you in the process. You saw in me what I could never see – a strong, influential and resilient woman who was capable of attaining so much more than she could ever fathom. I have learned some of the most valuable lessons of life because of you and I will forever be grateful to you for that.

Ash – You have been the inspiration behind my entire journey to self-love and acceptance. I learned so much about myself through your influence and example. My number one cheerleader, my safe space, the yin to my yang. None of this would be possible without your love and support.

Weston – You were the first person who ever saw me for who I was and accepted all of me – the first person to ever make me feel loved unconditionally. You stuck by my side and protected me in the times that I was most vulnerable, and I will forever be grateful to you. The role you have played in my life goes beyond what any words can ever explain.

Thank you for holding space for me to share my story. If it impacts only one person's life, it will be worth every ounce of affliction.

Foreword

Reflecting plays a large role in the lives we lead. Whether we know it or not, we constantly reflect on our days, experiences, and relationships. Remembering is healthy and crucial to personal growth and learning. It can be as easy as reliving a moment in your head and contemplating the outcome. Reflection can also come in physical forms, including diaries and journals.

The ability to reflect, adjust, and learn is what makes us human.

I remember reflection being drilled into my head as a child. The elementary school saw the value in the act, and from a young age, my classmates and I reflected on our assignments and experiences. During the moment, this felt like a waste of time. Why should I write about a project I have already completed? Should that not signal the end? As I transitioned to higher educations, reflection was even more prominent. And while the reflective essays were redundant, they taught a valuable skill to us, teenagers.

Writing down your reflective thoughts lets us flesh out the process, allowing room to grow, learn, and become better people.

As this incredible book puts it, we all have a story. No two people live identical lives, and every single person has unique experiences that make their story truly their own. I have always said that everyone has their version of success, and the same goes for stories. This stems directly from every one of us possessing a unique situation, background, and personality. A family from the projects of Chicago will have a different story than a wealthy family from Malibu. There's no shame in having differing stories from those around you; it's actually awesome!

My story will be different than your story. Tragedies, opportunities, experiences, and chance all play a role in shaping our stories. What is incredible about our storybooks is that not only are we the audience, but we are also the authors! Every decision we make begins with a new plot, and every plot comes with its own tree of decisions. Perhaps you ask your co-worker out for dinner. Regardless of their response, a whole new chapter will begin to write itself. If they say yes, you'll open yourself up to a new partner and possibly a spouse down the road. If you get rejected, at least you can move on to other potential partners. Again, every decision brings a new plot.

So what's the point of all this? First, of course, we all have our own stories. We are all our own people! So this idea that each decision breeds more decisions is not some profound philosophical discovery, and if it was, I certainly did not think of it first. But it is important to understand that our stories, and our books of life, can be written however we want them to be. Fortune and misfortune play their role, and many events in our lives are prewritten for us. But understanding that we can take charge of our lives is, well, life-changing.

This is all why it is so important to reflect. Analyzing our decisions and experiences lets us learn and make better choices in the long run. If you keep repeating the same mistakes over and over, you'll become unhappy. By refusing to reflect, you will never turn the page into the next chapter of your book of life. Whether you prefer mental or physical reflection, make an effort to do so at least once a day. I do it, successful people do it, and you can too.

That is what makes this book so spectacular. It motivates those in a dark place and a light at the end of a long and gloomy tunnel. The following pages prove that we can all write our own stories. Nobody is dealt the same hand at birth, and many of us are disadvantaged. But success stories do not randomly appear but are built and built by hard work, endurance, and a never-give-up attitude. Everyone can have a success story if they so choose to write one. And while this book may not outwardly scream victory, it presents success in its own right. This book is a self-reflection.

I am beyond honored to have the opportunity to set you off on your journey through this book. And while our time together will be short, I want you to have the right mindsight before you begin. This book is not your traditional success story, and the author may not consider it a success story at all. But what impresses me so much is the courage, bravery, and shamelessness throughout the book. This book won't build you up with motivating words, but it will motivate you. The pages to come, hold a story of towering highs and deep lows, but the author wrote their own story through it.

We all have our own stories, and eventually, we will all tell them. Whether it is to our close friends and family, a worldwide audience (like this book), or a stranger at a bar, we will all share our experiences with another human being. This process is the ultimate form of reflection. Every life story is full of mistakes, but shedding shame makes a true success story. There is no embarrassment in making a wrong choice but failing to learn from your missteps. And when you truly understand that, you will be able to share your life story with anyone.

If you take away just one message from this foreword, let it be this: write your own story. It is easy to coast through the years, blaming circumstances and harmful situations for a lackluster life. Instead, take control, reflect on your mistakes, and become a better person. You hold the pen to your book of life, now start writing.

Jon Talarico

CHAPTER ONE

Dust in the Wind

"Being unwanted, unloved, uncared for, forgotten by everybody, I think that is a much greater hunger, a much greater poverty than the person who has nothing to eat."

– Mother Teresa

I have no idea what to think or how to feel.

I wish I had written everything down last night. There is no way I can possibly explain what felt like an eternity of uncertainty and delusion; in a complete trance - a warped state of mind where the person you know yourself to be has vanished. Then, in an instant and without explanation, everything makes sense again.

When I find myself, I laugh out loud because I feel absolutely ridiculous for being so lost. Before I have time to appreciate the realization, I'm gone again; this time further away than before.

My soul becomes overwhelmed with feelings of deceit, fear, and turmoil.

Let me explain.

It's been almost twenty-one hours since I lost myself. It's crazy because I didn't think my mind was capable of escaping so deeply. Yet, I don't feel like I escaped at all.

What's real? What's real? What's real?

These powerful chants loop in my conscience.

What's real? What's real? What's real?

I'll start from the beginning.

I eat some mushrooms. Intensified emotions succumb my body. I sway to the mesmerizing beat of music. Everything is wonderful. I'm in sheer bliss. The all-consuming beat makes my heart pound, like majestic Indian drum circles. I am one with the music.

I smoke a bong and my buzz lowers, so I sniff a line of cocaine.

Nothing.

Alright, another mushroom cap should do the trick.

I observe the room around me, but my mind is blank. The intense high feels good, so I decide to heighten it further by eating the rest of my mushrooms, sniffing a few more rails of blow, and smoking a few more bongs.

I come back to reality and look up to see my best friend, Kayne, is in a state of psychosis. He paces rapidly back and forth throughout the living room; eyes completely focused yet gazing into nothingness. He is mumbling passionately to someone in a tongue I cannot understand.

God.

He is talking to God. Yet, a dark energy consumes him. Every so often he drops to his knees and begins giving praise, hands clasped, head to the sky. I cannot grasp what's happening. His energy is overpowering my vulnerable state and I become overwhelmed with anxiety while watching him.

"Kayne!" I stand in front of him, my hands on his shoulders, staring into his soul trying to bring him back to reality. He stares right through me, offering empty, soulless eyes and no response.

The phone rings.

It's Kayne's girlfriend, Macy. I tell her what's going on.

She begins crying in worry and fear, "How long ago did he eat them?"

"Hours ago..." I tell her.

Then it hits me. I just ate all of mine. I accept at that moment that I'm in for one bumpy ride. My trip hasn't even begun, and I'm already afraid of what's coming.

D promises me that he'll take care of me and that everything will be okay. I trust him. He always takes care of me.

Then I fade out and my mind goes blank. There are no thoughts in my head. Adrenaline races through my body. I want to be alone. I leave the overwhelming space and enter my bedroom.

That's where it all begins.

I sit on the edge of my bed, knees to my chest, hugging my legs as I rock back and forth, lost in a trance. I feel lost, confused, overwhelmed, sad, scared, hurt. I have no idea why. I ask myself over and over, expecting an answer. My brain can't think with all of the chemicals surging through it. I am present in the moment and afraid that if I leave this state of mind, I may never return.

With no control over my thoughts, slowly my mind trails off. Images flash through me like scenes from a movie.

Faces. Memories. Regrets.

I come back. Everything that catches my eye tells a story. I look at my big, fleece blanket that drapes the bed I sit on, and my mind rewinds to the Christmas I received it. My family and I are sitting around the tree opening gifts. I see my grandfather smiling as he hands me a present. Then I remember, I wasn't invited to his funeral and dementia caused my grandmother to forget me a long time ago.

My mind keeps replaying memories, each time so realistic, so vivid, causing me to relive every painful moment. Faces roll through my head. FLASH! FLASH! FLASH!

I'm pained to see so many people I have left in the past, but they would never understand. They would never accept the life I live. I'm lost, confused, and fucked up. How do I help anyone else?

My burning eyes become faucets of flooding water. I shake violently as anxiety encompasses me. I lay down and spread my body across my bed, moving around like a worm in search of a more comfortable, relaxed state of mind.

Without warning, without control, I jolt up!

I gaze around me. Everything is so illustrated, so unrealistic, so unimportant. It is all an illusion.

With each tear that rolls in slow motion down my face, I feel my purity and innocence. I am a good person who has undoubtedly made many painful mistakes. I try to learn from them. I use my knowledge to help people.

I scrunch my eyes tightly and feel each warm tear travel down my cheek, each in memory of a lost soul. All the poor, the hungry, the abused, the sick, the unloved. Each teardrop feels like a dagger in my heart.

I need to leave this state.

I am drawn to observe my left hand, which is swollen and has a large, purple vein I have never seen before. My knuckles are bruised. I feel poison, toxins, taking over my body.

Will I leave this world tonight? This fate is now out of my hands. Is fate even real? What's real? What's real? What's real?

I feel so insignificant sitting on this bed, in this room, in this apartment building, in this town, province, country, on this earth, in this solar system, in this galaxy among millions in our universe. I witness my soul exit my body and float outward at the speed of light, into the midst of the galaxies. A perspective I have never witnessed. As quickly as I got there, I returned to the flesh my soul inhabits.

I open my eyes. I truly am nothing. Like a grain of sand in the ocean. Nothing I see or have or feel is real. I know there is more to life. But what?

I keep asking myself what's real, but again, no response.

I look at the clock. I've been alone in this room for four hours now. I close my eyes and I'm gone again. This time, I have no idea where I'm going or if I'm coming back.

What the fuck?! I thought to myself as I finished reading the journal entry I had written a few years back.

What the hell was wrong with me?

It was like someone else lived an entire lifetime in my body before I got here. An unsettled feeling in the pit of my stomach; it was a hard mix of pain and shame chased with a million unanswered questions.

For the longest time, those feelings have haunted me, but I've come to realize that in life, you won't always find the answers you're looking for. Sometimes you just have to accept what was, and focus on what is and what can be. Everything makes sense when the time is right.

We all have a story. Mine isn't out of the ordinary compared to all of the chaos and tragedy in the world. My experiences are no more painful than the next person, but when I reflect on all the shit I've seen, all the shit I've endured, and most importantly, all of the shit I've overcome and learned– I think it's a story worth sharing. Regardless of what you're hoping this book is about, there is probably a little something for you. Whether it's the thrill of reading about someone's messed up life, you just like the drama of a good story, or whether it's deeper than that – understanding the power of the mind – I'll confidently bet that those of you who aren't simple-minded will enjoy the contents of this book.

It all started when … well actually, I have no idea when it started. Life's kind of interesting that way, isn't it? You spend your childhood thinking that things are normal (whatever that means) and then one day it just hits you. How twisted and painful life really is. For me, that day was the first time I cut my wrists.

I was thirteen. I had been in a deep state of depression for about two years. I didn't know that's what was happening to me, I just thought that the pain I was enduring was a part of life. I mean really though, what kid that age would know what the hell *depression* is?

No one noticed that after I went to bed at 8 p.m., I laid awake for hours and hours every single night, watching my digital clock change one number at a time; my mind perplexed with confusion, heartache, and pain. With only a couple of hours of sleep, I would head to school in the morning as a walking zombie. Still, no one noticed. Nobody noticed that I was bullied every day of my life, and had to come home to an even worse reality. No one heard me weeping into my pillow every night, or praying to God to give me answers. There was no one to listen, no one to comfort me. I felt completely invisible and unloved.

My parents were naïve kids when Mom got pregnant. My mom told me that my dad left when he found out about me and remained uninvolved for quite some time. That's usually how it goes with things like that though, right?

Eventually, he was married to a well-respected nurse named Janice and they started a family of their own. They had two kids, Emily and Anne. Janice also had another daughter, Jayne, from her previous marriage. I would typically visit them every other weekend, so it wasn't like they were complete strangers when I was eventually shipped off to live with them. However, I never felt like I was a part of their family. I loved their children, my sisters, very much. Though, I envied the love they'd get from my father that I never received. I just didn't fit in. Maybe it was because of who I was, or where I was from. My mother was a single parent on government assistance, with three children, by three different fathers. She didn't have many rules for us, and from an early age, I ran the streets as I pleased. My dad would constantly demean her in front of me, telling me: she was a lowlife who had no ambition, she was a slut because she had three children by three different men, and she was a poor excuse for a mother who took handouts and relied on the government to support her when she was fully capable of working. It may have been his intention to ensure I recognized her faults and led a better life, but all it did was make me lose more respect for him. I was very protective of my mother. The woman literally went days sometimes without a meal, just to make sure that my younger siblings, Chuck and Danielle, and I had three square meals every day. She slept on the couch most of my childhood because we could only afford small two-bedroom apartments. It was hard for her, and I see that now. She sacrificed many things to make sure we had what we needed.

We never lived anywhere longer than a year or two without being evicted, so we moved around more times than I can count. Bills quickly became unmanageable for her as she raised three children alone with little to no support from any of our fathers. We didn't get to do or have any of the things that *normal* families did. I can't tell you how many nights I listened to Mom cry herself to sleep. It tore me apart. So, I did everything I could to help her. I took on responsibility for my brother and sister, more than a kid my age probably should have; from changing diapers, feeding them, and keeping them entertained, to getting them ready for and walking them to school in the mornings as they got older. I would cook meals, babysit, teach them to read and do math, and even check in on them when we were at school. I grew very attached and very protective of them, and instinctively became more of a mother figure to them than an older sister. I recall my mom reminding me on multiple occasions that I was not their mother.

As much pressure as it was, they were my everything, and I would give anything to make sure they were happy and safe.

My mom always went out of her way to make sure we were happy. Even though she couldn't afford much, she would do many extra little things most parents didn't, like take us for walks every night before bed, and bring us to different parks every other day. We'd go on adventures and sing songs together, and stay up late watching movies on school nights. She would wake us up in the middle of the night to watch thunderstorms, or to watch a good Christmas movie if one was showing on one of the few channels we had on our TV. Naturally, I didn't know anything other than the life we had. Coming from nothing, I appreciated the amazing bonds I had with the people I loved, and all that my mother did for us.

My Mom would always tell me to be grateful for the things I had because no matter how bad we had it, there was always someone in the world who had it worse. She was right.

One day my world came crashing down.

I was eleven. It was a school night. My mom was angry with me because I had been caught vandalizing a local park that day with some of the other kids in the neighborhood. That same week I was also caught stealing from the supermarket up the road and smoking cigarettes I stole from her. Neither of us recognized it at the time, but I was acting out after finding out that she smoked weed. I was taught my whole life that drugs kill you and that weed is a drug. So, every time I knew she was smoking it I would throw a raging fit. I would bang on the door in agony, screaming and crying for her to stop, because I thought she was going to die. I began having nightmares regularly about her dying. The fear tormented me.

It sounds silly now of course, but I didn't understand at that age. She tried to explain to me that smoking weed wasn't that bad – that it calmed her anxiety, and that I was overreacting. I couldn't help the way I felt – angry, betrayed, and powerless. How could she be such a hypocrite and do the one thing she preached to me my entire life not to do?

As a defense, I started lashing out, talking back, and rebelling. I would run the streets and hang out with older teenagers who were far from good examples. As a result, I was exposed to many things a child should never witness – endless street fights, drug use, people engaging in sexual acts, pornography, girls prostituting themselves for drugs… you name it. Of course, all of those things began to influence my behavior.

Smoking and stealing only touched the surface of my rebelling.

Mom was at her wit's end with me and had no help. I guess that's why, after years of zero communication, she called my dad. I was in complete shock when I heard a knock on the door late that night, followed by my dad's voice entering our apartment. I knew something was wrong. They hated each other, and literally had no contact until then. Any communication between them was done through me.

I couldn't make out what they were saying, but I heard the stress in my mom's voice before she started crying. She couldn't handle me anymore. She feared I would influence my brother and sister, since they looked up to me as a role model.

I remember falling asleep that night, afraid of the consequences. I had no idea just how much my life was about to change.

The next day after school, my mom sat me down to talk. She explained that she didn't know what to do with me anymore. She said that money was getting extremely tight, and she needed some time to get back on her feet. She and my dad came to an agreement that I would live with him on a "trial basis."

I was completely devastated. I begged her not to send me away, but she insisted that it was only temporary and that it wouldn't be that bad. I knew I had no control and that the decision was made. I would move the following weekend.

Over the next week or so, I was on my best behavior. I wanted to prove to Mom that I could smarten up. I helped out with anything and everything, I didn't talk back and did everything I was asked without any arguments.

The night before it was time for me to go, I pleaded hysterically with my mom not to make me leave and reminded her of how well I had been behaving. There was no swaying her.

Saying goodbye to my brother and sister was the hardest thing I had ever done up until that point in my life. I felt like I was saying goodbye forever. Of course, we had no cell phones or social media back then. I felt like I would never see them again, and that they would be in danger without my guidance and protection. It became a huge weight on my shoulders and I carried it with me for many years to come.

When I arrived at my dad's everything felt like a nightmare. There was no way it could be real. I told myself that after a week, Mom would realize that she felt better and want me to come back home.

Boy, was I ever wrong!

That night would mark the first of hundreds of nights I would cry myself to sleep. It would be the first of many times to come that I would convince myself I wasn't good enough. The hardest part of it all was seeing Chuck and Danielle at school each day, knowing that they got to go home to my mom and all be together, and I would be going back to a place where I felt completely alone and unloved. I would have them go home to Mom and beg for me to come home. It didn't work.

Weeks went by. Weeks turned into months. I think I visited a couple of times after school or the odd weekend … I can't really remember to be honest. What I do remember was that in the beginning, I would call Mom constantly and cry to her on the phone about how much I missed them. As more time passed, she didn't answer the phone as often. Eventually, she stopped answering altogether. Alas, one day I called and the operator announced that the line was no longer in service. Her phone had been cut off due to non-payment. Every day after school I would wait for her to call. I had a brief moment of hope each time the phone rang, only to be disappointed again and again. It was months before I would speak to her. She never called. I told myself she forgot about me.

Back in those days, we had to use phone books to look up someone's number. Unfortunately, most of my mom's friends didn't have very stable lives and didn't have phone numbers listed. By the grace of God, I found one of her friend's phone numbers. We knew him by the name "Potato." I called Potato and asked if he had heard from her lately. He said that she had gone to visit him only a few days before and that he would tell her I was trying to get a hold of her when he saw her next. He gave me the phone numbers of a few of their mutual friends. Every day, I would call each of the numbers and ask if she was there. On occasion, she would be, and would briefly talk to me. She would tell me to be strong and that I should be happy that I had all the things she could not give to me. None of that mattered to me, I insisted that I just wanted to be with her, Chuck, and Danielle.

Eventually, she informed me that she was evicted yet again and had moved in with a guy she was dating. He had a very small house and there just wasn't enough room for me. She promised that she would get another apartment soon and that I could move back home.

So much time had passed that my dad had made a legal case of it and everything just became even more complicated. He would not let me go back.

When it became very apparent I was not going anywhere, my dad decided to build me a bedroom in the basement. It was the first time I felt like he maybe loved me. He worked long hours every day, and every night he would be hard at work building me a room of my own. I guess you could say I was excited (as excited as I could have been in the state I was in) to finally have my own room for the first time in my life. However, being in that room made me feel even more trapped and alone. There were no windows and no source of sunlight.

The rest of the family's rooms were upstairs. I could hear what was going on through the vent above my bed that connected with my sister's room. I would hear my sisters giggling as my father and step-mother would play around with them, or read them stories before they tucked them into bed. I remember how much it hurt —how much I wanted to be a part of that. I wasn't. No one came to tuck me in, or even to say goodnight. No one asked me how my day was or asked if I needed to talk about anything going on in my life. Occasionally, my dad would come to my room to lecture me about something I had done wrong that day, then slip in a "goodnight" before he closed the door and went back to work for the night. That was about it. Once or twice he gave me a kiss on the forehead, but I sensed that it was more out of obligation or guilt than out of love.

I was completely alone in the world.

I guess that's why I put that pin to my wrist in the first place. The only thing stopping me from cutting any deeper was the reality of my siblings' pain and suffering, because of my selfish choice. Still, the pain in that moment of slicing through my skin allowed me to focus only on that, and for that moment, every other pain vanished. It was the lesser of two evils. I continued to cut myself for months, hoping someone would maybe notice my slashed wrists, and recognize that I was in pain and needed someone to talk to. But, no one ever did.

In that house, and in life in general, I was just an outsider who no one gave two shits about. At least that's the story I told myself.

Finally, one summer's day when I was thirteen, my mom told me that I could come back home! She said she would come to pick me up with all my stuff in her boyfriend's truck that Friday. I had to be sneaky about it because my dad would not allow it to happen now that the courts were involved, and he was building a case against her. So, when Friday rolled around, I got up early like I normally would, creating the illusion that I was getting myself ready for the day. My dad gave me the breakdown of the chores I needed to get done, and he headed to work. I packed up all of the things I wanted to bring with me and waited nervously.

Since I had no way to contact my mother all I could do was wait patiently.

As the hours went by, I grew anxious, peeking out the window every few minutes hoping the neighbors wouldn't see me.

Ten o'clock … Noon … Two o'clock … Four o'clock … Soon, it was five-thirty. The sinking feeling in the pit of my stomach made me feel sick and pained beyond anything imaginable. I realized that she was not coming.

That was the second time I subconsciously embedded within myself that I was worthless. I wouldn't hear from her again for months.

Frantically, I brought all of my things back to my room and unpacked them so my dad wouldn't notice what happened. Then I scurried around to half-ass complete my chores so I wouldn't be punished for my laziness. I was relieved to discover that he didn't have a clue, but the betrayal I experienced that day triggered something deep within me that caused me to detach myself from any possibility of love for many years to come.

CHAPTER TWO

First Glimpse of Strength

"Never be bullied into silence. Never allow yourself to be made a victim. Accept no one's definition of your life; define yourself"

– Robert Frost

Fitting in was never my strong suit. From as early as I can remember, I never felt like I belonged in any group of people. I guess it was pretty apparent to everyone else because no one really seemed to want me around.

Elementary school was like something out of the movie *Mean Girls*. Literally. I'm sure many of you ladies know what I'm talking about. Young girls can be ruthless. When I say I endured it all, that's not up for question.

"Why are you so short?"

"You're so ugly, you look like a boy."

"You have no boobs, why are you even wearing a bra?"

"Why do you dress like that?"

"Haven't you had that backpack for like three years?"

"I heard your mom's on welfare and you live in that crack house up the road ..."

I felt like a million bucks if I made it through a day at school without being picked on or put down. In grade five, a girl from another school who was a year older than me and twice my size, decided she didn't like me for no apparent reason. Her route walking home from school crossed mine. One day she started yelling across the street, threatening to beat me up. I had never been in a fight. I was small, scrawny, and had zero confidence. Not to mention, I had no friends to back me up. I'd be lying if I said I wasn't scared. She harassed me for over a year. One day after school, she came around the corner when I was playing outside with Chuck and Danielle. She saw me and started for me, telling me she was going to knock me out.

I ran home faster than I've ever run before.

Being the small town that it was, the word spread pretty quickly. The next day at school, everyone made fun of me for running away like a chicken shit. I guess I was. That girl got such a thrill out of holding power over me – knowing I was terrified of her. One night, when I was walking home from the corner store, she and a group of her friends chased me home with crowbars trying to jump me. Luckily my adrenaline pushed me to outrun them.

It got so bad that when I would walk to and from school, I'd make Chuck and Danielle walk a block ahead of me to keep a lookout for her so they could warn me if she was coming. The times they saw her, I would either hide wherever I could take cover, or turn down a different street and take the long way home.

This became a way of life. Eventually, I became numb to it and just accepted that that's who I was. A loser who everyone hated and who would never fit in anywhere.

Now, typically in elementary school, there are the *popular kids* and then there are the *nerds*, or whatever you wish to label the stereotypes. You're either cool or you're not. I was an odd exception to the rules. I hung out with the popular girls, but I was definitely the outcast of that circle. These girls constantly belittled and made fun of me. I sat with them at lunch and hung out with them at recess, but when it came to hanging out after school or being invited to birthday parties and other activities, I was very rarely invited, besides the few times some of the nicer girls in the group took pity on me.

I was always the last to be picked for teams, and the odd one out when it came to partnering for activities. Of course, when it came to group projects, they all wanted me in their group because I was at the top of my class, and would gladly take on the greater workload. For some reason my ego preferred the façade of looking *cool* and not actually fitting in, to hanging out with the *losers* and probably making real friends.

The girls I hung out with were known as *The Group*, which consisted of an even number of people, because each girl had to have one *best* friend in the group. On certain days we had to sit beneath the big willow tree and watch the boys play basketball. Other days, we had to sit by the red door, each in designated spots. Once in a while there were *best friend days* where you had to spend each recess with your best friend only. Those were the rules. That's just the way it was. I'm not even sure who made them, but we all followed them. Oh, and God FORBID you missed a day of school, because you would not want to come back the next day! Any time you weren't around, the rest of the girls would gossip about you and try to turn everyone against you. The next day everyone would be whispering to each other and looking at you laughing.

In one instance I clearly recall, the school warned us about head lice spreading around. So, the girls in the group insisted that we spend recess checking through each other's hair. The girl who was looking through mine found a bug and started running around screaming "EW!! SHE

HAS HEAD LICE!" at the top of her lungs. The whole school heard, and no one would come near me for weeks.

That all sounds ridiculous now of course, but being a young girl having to go to school to endure that every day was a living hell. Especially when you knew no one really liked you in the first place. I guess that was why I immersed myself so much in my school work. Between the hell that was school and the hell that became my home life, I was always a straight "A" student.

Fast forward to high school. I decided to go to the same Catholic school the rest of my "friends" were going to. I figured I'd rather have "cool" people to hang out with than start fresh at a new school. If I did start fresh, I'd be forced into the "loser" category, or even worse, be completely alone. That would be social suicide (I laugh at myself for ever thinking such a thing)!

After the first few weeks, it became very obvious that I was no longer welcome in the group. Everyone started to act like I wasn't there. They didn't even pick on me anymore. They didn't look at me or even acknowledge my presence. I felt invisible. Like a little lost puppy following around it's owner begging for love. It must have put a damper on their image to have someone like me hanging around. They were all beautiful and charming, wore expensive clothing, and came from good families. I was nothing of that sort.

One day after the last bell, I was at my locker gathering all of my stuff to go home. Out of nowhere, a beautiful blonde girl with big, bright blue eyes, and a radiant smile popped out of the class across from where I was standing.

Cheerfully and confidently she looked right into my eyes and asked, "Are you here for cheerleading tryouts?!"

Hahaha! Yeah, right! Me? A cheerleader?! That was hilarious! Not only was I a tomboy with no sense of fashion, but I was ugly and awkward. Just the complete opposite of what you would picture a cheerleader to be.

"Uhmm …" I started, but before I could finish, the girl, who was at least two years older than I was and obviously very popular, cut me off.

"Come on! We could use you! You'd be a perfect flyer!"

I had been bullied enough to know when someone was being inauthentic, but this girl had a sincerity about her. It was the first time I had ever felt accepted at school, so I would have been stupid to decline. In fact, I didn't really have the chance to decline. It was like she saw right through me: an insecure girl with no place in the world, needing someone to give her a push.

"I'm Shay," she smiled as she took my hand and led me into the classroom. I had completely stepped out of my comfort zone – far out of it – but something about this girl put my worries to ease. I had no clue what I was doing, but I had nothing to lose.

There were about fifty girls who came to try out. The coach informed us that we would be reduced to twenty-five over the next few practices. I told myself I had no shot. I ended up making the first, second, and third cuts, and eventually became one of the best on the team. For once, my small stature was good for something! I fell in love with the sport. It wasn't like you see in the movies where you have girls in skanky outfits on the sidelines of basketball games chanting, "GO TEAM GO!" and all that crap. No, this was a mix of stunts, dance, and some hardcore workouts. We performed shows competitively – locally, provincially, and nationally.

Becoming part of a team for the first time really brought out a confidence in me that I probably never would have attained otherwise. I began to dress differently. I would do my makeup and put my hair up. I walked tall and proud, instead of staring at the floor to avoid eye contact like I had done my whole life prior. I didn't care what people thought of me. In fact, I walked right past all of those mean girls and smiled at them with pride. I'd hear them whispering about me, but I honestly didn't give a shit anymore. Boys started to look at me for the first time ever. I even formed an incredible friendship with Tiffany, a girl on the team. We became inseparable and would go on to spend almost every single day together over the next three years while I attended that school.

So many of my firsts were with Tiffany. My first job, my first parties, my first dates, and eventually, my first time getting high. We had always promised each other that we would never smoke weed, but as we got older, and everyone we knew started trying it, I guess we just felt juvenile. She tried it first, and in fear of drifting away from the best friend I had ever had, I decided to try it too.

One Friday night, Tiffany, her sister Leigha, our friend Lori, and I were sitting around in Tiff's basement trying to figure out what we wanted to do.

There was this cute guy named Brody, who Leigha knew, that lived a couple of blocks away and wanted us to come hang out. He was pretty well known in our small town and had a good-looking circle of friends. I knew that was where my friends had all first tried smoking weed, so I was a little uneasy, but I decided to suck it up and go anyway.

We walked up the driveway and past the house into the back yard where there was a tarped-in area. Brody and a few other cute guys I had never met, were inside sitting on couches and chairs that formed a circle, with a table in the middle that had a whole bunch of shit on it I had never seen before.

It looked drug related.

After everyone took their turn in the rotation, all eyes were on me to smoke a bong. They all knew I had never done it before, so I felt a lot of pressure. There was no way I was going back to being a loser. They were all high, and they seemed fine. In fact, I'd never seen anyone so happy or laugh so much before, so how bad could it really be?

Tiffany packed me a small bowl. She sparked the lighter, held it to the weed, and told me to just suck. Not having a clue what a bong even was or how it worked, I did what she said. Naturally, when I couldn't inhale anymore, I exhaled. Right into the bong! Dirty, sludgy, bong water shot everywhere! All over the table, the couch, and everyone's weed that was busted up on the table. To say I was embarrassed would be an understatement. I was mortified! To my surprise, they all burst into hysterical fits of laughter.

I coughed my lungs out for about five minutes. In that time, the topic changed and they had forgotten all about it.

I don't remember much else from that night, other than watching shadows of spiders projected onto a tarp, and thinking there were giant mutant spiders crawling around; or us all running twelve blocks to the store to get snacks, just to use the only five dollars we had to take a cab back home because we were too tired to walk back up the hill. It wasn't so bad after all.

At first, I didn't really smoke much. I was still living with my dad at that point in time and he would have slit my throat if he knew what I was doing. In fact, the very first time he was ever cool with me having a boyfriend (which was a huge deal because my dad was NOT about me dating), I went to the guy's house after school one day and decided to take a couple tokes off a joint. Knowing my dad was picking me up in a few hours and was going to find out anyway, I decided to just be honest about it when he called to check in on me. I figured, *hey, he knows everyone else does it, maybe if I'm honest he'll appreciate that*. HA! What a stupid thing to think. He was there within fifteen minutes to pick my sorry ass up, and let's just say I didn't get a chance to smoke again for a very long time afterwards.

When I messed up, he never let me live it down. Over the three and a half year period I ended up living with him, I learned to never cross him.

Dad's punishments were the worst. He was very strict and had very specific rules to abide by. I remember one time my sister and I had plans with the neighborhood kids to get together after supper to go in our friend's hot tub. We made the plans the day before, and our parents agreed to allow it. We were so excited that when we set the table for dinner that night, the plates and cutlery weren't placed properly. As punishment for being careless and lazy, we weren't allowed to go anymore.

Another time, just before Christmas, we decided to sneak some candies off of our gingerbread houses. Making gingerbread houses over the holidays was a family tradition, but we weren't allowed to eat them until Christmas. I mean, come on! We were kids, what do you expect? When my little sister Anne told on us that night, Dad quietly walked over to the gingerbread houses, picked them up, walked to the kitchen, angrily smashed them to pieces on the floor, and declared that we had "Two fucking minutes to clean up the mess."

He never laid a hand on any of us, but he scared the shit out of me. He made his rules very clear, and I learned very quickly not to question him.

There was no going out on school nights. Every day after school I was to come straight home, and my chores were to be done. If we managed to get our chores and everything done before my dad and stepmom got home from work, we were allowed out on our street to play. Of course, Emily and Anne had to agree to it, because we were responsible for them. When our parents got home, we'd have dinner. Then, we had to clean up after dinner, finish our homework, and then we could read, or – if we were lucky – watch some TV before bed. By watch TV, I mean sit quietly in the living room and watch whatever my dad was watching without interrupting.

It was the same routine, day in, day out – nothing compared to what I was accustomed to.

My sister Jayne, who was about a year and a half younger than me, was often exempt from those chores due to her after school activities, like volleyball practice and games. She was on the school team and eventually, a locally organized team. My stepmom would pick her up from all her practices, make sure she was at every game, bought her all new attire and equipment, and paid for the tournament expenses. When it came to my cheerleading, on the other hand, it was a completely different story. Oftentimes, I would have to miss practice, because Jayne would have practice the same night, and someone needed to watch our younger sisters. I was always that someone. Sometimes Dad would pick me up from practice on his way home from work, and I'd wait at least an hour in an empty school by myself, sometimes longer if he was working late! Other times, I'd walk an hour and a half to get home, even if it was a blizzard in the middle of the winter. My dad never came to a practice, nor to a competition. Dare I ask for money for clothing or competition fees. I got zero support. I was nothing more than a burden.

Then there were Saturdays. Oh, how I hated Saturdays. Every Saturday we were to complete a thorough clean of the entire house, which would generally take half the day. If it was not done properly, there went the rest of our weekend. Most times, Jayne would "have to go to the bathroom" five times, or would "clean" her room for two hours, so I would end up doing most of it myself, and it would take twice as long. If I tried either of those escapes, I'd get called out and lectured about it. I convinced myself I was nothing more than their Cinderella.

To top it all off, in the small increments of time that I saw Dad while he wasn't at work, he tended to bully me almost as much as I was bullied at school. He loved pointing out my flaws – like how all my friends had developed, and I was still flat-chested, or how I looked like a boy because I never put my hair up; how I was skin and bones and needed to eat more. Maybe it was his way of trying to toughen me up, but some of the ridicule he bestowed upon me followed me for many years to come. Maybe that ridicule instilled that I was never good enough for any man.

To sum it all up, there was no equality. I felt completely belittled all of the time, and I was denied the social life most of the kids my age were privileged to experience. I had few opportunities to figure out who I was or explore what I was capable of. I had no place in the world, like a drifter trying to find a place to call home, and people to call family.

When I was fourteen, something in me just snapped. With my new-found confidence and slight recognition of my self-worth, I couldn't bear to live like that anymore – degraded, used, unloved, and mistreated. My self-esteem was non-existent, and I was tired of giving my all to people who showed me no love or appreciation.

By this time, I had been visiting Mom again somewhat regularly. She, Danielle, and Chuck lived in a tiny two-bedroom apartment in a small, ghetto, hick town known as the Dot. It had a really bad reputation. Everyone I grew up around was afraid of the people who lived there. I guess you could say it was the "hood" of a small-town area. It had three small stores, a gas station, a post office, and a tiny library. I didn't care. Anything was better than where I was.

Within a few months of visiting her again regularly, I begged her to give me the chance to prove myself by letting me move back. She eventually agreed, and little by little, one visit at a time, I brought some of my things to her place so that my dad wouldn't notice. Then, one Sunday evening when he came to pick me up, we turned off all of the lights and locked the doors.

I heard his truck from three blocks away. As the sound of the engine got louder, I felt the immense pressure of my heart ferociously pounding in my chest. I was terrified. It was the first time I had ever crossed my dad and I was certain he would not let me get away with it. His headlights flashed into the window as he pulled into the driveway. He laid on the horn. I hid around the corner so that he wouldn't see my shadow. My body tense, I held my breath, praying that he would just leave.

The phone rang. It was him. It rang and rang until the voicemail picked up: "Sasha. I'm outside. Let's go." Everything in my body told me to go, but I resisted. The phone rang again. Another message. Again and again. Finally, I heard his engine roar and his tires screech out of the driveway. He was gone.

It was over a year before I saw him again.

This was the second major transition of my life. I became yet another version of myself. This version learned how to stand up for herself, but with that, my rebellious stage commenced. This would lead me down a path I am lucky to have survived.

CHAPTER THREE

Breaking Free

"You are confined only by the walls you build yourself"
– Andrew Murphy

Living in the Dot changed everything about me. It was there I found a sense of belonging. It was there I learned what struggle really looked like. It was there I started doing drugs and entered a world that many never return from.

Two things you should know before moving forward:

1. When you grow up in a small town – reputation is everything.

2. In small towns, everyone knows everyone.

The Dot was a place that I was taught to fear growing up. In past generations, the people of that town (or village as my grandmother called it) built their reputations on drugs, partying, hustling, fighting, and robbing. It was, for lack of better words, the ghetto. Instead of gun violence, the Dot promoted that a real man fights with his bare hands – that only a pussy needs a weapon.

When I invited friends from other towns to hang out, they'd shoot me down nine times out of ten, when they found out where I lived. Those who came refused to step foot on my school bus. I didn't blame them. One year we went through almost ten bus drivers. Within two weeks, we literally had a different driver every single day. Sometimes the driver after school would be different than the one we had in the morning. Why? Kids from the Dot were reckless. Our bus rides looked like a bunch of wild animals yelling, fighting, smoking bongs, and talking smack. They didn't give a damn about what anyone had to say about it. After so long, no one really said anything about it.

How did they get away with it? Suspensions didn't mean anything. It's not like many of them had to go home and face consequences from pissed off parents. Most of their parents were drug addicts or alcoholics. Really, it's not like many of them were even taking the bus to go to school in the first place. For the most part, taking the bus was just a free ride to town to hustle some weed, get high with friends, then catch a free ride back.

On the outside, it was clear why all anyone saw was a little shithole, waste of a town, full of delinquents and low lives. In my time living there, I gained insight I never would have attained anywhere else, and formed friendships that would last forever.

Since the very first experience I had visiting the Dot, I was intrigued by the way of life there. One summer day while still living with my dad, my neighbor, Mandi and I, decided to sneak out to the Dot. I guess we were being "rebellious" because our parents would have killed us if they caught us going to hang out in such a "dangerous" place. We found a little park across the street from where my mom lived and decided to hang out there. After about ten or fifteen minutes, we saw two guys who looked about our age emerging from a nearby bush. One of them had long, dark, messy hair covered with a toque and was rocking the whole "skater boy" look. The other had shaggy brown hair with a hat on backwards and headphones around his neck. He had more of a Vanilla Ice look going on.

They walked with attitude, with confidence. I could tell they weren't like any of the guys I had met before. I was a little nervous because of the status the Dot Boys had, but more so I was intrigued.

They approached us with smug grins on their faces. It was pretty obvious we weren't from around there.

"Who are you guys?" one of them asked bluntly.

"I'm Sasha. This is Mandi," I replied, wearily.

"What are you guys doing here?" the other one chuckled.

I explained that my mom lived up the street and I was just visiting. They introduced themselves as Kayne and LT. I had heard of LT before; everyone knew who he was.

They hung around a while, just goofing around and cracking jokes. To my surprise, they were really nice and seemed really cool. There was something fascinating about them. When we reluctantly decided it was time to start on our trek back home, LT said whenever I was back in town visiting my mom, to just ask around for him and he would show me what the Dot was all about.

A couple of weeks later, I was visiting my mom again and decided to test my luck to see if I could find LT or Kayne. I ventured out down the hill to the two-block-long main street. I walked up and down the road a few times, but it was nothing but a ghost town. Not a soul in sight.

Just when I started walking home, someone pulled up beside me on a bicycle.

"Hey," said a gentle voice.

I turned to look at him. He was really cute!

"Hey," I replied as coolly as I could manage.

"I'm Corey. What's up? I've never seen you around here before." He had the most welcoming eyes and warm smile. I instantly felt at ease.

"I'm Sasha. My mom lives here. I'm just visiting," I told him. "Do you know LT?"

"Yeah of course," he snickered. "How do you know him?"

"I don't really," I realized I probably sounded a little weird. "I met him a few weeks ago at the park. He told me to ask around for him when I was back in town. Do you know where I can find him?" I explained I didn't know anyone here and was just looking to meet some people to hang out with.

"Yeah for sure. I'll rip up to his place now and see if he's home." He took off. Only, he didn't come back. Guess I weirded him out a bit.

With nothing else to do, and nobody to hang out with, I sat on top of a mailbox out front of the liquor store and waited to see if I would see anyone around my age. After a short while, I saw a guy casually walking down the street coming my way. As he got closer, I recognized him.

"Hey! Are you Kayne?" I yelled excitedly as he got close enough to hear me.

He looked at me in utter confusion.

"Um … Yeah …" he replied, still trying to figure out who the hell I was.

I noticed that he was walking in the same direction that Corey went to go to LT's house.

"Are you going to LT's?" I asked, without the slightest acknowledgment of how crazy I probably sounded.

"Um … Yeah …" he remarked, again, looking a little lost.

"I'm coming with you!" I jumped off the mailbox and proceeded to walk with him up the street. He didn't oppose my joining him.

We walked for a few short minutes (it only took a few minutes to walk anywhere in that town because it was about ten square blocks), and came to a dead-end street with a few houses on it. We walked up a loose gravel driveway to the side door of a cute little house. LT answered the door, and seemed very surprised to see me again.

"Yo! What's good!?" He greeted us charismatically, and summoned us to come inside. Being only fourteen at the time, I thought it was pretty cool he had his own separate entrance to the basement where his room was.

Kayne and LT were really down to earth. Nothing like I expected Dot boys to be. They were goofy, funny, weird, and weren't trying to be anything other than themselves. They asked me questions about myself and were genuinely interested in what I had to say. No one ever cared about what I had to say before. It gave me a sense of inclusion like I had never felt.

Over the next few months, I visited my mom as much as possible so I could hang out with my new friends. I met more Dot boys in that time, all of whom made a lasting impression on me and inspired me to break out of my shell. They were real. I'd never met real people before.

There was Danzie, an intelligent outcast who knew a little something about everything; Myles – a loud-mouth country-boy who was obnoxious and goofy; Kuba – a chubby German kid with long blonde hair. He was sweet and quiet until something pissed him off, then it was like Dr. Jekyl and Mr. Hyde; JJ– the prick of the group who loved playfully teasing me any time he had a chance; Carl, a very quiet and socially awkward kid who was quirky and lovable; Tommy – who you'd never see without a beer in his hand cracking red-neck jokes; Ashton – who was always smiling, singing off-key and playing his guitar; and of course Kayne, LT, and Corey. They were a fun and intelligent group of guys that I grew to adore very quickly.

It was evident that everyone in that town was like family, whether they saw each other every day or once a month, and I wished to one day be a part of that. They accepted me for who I was; I never had to put on an act to try and fit in. I could be my weird, quirky, socially awkward self and they liked that. They were there for me in times of need, and always treated me with respect.

It was their friendships, I see now, that gave me the courage to feel confident in myself, to feel like I mattered.

The girls were another story, maybe because I'd never had good experiences with females my age in the past. They all had this bad-girl, I don't give a fuck, attitude that intimidated me at first. Dot girls were known for brawling. They stuck together and would fuck up anyone who crossed them. The last thing I wanted was to step on their toes. I was afraid to even look at them the wrong way.

I saw Shenice for the first time at my bus stop. She went to a different school, and her stop was right across the street from mine. My first day catching the bus she watched me closely like she was wondering who the hell I was and why I was in her town.

I saw her later that week at Kayne's one night and she insisted on walking home with me. I thought to myself, *Shit. This girl is gunna punch me out.*

The walk turned into our whole weekend spent together. We formed an inseparable bond and later I would become her son's Godmother. Funny how things work out.

Then there was Bea. She was the powerhouse of them all. She was loud, cocky and confident. She was a menace on the surface, but as I got to know her, she turned out to be a lot of fun, and a good friend when needed. I still wouldn't mess with her because that girl was nuts.

And little Fay. She was a tiny and mighty girl. Always high as a kite with permanently squinty eyes and had a laugh that you could hear for miles. She was sweet to everyone, but at the flip of a switch, could turn into the most psychotic female you'd ever crossed.

Lee and Maggie were two of three triplets (Ashton was the third). Both had reputations of girls you didn't want on your bad side. They were intelligent, beautiful, and came from what was probably the only good home in the town. I never got that close with them, but they were always very nice in the time I did spend with them.

Lastly there was Beth. She was a heavy set girl who always wore dark make up and had a ton of piercings. She had that resting bitch face and a no-fucks-given attitude. She had no filter, and spoke what was on her mind no matter who she offended. She was real, and I liked that.

There were a few others, but they weren't around quite as frequently.

When I initially moved to the Dot, I became really close with Corey. He lived right around the corner from me, and oddly enough, our moms knew each other from years before. We had actually hung out a few times when we were very young. He and I clicked right away, and would meet almost every day after school to go over to Kayne's place together, which is where everyone hung out. It always felt like there were twenty people deep in his little two-bedroom apartment, located on top of a little variety store downtown. The apartment was constantly overcrowded with people, filled with loud voices telling stories, sharing laughter, and hot boxed with marijuana smoke.

I smoked the odd bong or joint when I went over, nothing too crazy, and always waited until the high wore off before heading back home. My mom never really had rules for me, so she didn't seem to mind that I spent most of my time there. If I wasn't home for dinner, I didn't get to eat, simple as that. I had a curfew of 10 p.m., so I just made sure to be back by then each night.

At least I did, in the beginning.

I was pretty naïve, so it took me a bit to catch on that Kayne and his mom were weed dealers. I didn't care. In fact, it gave me an unexplainable sense of security when I put two and two together. I had grown up in a school surrounded by so many goody-goodies who feared people that lived the lifestyle they did, and here I was friends with them. I had the "bad guys" on my side. I knew that if anyone ever fucked with me again, I had a lot of people who cared about me that had my back.

For the first time in my life, I felt safe, even in a place and time where "safe" was the last thing I actually was.

As amazing as the people I met were, the mentality they had was destructive. It was not an ideal place for a child to grow up. A majority of the town lived in poverty, and came from many past generations of poverty . They were all trapped in survival mode. By that I mean they did what they had to do to get by and to protect themselves – no matter the cost. Most of them had no aspiration to do anything purposeful in life.

Almost everyone there had a gang mentality. Nothing mattered more than respect and loyalty. To defend your reputation and your respect, you fought for it.

In the first few months living there, it was like God was trying to show me signs of what was in store for my life if I decided to take this path without foresight. I was blind to Him.

One morning, my sister Danielle, who was maybe eleven at the time, was brought home by the police. She stayed the night at a friend's place up the road, and the little girl's dad overdosed and died that night. They found his body in the morning.

A few weeks later, I was hanging out with a few friends when an older girl named Lish (the most hardcore, gangster looking chick I'd ever seen in real life) ran up on us, and beat the crap out of Beth. It was on the side of the road in broad daylight. People passed by without stopping to intervene. It was just a way of life there.

Another evening I was on my routine trek to Kayne's when, all of a sudden, ambulances, fire trucks, paramedics, police cruisers, and even a rescue helicopter sped down to the waterfront where a massive, abandoned grain elevator stood. Some intoxicated, mentally unstable chick was standing on the roof of the elevator threatening to jump off.

Then came the day I was at the corner store and Kay (who was a year older than me and went to school with me my whole life) abruptly burst into the store pleading for me to hide her. She ripped off two drug dealers from the city for some coke and they were driving around with guns looking for her. Just as she finished telling me what was going on, a white truck peeled into the parking lot, and three grungy-looking drug addicts jumped out and surrounded the store. I told one of them I'd just seen her go down the road, and proceeded to sneak her out and hide her.

It was like something out of a movie to me. I couldn't even comprehend the danger I put myself in. I just wanted to be accepted at any cost necessary.

The first time I was nearly kidnapped was when I realized the threats were very real. I say the first time, because I was nearly abducted on more than one occasion in that town.

I had been sneaking out of my bedroom window at night to an older guy's place. My mom didn't approve of him. I'd stuff pillows under my blanket so that if my mom came to check up on me, she'd see a lump under my blankets and think I was asleep. Chuck and Danielle would cover for me, even though I knew they weren't comfortable with it.

Said older guy lived up a long, dark road that had no street lights and was surrounded by bushes. One night while partying at his house, I lost track of time and noticed that it was almost 4 a.m. I had to get back home before my mom woke up, or she'd be bolting my windows and I'd have no way out again.

I was half-way down the dark, deserted road when I heard the bass of loud music from an approaching car. Normally that wouldn't concern me, but something that night gave me an unsettled feeling, so I hid. After all, I was a fifteen-year-old girl who looked like she was maybe thirteen, walking alone down a long, dark road at four in the morning, plastered.

Before the car was in sight, I leapt into the bushes and squatted down amidst the darkness to conceal myself. I didn't consider the wide span that headlights cover, so as the car drove by, the lights shone into the bush where I was hiding. I made eye contact with the driver, whose creepy smirk sent chills up my spine. There were other males in the car as well, but I couldn't tell exactly how many or what age they were.

The car kept driving, so I assumed I was safe.

I listened to the pounding bass fade away as the car drove down the hill ahead. Being a little on edge, I picked up my pace and started jogging. As I approached my street, the sound of the bass grew louder. The car was coming back up the hill toward me!

I ran as fast as I could.

They must have caught a glimpse of me turning down my road, because they stopped the car in the middle of the intersection where I had turned and waited for quite some time to see if I would reappear.

Out of fear and desperation, I crouched down behind a small tree in someone's front yard. My heart hammered into my chest as I struggled to gasp for air.

Finally, they started to drive away slowly.

The second the car was out of sight, I darted up the street toward my house. Within a split second, the tires screeched as the men put the car into reverse and turned down my street after me full speed. With still two blocks to run, my mind went blank as my feet took over. Just as they came up alongside me, I lunged into the six-foot-tall hedges that surrounded my house!

I'm not sure whether the car proceeded to drive away, or whether they stopped and waited. Time stood still as it usually does when you're in complete shock. I must have stayed in those hedges for a good twenty minutes before gathering the courage to walk through my pitch-black back yard, climb up a make-shift ladder to the lower roof, jump across a gap to the higher-level roof, and go back in through the window.

The adrenaline was indescribable.

Instead of feeling traumatized, it left me with a sense of power – like I was untouchable.

CHAPTER FOUR

Good Girl Gone Bad

"Once upon a time I was sweet and innocent, and then shit happened"

– Anonymous

One of the greatest challenges we face growing up is the struggle between trying to find a place where we fit in in the world, and trying to figure out who we actually are.

Some of us are fortunate enough to be brought up in households and families that offer abundant opportunities to explore dreams and talents for our best shot at success. For the rest of us, it usually takes a lot longer to make something of ourselves. That's if we even believe there is something more out there to aspire for.

Many of us never reach a fraction of our potential, because as the law of nature suggests, we gravitate toward the influences that surround us. Our environments and experiences shape the way we view the world, and the way we perceive things.

A wise man named Mahatma Gandhi once said, "A man is but the product of his thoughts; what he thinks, he becomes."

The problem is, as children, we don't choose our environments. We are programmed based on what surrounds us, not able to fathom that something other than how we perceive the world could be possible.

When we are brought up around people who are all like-minded, with no diversity, we adopt the views of those people and often remain closed-minded to all other possibilities and perceptions.

In my case, for example, I grew up poor, always in the presence of people who had little to no ambition and were trapped in survival mode – people who relied on drugs and alcohol as a means of coping with their fears and sorrows. As intelligent as I may have been, my experiences and influences pulled me down a path contrary to my own beliefs. The further down that path I strayed, the further I drifted from the person I thought I was.

I became someone I never imagined myself to be.

I became my situation.

****

"Hey Corey! It's me. I didn't see you get off the bus today. Everything alright?"

"Yeah I'm fine, just stayed home today. Not feelin' so great," Corey explained when I called him after school one day.

"Oh … ok … so I guess you don't wanna go down to Kayne's tonight?" I asked him.

"Nah. Probably not tonight. I'll catch you tomorrow or something k?"

"Alright," I replied in disappointment. "Feel better."

Now what am I supposed to do? I thought to myself. I had become so used to being surrounded by people that I felt disempowered being alone.

I felt a little weird just showing up at Kayne's by myself, but I had overcome so many of my fears lately that I started to develop the courage to step out of my comfort zone.

I asked my mom for five dollars to get something from the store and made my way down. Kayne was a little surprised to see me at his door without Corey, but welcomed me in with a playful smile when I asked if I could buy a joint and hang out for a while.

It was that day he confessed to me that he was envious of the male-female friendship Corey and I had – that he always wanted a female best friend. He thought it was so cool that a male and female could hang out and form such a strong bond without it being of an intimate nature. I'd never thought of it like that. I guess it was pretty cool.

I told him that I would be his best friend. Strangely enough, from that moment on, we became inseparable. We were together every single day after school, and spent every weekend hanging out and partying together. We connected on a deep spiritual and intellectual level, sharing our stories, our secrets, and all of our thoughts about life. We got to know each other from the inside out.

Kayne and I always had fun together, regardless of whether we were out adventuring with all of our friends, or sitting around doing nothing, just the two of us. We made the best of every day, and our friendship flourished like I never imagined. He taught me the value of what being a true friend meant.

It wasn't long before I decided to switch schools to be with him and the rest of the Dot Kids, and say good-bye to anything connecting me to my old life once and for all.

Transitioning to a public school where there were few rules and morals after attending strict Catholic schools my entire life was a substantial transformation. As much as my confidence had grown over the past few years, I still felt like an outcast in the grand scheme of things – until my first day at my new school. When I arrived there, people were literally cheering when they saw me. I didn't get it. How was it that after being rejected my whole life, all of a sudden so many people loved me? What was I doing differently?

Everywhere I went someone greeted me excitedly. Girls were running to me and tackling me with giddy hugs. My boys surrounded me, welcoming me with open arms and introducing me to new friends. Before long, everyone seemed to know who I was – even people I had never seen before. It became apparent right away that my new friends belonged to the group of people who were superior in that school.

I felt like a boss, and it got to my head quickly.

Suddenly, I was superior for the first time in my life.

In a place where ghetto mentality resides, loyalty and respect were everything. I knew I had a tight circle that other people felt intimidated by, and with that, I developed a cockiness that told people not to fuck with me. I rolled through the school like I owned it! For once, people walked by me with their heads down, instead of the other way around. I observed as people approached me in a new light, like it was their privilege if I befriended them.

The whole school system itself was different. At my old school, if you were caught skipping class, our six foot, two hundred pound principal, who looked like Steve Wilkos, would chase you down and drag your ass to class. He was always lurking the halls, the property, and even surrounding areas. There was no running, he would catch you. Literally, chase you and catch you! If for some reason he didn't, it wouldn't take long for him to find out exactly who you were so he could issue an in-school suspension. Yes, in-school. He realized that suspensions for skipping were counterproductive because the whole reason people skipped was to NOT be at school. Brainy he was. Instead of having to only deal with your pissed off parents, you'd also be stuck in the principal's office for the next few days with him breathing down your neck.

Let's just say that school had a very high record for perfect attendance.

At my new school, we would stand just off the perimeter of the school property when we skipped class, accumulating large groups of other people who were skipping. When the principal came out to tell us to get to class, kids would tell him to "go fuck himself," and blow smoke at him. He did nothing. Literally nothing. Empty threats were all he could conjure up to try and intimidate us. Knowing he had no power, he'd eventually give up and go back into the school. He had no idea what any of the student's names were, so nobody feared any sort of consequence. The school was a prime example of how *not* to run a learning facility. The staff had zero control.

There were fights every other day. Sometimes it was petty high school girls fighting over boys, others it was a lot more extreme. There was one fight in particular where a girl got beat up pretty bad (during a fight she instigated). The next day her crack-addicted mother rampaged through the halls going class to class, screaming like a psychopath trying to find the girl who beat up her daughter.

Another time a group of guys flew all the way from India and ransacked our school in search of a student who was hanging out with one of their girlfriends.

I think the most memorable story of all was when an older Dot Boy punched out our principal in front of half the student body.

Every day was a different story.

At first, I didn't know what to think of it all. Within a very short period of time, it became normal to me, and often I was involved in one way or another.

Then there were the drugs. Every day big groups of us hung out in a nearby bush that we referred to as *The Greens* to smoke weed. I can't deny, some of the best memories we made at school were back there. Teachers watched swarms of us going to and from The Greens, knowing we were all high and in possession of bongs and weed. If it were my old school, we'd be expelled immediately and the police would be involved. At the new school, the teachers would still expect us to attend class, not making a big deal about it. Kids would come to school wasted and high on all sorts of drugs on a regular basis.

To see someone green out, trip out on drugs, or be fall-down drunk on school property was nothing out of the ordinary. Drug busts became frequent. In fact, our school was listed in *High Times Magazine* for a record amount of drug busts in a year. I thought that was pretty cool.

There were multiple times that we were smoking in the bush and heard someone yell "PIGS!" We'd all scramble to collect our belongings and try to find an exit without being caught by the cops.

I will never forget my first experience in a bust. I was having a really rough day for whatever reason, and I JUST sparked the lighter to smoke my first bong of the day when I heard someone yell, "Five-Oh!"

No way I'm wasting this popper! I thought to myself.

I ran through the ungroomed forest in four-inch heels smoking my bong. I tossed the bong aside when I finished, kicked my heels off so I could run faster, and blew out a cloud of smoke behind me knowing the cops were closing in.

What a rush!

I made it to a nearby road just as one of my girls ran out of the bush yelling, "Ay bitch! These yours?!"

She was carrying my shoes!

We all had a good laugh as we walked back to school, strutting cockily right past the police. They knew we were guilty, but had no probable cause to search us since they didn't actually see us emerge from the bushes.

The adrenaline of breaking the law and almost getting caught was intense. It was like a game to me; a game I fell in love with. I started to believe that I was invincible, and soon every fear I'd ever had vanished. I was completely fearless. Untouchable.

Being young, naïve, and fearless is a beautiful and lethal combination.

I carried my bad attitude home with me, and it wasn't long before I stopped trying to hide the fact that I was a stoner. Everyone smoked it anyways. But I wasn't smoking just straight weed. I got hooked on poppers, which are a mix of unfiltered tobacco and marijuana, smoked out of a straight shaft in a bong. It hits you completely differently than straight weed does. Tobacco and weed create a chemical reaction that affects you much more intensely. The first one I ever smoked hit me so hard I thought I was going to die. I greened out within seconds.

Before long, I'd need multiple just to get high. My days all blurred together. Many mornings, I woke up not remembering what I did the night before. My mentality shifted completely, and I lost sight of many of my morals and values.

I expanded my circle and started to hang out with certain individuals I knew were trouble. Mom and I began fighting every night. I was back with her, not even a year, and we were already ready to rip each other's heads off! The cockier I became, the worse our fights got too. I didn't see it like that at the time of course. What know-it-all teenager is ever the one to blame? It was all her fault. Who was she to give me rules after abandoning me for three years? Who was she to tell me not to do the things I did when she lived a life that was no better? I was in control of my life for once, and she wasn't taking that away from me!

After months and months of a constant power struggle between the two of us, and multiple threats of her threatening to kick me out, things hit a breaking point.

"Get the fuck out of my house you ungrateful little bitch!" Mom cursed at me after throwing a cup across the room at me.

"Fuck you! I hate you! I wish you weren't my mother!" I yelled back, years of unresolved pain and resentment taking over.

Chuck and Danielle peered from behind their bedroom doors. Danielle was crying just as she usually did when we got into it. She was always really sensitive.

"Good! I hate you too! Now get out before I put you out!"

She backed me in toward the door as I fought back, furiously screaming in her face with my packed bags over my shoulder. She pushed me out of the doorway, slammed the door in my face and locked it.

I realized I'd forgotten my boots, and it was the middle of the winter. I banged on the door demanding that she give them to me, but she insisted that I go.

Finally, I had no choice but to leave.

My mom was as stubborn as they came and she wasn't going to give in.

Just like that, at fifteen years old, I was on my own to fend for myself.

I ran seven blocks in my socks through the slush and snow to Kayne's.

When I showed up at his house, my socks were drenched in dirt and icy water, and black makeup ran down my red face from crying. I was still shaking from the adrenaline.

Upon opening the door, I saw the sincere pain in his eyes as he immediately grabbed me and hugged me firmly. He already presumed what had happened because it wasn't the first time I'd run to him like that. He was my comfort zone. The only person in the world who understood me. Over the months of our growing closeness, I opened up more to him about my life than I ever had to anyone before. He made me feel unjudged. Understood. Safe.

Since my dad was no longer in the picture, and my family was never close, I had nowhere else to go. With the approval of his mother, Kayne insisted that I stay with them. His younger sister Keisha was overjoyed to have me stay there, and even offered to share her room with me. Her bed consisted of two single sized mattresses stacked on top of one another. She placed them side by side on the floor so that I would have a bed to sleep on.

I was so grateful to their family for welcoming me the way they did, especially when they didn't have a lot of money as it was.

I had no job and no income. I thought I could make it on my own, but didn't consider what it actually took to support myself.

Kayne completely took me under his wing and took care of me (as best a fourteen-year-old boy possibly could). Any time he bought himself something to eat, he would buy extra for me, or at least share what he had. We lived off of beef jerky, mini pizzas, and chocolate milk for months. If his mom made dinner, he'd offer me some, and if there wasn't enough, he would save me some of his. He would also hook me up with weed to clean his room most days (which got messy fast with all the traffic in and out of there), and he was such a gentleman, he eventually crammed his tiny, single-sized mattress and box spring into his closet so that I could have his room.

I never would have survived without his love, support and kindness.

At school I didn't really eat much, since I had no food or money. Sometimes people would feel sorry for me and offer to share their lunches with me, or give me a few dollars to buy something from the cafeteria. It grew to be extremely embarrassing, so I'd pretend I wasn't hungry so that people would stop offering me free handouts.

As insane as it might sound, I was grateful. The physical suffering from not eating properly was less significant than the mental and emotional suffering I endured with everything that went on at home. I was happy to be away from it all. I got to wake up in a room full of friends every single morning; people who were genuinely happy to see me, people who had my back. What more could a lonely fifteen-year old girl ask for?

I had no one to answer to, and no one who could hurt me anymore. I could do whatever I wanted without any repercussions.

Being young, naïve, and fearless is a beautiful and lethal combination.

CHAPTER FIVE

A Recipe for Disaster

"Hell is empty and the devils are here."
– William Shakespeare

A concept that astounds me still to this day, is the self-devaluation that stems from insecurity. How things that happen to us can embed so deeply into our subconscious that we are never the same again. Very often we don't even recognize how it happens or the levels that we are affected by it. It changes the way we view ourselves. The way we view ourselves completely alters the way we perceive the world and how we show up in the world, manifesting everything that happens to us from that moment on. I know, I thought it all sounded crazy at one point too. But the thing is, when we are betrayed repeatedly, and filled with distrust and resentment, we lower our standards because we don't believe anything better exists for us. Our self-worth diminishes, and we learn to accept pain as the norm. We allow substandard treatment by others and say that is "the way things are."

I've always pictured myself falling in love with a tall, dark, and handsome man and living that happily ever after I saw in the Disney movies growing up. Obviously, relationships aren't so black and white, and it's naïve to believe that love is so perfect, but never in a million years did I expect to encounter the hell I went through with men.

It might have been a combination of abandonment issues and the sense of false love from my parents, or never fitting in growing up that made me lower my standards when it came to love. It couldn't have helped that the exposure I had to men and relationships were all so warped. Maybe it caused me to be attracted to all the wrong guys.

My insecurities may have been derived from the ten-plus times I moved around as a child, and never having any stability in my life. Maybe it was watching my mom go from man to man trying to find happiness, or seeing my brother grow up without his father. It could have been knowing my own father cheated on every woman he was ever with. Perhaps it was the time I saw Mom being strangled by my sister's dad when I was little, or knowing that my brother's dad locked him in the closet so he didn't have to hear him cry. It could have been one of the times her boyfriend banged on our door all night, maliciously howling threats at her. It could have had something to do with the drunk guy that lived downstairs from us who would throw rocks at peoples' windows and yell threats at them; I watched from my bedroom window conspicuously as he would fight off cops night after night and get thrown in the back of the cruiser in cuffs. Surely it stemmed from the time I was outside of my building playing after dark when a fight broke out, and I witnessed a young man get beat helplessly with a baseball bat.

A majority of the 'men' I was exposed to growing up were low-life, gangster wannabes, and thugs. It painted a picture in my head of what a man was supposed to be: feared, violent, and powerful.

I think what set me up for disaster the most was something I came face to face with when I was twelve. A memory that came to me laying in bed one night, almost in a dream-like state. I was a five-year-old girl and was molested by my babysitter; a young man who was a trusted friend. I didn't tell anyone for years, until one summer day when I was fifteen.

I received a Facebook message from Eduardo Bunnito. When I saw his profile picture pop up in my messenger, I wanted to puke. I'm not sure exactly why I did, but I clicked on the message and read:

Hi, Sasha.

> I don't know if you remember me or not. I used to babysit you when you were little. Wow what a beautiful young lady you've become. If I were only half my age ...

Unable to hide the turmoil within, I broke down and told two of my girlfriends. They insisted that I call the police. The fear and the shame wouldn't allow me. Where I came from, everyone hated the cops. I had no reason to believe that reporting this sicko would do anything other than make my life more difficult. So much time had passed, and all I had was one groggy memory without solid details. I didn't think I had enough proof to open a case. So instead, I responded to his message:

Yeah, I do remember you. And I remember what you did. Message me again and I'll contact the police you sick fuck.

He blocked me.

About a year later, a girl at school approached me cautiously with intense discontent and ultimate compassion in her face.

"Sash? Do you know someone by the name of Eduardo Bunnito?"

My throat clenched. My body tensed. My heart raced furiously.

"Uhm ... no ... why do you ask?" I lied ... Not really a story I wanted to share with someone I went to school with and barely knew.

"He lives in my building, just a couple apartments down. His place was just raided by the police. They seized his computers and arrested him. I overheard something about him being a pedophile. Sash, he had pictures of you from your Facebook page all over his walls."

I instantaneously understood the extreme depth of the term violation.

Still, I didn't go to the police.

I wanted to. But I didn't.

Instead, a couple of my friends and I suited up in black attire and trashed his van late one night. It made me feel better for a brief moment.

Months later, I stopped at a convenience store one evening, and stood in line to pay for my things. The man ahead of me in line turned around, and when our eyes met, we both froze. It was him. Eduardo. The sadistic man was placed into a mental health institution after what happened and had already been released.

He smiled at me and even had the audacity to say hello. I pretended I didn't know him and went on to pay for my things and left. My coping mechanism was to pretend he didn't exist. I was so used to suppressing my feelings that I just brushed it off and went on with my life. Still, a feeling of uneasiness and vulnerability stayed with me.

As I reflect on the events I've encountered throughout my life, it makes sense to me now why I was attracted to the types of guys I was. I had no idea what a man was supposed to be, and I didn't know what a relationship was supposed to look like – I'd never seen a stable one. Nobody ever taught me what was healthy in a relationship or that if you weren't treated properly to move on with dignity. I thought it was like in the movies where you fall in love with someone and love them forever, no matter the circumstances.

As I grew older, I learned everything I thought I needed to know about men and relationships through music. The issue with that is that I listened to rap.

I wish I knew then what I realize now, because it probably would have saved me many more years of torment and misery.

As I stated earlier on, I didn't have much luck with boys growing up. Any time I had a crush on someone, they rarely even noticed me. It wasn't until high school when I finally began to develop that I actually started to date. I went out with a couple of guys who I quickly grew bored of because they were "too nice" or "pushovers." As far as I had learned, that meant they were weak and inferior.

Then I met JT. He was the first boy who made my heart flutter when he looked at me. He was that butterflies-in-the-stomach, knees-weak-every-time-I-looked-at-him boy. He had this rebellious demeanor about him, with his shaggy blonde hair and lip piercings. All the girls went crazy over him. I'm not really sure what he saw in me, but he made it clear to all the other girls that it was me he wanted. There was something so empowering about that.

We always sat together in class, even though we were assigned to other seats. We constantly flirted and joked around with each other – we just clicked. He walked me to all my classes, held my hand through the hallways, stayed to watch my cheerleading practices, and wasn't afraid to show me affection anywhere or anytime. I fell for him hard and fast.

There was only one problem. I was a virgin. He was far from being one, and everyone knew it.

Over the months, he grew frustrated, but I just wasn't ready. I guess he got tired of waiting because on Valentine's Day when I found him at school to give him his gift, he apologized and said he couldn't accept it. He told me things just weren't working out.

The very next day I saw him with another girl, treating her the way he treated me and looking at her with that same look. It broke my heart.

Thus, an illusion was created in my subconscious that guys won't like you unless you put out. That you had to keep a man happy by giving him what he wanted or he would leave you.

Without intention or acknowledgement of how I was acting, I started becoming more promiscuous.

A couple of weeks after losing my first real boyfriend, I was at a local convenience store when the door swung open, and in strutted a familiar face.

His name was Kyler. He was four years older than I was. I had seen him at a party at my cousin Jaxon's one night not too long before. He stuck out to me because he was the only guy spitting verses in the middle of the party, and had a handful of beautiful girls surrounding him. He was outgoing, confident, and everyone seemed to respect him. He dressed like a thug and walked and talked with swag, like he ran shit. Totally my type. I didn't try to talk to him because, I mean, why would he talk to me with all those gorgeous girls on his arm?

So, when he came up beside me at the register and asked me what I was doing that night, I was stunned.

"Just chillin out," I played it cool.

"True, well you should come down to Jaxon's tonight," he gave me a little half-smile. "Big party."

"Yeah, maybe," I replied smoothly, "I'll see what's good."

"Aight cool, hope to see you there."

There was something so intriguing about him. There was no way I wasn't going! I went home immediately to get ready. I put on my tight, low-waisted jeans that really accentuated my bubble butt, and a nice tank top that hugged my body firmly. I wanted him to want me. I had to look sexy to compete with those other women, otherwise, why would he even notice me?

I stopped in at Kayne's place and had a few drinks with my friends so that I wouldn't show up right away (seeming desperate). After an hour or two, and already a little tipsy, I made my way over to Jaxon's, who lived not too far from Kayne's.

Jaxon wasn't really my biological cousin. His mom was dating my cousin's father, so we just called each other cousins. We were extremely close; he became like a big brother to me. He was tall, lean, and very strong. Not too many people got on his bad side. In all the street fights I saw him get into, he lost not one. One time he bit a guy's ear almost completely off, and left another guy in a wheelchair for life. He was psychotic like nothing I'd ever seen, but he always protected me. If anyone so much as said a bad thing about me, he wouldn't let them live it down. My own personal bodyguard.

When I got to his house, I went down to the basement where everyone was partying, and the first thing I saw was Kyler, sitting on the couch with a pretty girl on his lap.

Damnit. I thought. *I shouldn't have waited so long! Whatever. Fuck it. I'm here now, might as well have a good time.*

I made friends with some of the girls there and made the best of the night. From time to time, I glanced over at Kyler and noticed him watching me like a hawk with pure lust in his eyes. He and a few other guys broke out in a little rap battle, just like they usually did. When he started spitting a freestyle about me, I felt the stars in my eyes. Out of all of the beautiful girls at that party, I obviously stood out to him. For once in my life, I felt like I actually belonged in a group of good-looking people.

Before I knew it, I was sitting on his lap and he was kissing on my neck. He poured me a few drinks. In what seemed like only moments after, the room was spinning. Most of the party had cleared out. The music was off and I could see a few bodies passed out on the floor.

Everything was a blur.

I couldn't walk or talk.

The last thing I remember was laying down on the couch to pass out, unable to control myself. Then everything went black.

At some point, I woke up – if that's what you want to call it. I could barely gather the strength to open my eyes, but when I did, everything was foggy. I could tell that my pants were off, but the only thing I could make out was the faint silhouette of someone's face between my legs. Then it all went black again.

When I woke up in the morning, my pants were pulled back up but were unzipped. Kyler was asleep at the other end of the couch.

I was sore. Really sore. And so disoriented.

I still don't know if that was the night I lost my virginity.

I never asked him what happened. I was too embarrassed and ashamed. I told myself it was my fault, that I was leading him on all night so I must have wanted it.

I hung around for a few hours, not having a clue about how to deal with what had just happened, and not wanting Jaxon to find out what was going on. Kyler was his best friend.

All morning Kyler acted like everything was normal. He treated me like we were together or something, sitting close to me with his arm around me, and playfully flirting like he was into me. I convinced myself that whatever happened must have been consensual, since I didn't remember. I must have just drank too much.

So, like every other complex situation that occurred in my crazy life, I buried my feelings and went on with my day.

Over the next few weeks, he did everything in his power to woo me. He wrote me songs and left love notes at my door. He wasn't as affectionate when people were around, but behind closed doors, he acted like we were together. It infuriates me now thinking about it, because

I was so delusional and confused when it came to love that I actually started to fall for him.

We never had intercourse during the months I spent with him. It was just a lot of cuddling, making out, and some foreplay. He tried many times but wasn't pushy about it. I respected that. I persuaded myself to believe that he couldn't have raped me, that he genuinely loved and cared for me.

It wasn't long before others started catching on to what was happening. People started talking, and I was confronted by some of his female friends who told me that what we were doing was not okay, that he was too old for me. The more they tried to tell me what to do, the more I did the opposite. I didn't even blink twice when his best friend told me he was only pretending to be with me, because he was afraid I was going to press charges against him for soliciting a minor. He denied it of course. And I believed him.

He must have grown frightened because every time I pulled away from him, he fought for me to stay. I thought he was fighting for me out of love.

He even went to the lengths of giving me a beautiful diamond necklace and telling me he loved me. What's more, he chased me down the street in his socks in the pouring rain one morning when I awoke on his living room floor to find him in bed with another girl. I threw the necklace at him and stormed out of his apartment, running through the storm as fast as I could in complete devastation. He caught up to me and pleaded for me not to go, insisting that nothing happened. He swore up and down that she must have crawled into his bed after he passed out and fell asleep. I believed him.

Such occurrences continued for months.

There were so many red flags, and I was ignorant to every single one of them. I lowered my standards so greatly, all due to my deep, burning desire to be loved.

The way Kyler and his friends partied was much different than what I was used to. The fights that broke out were on another level, often resulting in very serious injuries. The very first night I spent partying with them, a huge fight broke out with at least twenty people brawling all over the house and parking lot. It was terrifying and exhilarating all in one.

On another occasion, my hand was sliced open while prying a knife out of Jaxon's hand while trying to deter him from stabbing someone he and Kyler were fighting.

Still, I stuck around. It was a lifestyle I became accustomed to, and was infatuated by.

One night, I overheard Kyler and Jaxon joking about spiking drinks with date rape drugs. Being as naïve as I was, I didn't think there was any seriousness to the conversation. Jaxon was extremely mentally unstable, but very protective of me. I told myself that he would never allow anything bad to happen to me, as he had proved in countless prior situations.

The thought crossed my mind for only a split second that I could have been one of Kyler's date-rape victims. To this day, I have still never confronted him about it. But I know deep in my soul that the "drunkenness" I felt that night was incomparable to any other night during the years that followed my heavy partying lifestyle.

Even without the details about what had happened, my mom was repulsed by my hanging around him. I was still living under her roof at that time. She must have felt that something was horribly wrong. She attempted with all of her might to keep me away from him, but her efforts only caused me to start sneaking out of my window after she went to bed.

One night after sneaking up to Kyler's, my mom finally noticed that I was gone in the middle of the night, and resorted to calling my father. And the police.

I was laying in Kyler's bed with him watching movies when someone started beating on his door:

"Open the fucking door you slimy piece of shit! I know she's in there!"

It was my dad.

Holy shit.

"Jump out the window, now!" Kyler insisted.

I had never seen fear in him until then. He closed his bedroom door behind him as he went to answer the front door. I heard him deny my being there and offer my dad to come in and look for himself.

Within that time, I did what I was told. I ran through the forest and fields to get home as fast as I could.

We had a tent set up in the front yard for the summer for sleepovers with our friends. I snuck into the tent and passed out.

The next morning, I woke up to texts and voicemails from my friends telling me that they had police showing up to their houses all hours of the night looking for me.

I gathered my courage and casually walked inside my house, pretending I had no clue as to what was going on. My mom lost her mind! She had been up all night worrying.

"Where the hell were you all night?!" She demanded as soon as I stepped through the door.

"Huh?" I played stupid. "What are you talking about you spaz? I slept in the tent."

"Don't play that shit with me Sasha! I checked in there! You were not in there! I know you were up at that Kyler guy's house! Stay the fuck away from him or it's not gunna end well for either of you! He's bad news! I know ALL about him and his cokehead friends!"

Cokehead? I started to put the pieces together. Every time we partied at his house, he spent intervals of time sitting in his room with the door closed with his buddies. I never questioned what they were doing. I knew he sold weed, so I figured it was just business. There were times where I saw other people sniffing lines out in the open, but never Kyler, so I paid no mind.

When I called Kyler later that day, he told me we should probably lay low. That all this drama was bringing too much heat to his house.

Instead of seeing the situation for what it really was, I blamed my parents for ruining things, and more anger ignited within me. I developed a very twisted reliance on Kyler and felt that familiar sense of abandonment when he began to push me away.

My mom started keeping close reins on me, having to know where I was at all times. When nearly a week had passed, I couldn't take it anymore. I needed to see him. I asked my mom to take Chuck to the library so that I could get out of the house. She agreed. I made my brother promise not to tell my mom and took him up to Kyler's with me. Deep down she knew me all too well. When I failed to answer my phone, she called up the only person she knew I feared.

We tried to remain relatively discrete as Kyler walked me back home down the long stretch of road between our houses. I think we both sensed something was about to happen, and collectively decided I would walk the rest of the way without him. As he leaned in to kiss me goodbye, a big black truck roared up and missed running him over by inches.

"Get in the fucking truck!! NOW!"

I gasped.

It was my father.

Here was the man who was never there for me a day in my life, and all of a sudden he wanted to waltz in and play hero. I was beyond pissed off and embarrassed, but fearing this man the way I did, I grabbed my brother and got into the back seat immediately.

"And YOU!" he started at Kyler through the open window of his truck, "You EVER go near her again and I will fucking kill you! What the fuck is wrong with you? She's FIFTEEN!"

Kyler leaned in through the window, looked directly at me, said, "Call me later babe," then turned and walked away. But there would be no calling him, or seeing him, for weeks. I had security up the ass after my little deceiving stunt.

By the time I had contact with him again, he had a new girlfriend. I told myself I had caused enough problems for him and that I needed to finally let go.

God works in mysterious ways.

I was shattered to pieces again. This time, even more lost and confused than ever before. I knew in my heart that I fell in "love" with a twisted fuck who took advantage of me in every way possible. I never told anyone what happened.

My perception of love and relationships became warped beyond recognition.

CHAPTER SIX

Warped Reality

"Trauma steals your voice"
– Nikita Gill

After my experience with Kyler, I withdrew from the possibility of love for quite a while. I spent more time with Tiffany, who I had really distanced myself from during my ordeals. During the weekdays, my focus was on school and keeping my grades up, but come the weekends, I did nothing short of let loose.

We drank like we had nothing to lose. We went hard like every day was our last, and we never missed a party. Within a short period of time, I met hundreds of new people, and formed some truly amazing (what I thought to be) friendships.

One of those parties brought me a temptation sent by the Devil himself; a temptation I failed to deny.

Tiffany and I had been spending a lot of time over at Brody's house. You know, the first place I got high? He was a really close friend of Tiff's sister Leigha, so naturally, we all grew to be very close. It became like a second home to us.

It was a very unordinary household. His mom was a nudist and outwardly expressive dominatrix. I enjoyed being in a place of complete openness and non-judgement, and was intrigued by her openness about sex.

Having the expressive, cool mom he did, Brody always had friends staying with him.

One day while Tiffany and I were laying out by the pool, I noticed some older guys moving furniture into the basement.

"Someone moving in down there?" I asked Brody's mom, Katryna.

"Oh yes, Brody's friend Gage is going to be renting a room down there."

I thought nothing of it.

Tiffany told me that she knew of Gage. He was a few years older than us, and was by far the sexiest guy she had ever seen – all tatted up with a beautiful face and perfectly defined body– but was more twisted than anyone could imagine. She added that he was a diagnosed nymphomaniac and had fucked half the girls in town. I didn't really understand the concept of a nymphomaniac, but "powerful" and "twisted" seemed to always draw me in.

Then came that party.

We were taking back shots in the hot boxed house, singing at the top of our lungs and dancing the night away, having a great time like we always did. Suddenly, as electric as lightning striking, a compelling force overtook the room.

"YO GAGE!! What's good bro?!" I heard a voice shout enthusiastically.

I turned around to face the most gorgeous human being I had ever seen in real life. Tiffany was right. He was perfect. Beyond perfect. He looked like a fucking god.

Everyone was drawn to his energy. There was something about him that made the room submit to him. People were fighting for his attention, offering him drinks and weed and even their seats. I couldn't take my eyes off of him.

In the overcrowded room, he didn't even acknowledge me.

Hours passed. No matter what I was doing, my attention was completely fixed on him. I had never been so drawn to someone before. Still, he hadn't even looked my way. I told myself he was way out of my league anyways. He could have any girl he wanted.

As dusk became dawn, my energy faded out. I grabbed a pillow, laid down on the floor and started to drift off.

"Need a hand?" I heard an unfamiliar voice ask nonchalantly.

I looked up.

It was him!

"I'm alright," I said shyly, feeling my face turn red. I was astounded that he was even talking to me. "Just tired."

"Here, get up off the floor," he insisted, and reached his hand out to help me up.

I took his hand and sat up.

"You just moved in downstairs right?"

"Yeah," he smiled innocently, with a touch of seduction in his eyes. "You wanna come check out my spot? It's pretty tight."

I was thrown off by his bluntness, and a little hesitant about his intentions, but there were still a lot of people at the house, so what could really happen?

"Alright," I replied uneasily, and I followed him down a set of stairs, through a hallway, and into a small room that consisted of only a bed, a dresser, a desk and an office chair.

"What do you think?"

"Pretty sweet" I lied. There really was nothing special about it.

"Smoke a bong with me?" He looked sweetly into my eyes. I was mesmerized.

I couldn't believe I was alone with this unbelievably sexy guy in his room. I wasn't thinking about sex. I was still a virgin (as far as I remembered).

It was pure infatuation and lust.

"I guess I could hit one before I go pass out." I decided to play hard to get.

He pulled out the chair and kindly gestured for me to sit down. As he turned back around, he locked his eyes on mine with a look that told me he was trouble. It turned me on. He slowly walked to the back of my chair, spun me around and kissed me with great intensity and passion.

We kissed for what seemed like an eternity, until we were interrupted by someone walking into the room. It was Brody.

"Yo bro! Get back up there!"

"Aight, I'm coming" he smirked at me. "After you babe."

We went our separate ways – he went to chill with his boys, and I left with Tiffany and Leigha.

Tiffany saw me come back up with Gage, so she knew I had been alone with him downstairs.

The second we walked out the door, she blurted out, "Sash, he's fucked. I'm telling you. Don't get involved with that shit."

She enticed me even more. Fear and power. He was the perfect mix of both. I convinced myself she must have just been jealous that he wanted me and not her.

Some time went by, and I went on with my life. I thought often of the passionate kiss that Gage and I shared, but accepted that it was just one of those things that happens when two people are really wasted. I hadn't seen him or heard from him since.

Until one boring, lazy day, I was scrolling through my social media when a message popped up on my screen. It was Gage!

Hey beautiful. I've been thinking about that kiss. Have you?

I stopped and analyzed the message for a few moments and came to the conclusion that he was running game on me. I mean, come on, who starts a conversation like that? Two can play the same game right?

Pfft ... don't flatter yourself Mr. Big Shot. It wasn't THAT good.

Who was I kidding? It was unbelievable.

Ouch. He replied shortly.

I waited to see if he was going to follow it up with anything else, but after a few minutes, there was still nothing. I kept replaying my words, overanalyzing what he must have been thinking.

Did I offend him?

It wasn't like me to be such a bitch. I felt guilty.

I'm just teasing. I continued. It was a very memorable kiss if you really must know.

Oh yeah? How memorable? He insisted.

I wasn't really sure how to answer, so I just sent a wink face.

Wanna hang out sometime?

I was blown away that he wanted to see me again. Perhaps it wasn't some drunken thing. Was he actually into me?

Me: I'd be down for that, I guess.

Gage: Oh yeah? Well what are you up to right now? I could come pick you up and we can just go for a drive and smoke a blunt or something?

Me: Alright, sounds chill.

I sent him my address and quickly applied some makeup, tossed my hair up in a cute messy bun, and threw on a nice outfit that screamed casual but sexy. I didn't want to look too interested. Guys seem to be more into you when you play hard to get.

About fifteen minutes later, he picked me up. His energy was very awkward. He made almost no eye contact with me, and was very short with his words. He seemed nervous. I wasn't sure why he would be nervous. Had he seen himself?!

Turns out the nerves were a byproduct of his sadistic mind conjuring up a plan.

Within a few short minutes he sighed in frustration and informed me that he had forgotten his weed at home. He asked if I wanted to just go to his house and blaze instead.

It seemed harmless, so I agreed.

He had moved since the last time I saw him. When we got to his apartment, he introduced me to an old, frail-looking woman who was sitting downstairs. She kindly greeted me and went on to finish cleaning up the kitchen. I was a lot less nervous knowing that there was someone else at the house, especially an old woman. I didn't think anything bad could possibly happen.

He led me upstairs to a bright room with a large window overlooking the main street. A queen-sized bed was set up beside the window, and just beside that was a sitting area which consisted of a loveseat, a few chairs, and a table in the middle that held a couple of bongs and pipes, as well as a bowl of weed.

He switched on the TV, busted up some weed and told me I could smoke a bong. We each smoked a couple, both fixated on the movie, and not conversing very much. The tension and energy between us was fierce. I was so nervous that my palms were sweating.

His head seemed to be somewhere else, like he was lost in thought about something very serious. He proceeded to get up off the couch and laid on his bed, looking out the window with something consuming his mind.

"Holy fuck," he said in surprise, "some dudes getting arrested out here. Looks like they found drugs on him."

It didn't surprise me the least bit. That kind of thing was normal around there.

"Oh my God!" he continued with immense exaggeration in his voice. "Dude's running away! They're chasing him … They got him … They're beating the shit out of him!!"

There was something about the way he portrayed the story that made me uneasy. It seemed very imaginative. I wondered if he was just trying to get me in his bed.

"You gotta see this!" he went on, "I can't believe you're missing it!"

Still, I stayed where I was, laughing hesitantly and playing along with it. His story expanded to the cops throwing the guy in cuffs and driving away with him in the back seat.

I didn't want to seem rude, but I had no intention of climbing into his bed. I didn't want to give him the wrong impression.

After his five-minute narrative, he looked extremely disappointed with my lack of interest in his story. I watched as he pondered for a few moments, then looked at me with emotion I had never seen in someone's eyes before.

"I gotta be honest," he admitted finally, "I made up that whole story to try and get you in my bed."

What a fucking weirdo! I thought to myself.

But even after acknowledging what my gut was telling me, I disregarded the thoughts I had as being ridiculous. I was completely ignorant of his real intentions. No one had ever taught me about dating, relationships, or sex for that matter, so I had no idea what was considered normal. I was figuring it out as I went.

I persuaded myself into believing that he was just an awkward person who was probably just as nervous as I was in order for him to have said something so odd. I too had done some pretty weird things in the past to try and get someone's attention or approval.

That justification lasted for a whole five seconds.

"Come over here. I want to fuck you."

There was no sign of any kind of sarcasm in his tone. Surely, he didn't expect that to appeal to me … did he?

I chuckled out of uncomfortableness, intimidated by his blunt and straightforward comment. I had no clue how to respond.

So many thoughts raced through my mind.

Did I give him the wrong idea by coming here with him after kissing him the way I did?

I really wanted him to like me. But I was seeking love, not a fuck and chuck. I was afraid for what I had gotten myself into, and embarrassed that I had led him on. I did not see what his real intentions were.

Still searching for the right way to handle the situation, he continued, "I said come over here."

I tried to appear confident and stand my ground without having to verbally defend myself. I should have just got up and left, but in that moment, I was naïve, inexperienced, and uncertain of myself.

"If you don't come over here by the count of three, I'm coming over there to get you myself."

Is this guy serious right now?

Too fearful to run, or even react in any way to what was going on, I remained sitting tensely where I was.

"One…two…three." He slowly got up off the bed, holding eye contact as he approached me invasively. He swooped me up into his arms and brought me over to his bed. He sat down, and placed me on his lap facing toward him with my legs wrapped around him.

He kissed me on my lips, down my neck and across my shoulder. I remained tense, my mind and body on autopilot.

"Why are you resisting me? I know you want me," he tried to entice me.

He was right, I did want him. But not like this …

With every moment that passed, I fell deeper and deeper into his trap, pressured into giving him what he wanted.

Then, as if he could see into my soul and read my mind, he stopped kissing me and looked me dead in the eye with a sinister grin and asked me if I was a virgin.

Again, I had no idea how to answer.

"Ah, okay. I get it," he said - seemingly amused. "Don't be scared baby."

His words gave me chills.

With complete power over me, he began unbuttoning my shorts. I grabbed his hand playfully to redirect it elsewhere. He brushed off my multiple attempts to stop him and proceeded to unzip them.

"Take your pants off," he demanded.

When I didn't act on his command, he aggressively pulled them off himself and placed me back onto his lap.

"I really don't …", I didn't have time to finish my sentence when he interrupted me.

"Shhhhhhh," he held his finger to my lips to silence me, "relax."

He forcefully thrust himself into me.

I stayed there, motionless, unable to process what was happening. The world around me went black, a familiar subconscious reaction I had to blocking out trauma.

Immediately after he finished, he stood up, pulled his pants back up, and told me to get dressed so he could bring me home.

There are no words to describe the all-consuming embarrassment, shame, guilt, vulnerability, confusion, and deceit that devoured me in that moment. I wanted to run away crying.

Still on autopilot, I put my pants back on, grabbed my things, and walked out of his room shamefully, down the stairs and out to his car. We did not speak to each other the entire ride back to my house.

"That was fun," Gage stated amusingly as we pulled up to my house. "Let's do it again sometime."

Without saying goodbye, I got out of his car and slammed the door behind me.

I didn't tell anyone. I told myself it was my own fault. I was warned about him, and I didn't listen. I put myself in that situation. So, I sucked it up, buried the memory in the deepest part of me, and went on with my life.

I was a master of suppressing memories.

Months passed as the memory long suppressed itself, anchoring those feelings of worthlessness even heavier into my soul.

Later that summer, there was a big pit party that Tiffany and I heard about. All of our friends and the people we partied with on a regular basis would be there. The pit was a spot where we all used to party throughout the summer because it was far enough away from civilization that no one could see us or hear us, no matter how wild things got. Cops couldn't drive their cars out there. You had to walk through a forest, down a huge hill, across an overgrown field, and there, in the middle of nowhere was a huge sand pit with a firepit fifteen feet down in the centre.

I drank more that night than I had ever consumed prior. I drank the equivalent of a full twenty-sixer to myself, of various types of alcohol: some whisky, rum, tequila, vodka … you name it. I also tried magic mushrooms for the first time that night. A buddy of ours from the Dot had a big bag of them and he was giving out handfuls to people. I had already planned on trying them, so I felt no unease about it. It was all good vibes, and good people.

Long into the night, under the light of the moon and by the heat of the raging fire, we partied like tomorrow would never come.

As the night progressed, I lost control of myself.

I was stumbling all over the place. When I nearly landed myself in the firepit, a close friend took it upon himself to look after me. He held me close, trying to keep me in check until someone was ready to take me home. That's how we rolled. We all had each other's backs and no one would ever be left behind.

I stood there in his arms, looking around, when all of a sudden, bam! There was Gage, watching my every move with a possessive and jealous energy about him. I tried to ignore his presence the best I could, which actually wasn't entirely difficult being in the state I was in at the time.

At some point, my buddy sat me down at a picnic table and told me to rest my head and sleep it off until someone was ready to go.

Being hard headed and never knowing when to call it quits, it wasn't long before I was up mingling again and sloppily falling all over the place. We all acted like fools when we partied, because none of us knew our limits. It was high school. We were young and dumb. It was fun to us. We thought we were cool.

Next thing I knew, I was face-down in the grass at the top of the pit, border-line blacking out, when I saw a blurry figure pick me up off the ground.

"You're way too fucked up Sasha. I can't watch you like this. I'm taking you home." Guess who? Yep. Gage.

I had absolutely no control over my body. My speech was so slurred that not even I could make out what I was trying to say. He and his cousin each took one of my arms and put it around their shoulders as they carried me to Gage's car. I nodded off the entire drive and came to as we pulled into a driveway. It wasn't my house.

"I'm not taking you home like this. You can sleep here and I'll bring you home in the morning." That was the last thing I remember from that night.

When I woke up the next morning, I was laying in his bed next to him with my pants off.

He did it again.

I got up, put my pants on, gathered my belongings silently in shame. He explained to me how lucky I was to have been able to sleep over because he never let any girl stay the entire night with him; that I was special to him.

Fucking psychopath.

I called a cab and waited outside until it came.

Reflecting on this now, I can't believe how damaged and naïve I was to put myself in such situations where things like this could have happened. That is, to get so intoxicated that someone could just take me away and do whatever they wanted to me.

No, what happened to me was not my fault. And yes, I do take responsibility for my part in putting myself into such vulnerable spaces.

But here's what I've come to realize: when you spend your whole life believing you have no value, no purpose, and no worth, you align yourself with dangerous and self-destructive behaviors. You have no worth, so what does it matter if anything bad were to happen to you?

I drank to the point of incapacitation because deep down, I really didn't care what happened to me. I suffered the pain that was the consequences of the circumstances I brought on myself, but it didn't stop me from making the same stupid choices again and again, victimizing myself into great despair.

Unfortunately, this was only the beginning.

The more trauma I encountered, the more I lowered my standards, forcing myself to reside in some of the darkest of places.

CHAPTER SEVEN

Special K

"Constantly choosing the lesser of two evils is still choosing evil."
– Jerry Garcia

Everyone says weed is a gateway drug, and I've always said that was the stupidest thing I've ever heard. Weed shouldn't even be categorized with other drugs, really. But then I ask myself, if I had never tried smoking weed, and becoming comfortable in – even dependent on – the mental escape in an alternate reality, would I ever have had the courage to indulge in a harsher drug, with no idea what to expect a "high" to be like?

I'm still not one hundred percent certain of the answer to that question, but I do know that I feared drugs for the entirety of my youth, and after I stepped past my boundaries and started smoking weed, it became a lot less scary to try other drugs.

I started to wonder what other highs might be like.

Just before I turned sixteen, I met a girl by the name of Stephanie through one of our mutual friends. She was absolutely beautiful: bleach blonde hair, bright blue eyes, perfect pearly white teeth, beautifully sculpted, and just all around gorgeous in every way (everyone referred to her as a Barbie because of how attractive she was).

Stephanie was quite the partier, just like I was, so of course we hit it off almost instantly. She was a year younger than I was but seemed a lot more experienced in the type of lifestyle I'd become accustomed to. She was a huge stoner, could drink more than most guys I knew, dabbled in harder drugs recreationally, and had dated many of the guys that most girls could only ever wish for. I suppose I was fascinated by, perhaps even envious of her. But we also connected on a deep and profound level. She was very book smart just as I was, and very self-expressive, as I was finally learning to be. We shared our deepest, darkest secrets, spending many sleepless nights in deep conversation. We empowered each other in many different ways, and I looked up to her in a lot of senses. When she moved to the Dot about a year after I did, we became best friends. In fact, we were inseparable. Oftentimes we would isolate ourselves from the rest of the world together for days at a time in her small little room, getting high, crying over heartbreak, and supporting each other through things that nobody else seemed to understand.

One Friday night, Steph informed me that she was going to stay at her sister's house for the weekend, who lived in a nearby city about forty-five minutes away. She begged me to come with her, expressing that she needed to get away but she didn't want to be alone. Naturally, I said yes without hesitation.

She mentioned that her sister was a pimp and ran a type of red-light district out of her house, but said it was nothing to worry about – we'd just be doing our own thing anyways. It was just a place to get away. I trusted Steph completely so I wasn't at all concerned. I was a little intrigued to be honest. I'd never seen something like that before.

When we arrived at her sister's house, nothing seemed abnormal. It was a regular house with two levels, set up like any other house would be. It had a casual living room, a few bedrooms down the hall, and a basement that we didn't really see much of.

Her sister was really cool, although I could tell right away that she was high on something a lot stronger than weed; her energy was high and her pupils dilated. She spoke so fast I could hardly understand what she was saying, and she kept grinding her teeth and rubbing her lips together aggressively.

We spent the day hanging out at the house getting day-drunk, bumping music, and smoking up. As it got later in the evening, some interesting people began showing up. I guess the way it all worked was that her sister (who will remain nameless) would set up dates in her house and take commission for renting out rooms hourly, nightly, or per weekend. She knew most of the girls personally and would seek their clients through various forms of networking.

When people started showing up, Steph and I decided to go out into the city to explore a bit. As we were getting ready to leave, half in the bag already, her sister handed her a small vial of a substance I didn't recognize.

Steph took the vial and led me into another room, closing the door behind us.

"Wanna try some?" she asked persuasively, eyes beaming into the rebellious part of my soul.

"What is it?"

"Special K."

She could read me like an open book. No way in hell did I want any part of that. But after a few moments when I still had not answered her, I noticed she had divided a line and a small bump from the rest of the pile.

"Here," she insisted, "this is nothing. Try it and see what you think?"

I don't know why I was so easily persuaded to do such stupid things. I guess I just didn't want to look like a pussy. I mean, there I was in a damn trap house hanging out with pimps and hookers … there was no room for weakness.

Being as impulsive and fearless as I was, I sniffed the bump without thinking twice about it. It burned a little as it entered my nostril, but it wasn't as bad as I thought it would be. Not too long after, the drip came.

The drip is when the substance reaches the back of the sinus and leaks into your throat.

I almost puked. It tasted disgusting. But I didn't feel any different so I decided that it couldn't be that bad.

"Duuuude. I'm sooo hungry. Let's go for an adventure and find food?"

Stephanie always knew just what to say. Adventure plus food? How could I say no?

It was still daylight when we left. Somewhere in the midst of the shots we took along the way, we lost track of our direction. By the time we found a McDonald's, the sun was beginning to set.

As we ordered our food, I noticed four guys sitting at a table gawking at us and whispering amongst each other. I thought nothing of it and watched them leave as we sat down to eat. Half an hour or so must have passed when we had finished eating and proceeded to walk outside to try and find our way back to the house.

"Hey ladies," said a male's smug voice coming from a parked truck.

Of course, Steph waltzed right on over in confidence. I realized right away that it was the four guys from inside who were staring at us. It was a little odd that they had waited half an hour for us to come out, but I didn't read too much into it.

"What are you guys sayin tonight?"

"Going to get fucked up!" Steph slurred in response. She was always so forward. That's what I loved most about her. What you see is what you get.

"Oh yeah? Can we join ya's?"

Steph took a paper from them that had a phone number and said we'd call them in about an hour. They took off and we started on our way back to the house. Only one problem … we realized we had no idea where the hell we were going. We were so *in the moment* on our mission to find McDonald's, that we completely lost track of the route we took to get there.

Steph suggested that we just find a cab and that they would know where the house was based on her description. I must have been more messed up than I thought I was to think that would actually be a plausible scenario.

We approached a few different cabs, all of whom told us they had no idea where the "house just over the bridge" was.

Finally, one cab driver who barely spoke English agreed to help us find it. We drove around for quite a long time. I watched as the meter soared higher and higher. Soon it reached $80, and neither of us had more than $10 to rub together.

"Right here!" Steph suddenly shouted. I looked around and did not recognize any of the houses. "Pull over!"

The cab driver pulled over and requested the eighty dollars we owed for the ride. Steph told him that she had to run inside and grab it from her sister.

Thank God. I thought to myself. I wasn't sure how we were going to pull $80.00 out of our asses.

We got out of the cab, and I followed behind Steph as she bolted toward a house on the other side of the street. I didn't recognize the house.

She kept running.

I realized in that moment her sister was not giving us the money for the cab. I began laughing hysterically, in such disbelief that we were seriously hopping a cab. A stupid and immature thing to do, but man, what a rush it was.

Luckily, Steph actually did recognize the neighborhood and had set it up so that we could sneakily make it to her sister's house without being caught. We darted inside and slammed the door, falling onto each other in fits of adrenaline-fueled laughter.

When the moment passed, Steph called up the guys from McDonald's and briefly gave them the address and hung up the phone.

"They'll be here in like half an hour," she said coolly.

Her sister overheard her and intervened, saying that she wasn't down for having random strangers in her house. I totally understood. Being the kind of place that it was, I wouldn't trust some random dudes brown nosing in my business either. We decided we'd just hang out outside when they showed up.

In the midst of getting ready, Steph busted out some more Special K, this time forming two lines – one about half the size of the other. She handed me the rolled-up bill, and I sniffed the smaller of the two lines without hesitation. I felt a little funny this time, but nothing overly concerning. My body felt relaxed and my heart rate slowed. It was kind of nice.

"They're here!" shouted Steph as the sound of a horn honked just outside the house.

We threw on our shoes, grabbed our purses, and went out to meet three of the four guys. Steph told them that her sister didn't want them in the house, so they suggested we just bring the bong out and chill in the truck for a bit.

Steph hopped in the front middle seat between two of them – Jay and Tony, and I got into the back with the third, Malik. For a little while, everything was cool. We just chilled, listening to music and smoking bongs. My mind was numb and blank.

When the truck engine started, and we were – without warning – reversing out of the driveway, a very unsettling feeling overcame me. I told myself it was just the K kicking in, I was probably just paranoid.

"Where are we going?" I asked, trying not to display my discomfort as Malik casually put his arm around me.

"We're just gunna go to my parent's place," said Jay, who was driving. "They're out of town for the weekend so we have the place to ourselves."

We drove for quite a while; past the outskirts of the city and into a more desolate area. We arrived at an old brown brick house that had lights on in the upstairs window. That was when the K *really* kicked in. Have you ever seen the *Truman Show* with Jim Carrey? It felt exactly like that. I was in some kind of horror movie from which I could not escape.

I don't think I said more than a few words in the time that we were there. In fact, I have no idea how long we even stayed. My mind was blank and my body numb. Nothing was coordinated. I couldn't find the words I was looking for. In fact, there were very few thoughts in my head at all – like I was merely a puppet.

I sat in silence on an old piano bench beside Steph. All of a sudden, my body began to swell like Harry Potter's aunt Marge in the *Sorcerer's Stone*. Everything within the room was sucked into my body – the table and chairs, the television, even the photos on the walls. Larger and larger

I grew until I could not expand any further. As I yawned, everything came back out of me and into its proper place in the room.

There it was, the yawn – the yawn that intensifies the high.

Jay emerged from the bathroom, telling us that there was a problem with the toilet, and he needed Malik to help him fix it. When fifteen or twenty minutes had passed, Tony exclaimed that he would go see if they needed help. I couldn't help but to feel that they were conspiring against us. It seemed like they were in there forever. Finally, we got up to see what was really going on.

The guys seemed a little startled to see us enter the bathroom but invited us in to hotbox it.

"So … we have to go pick up my friend from the bus terminal. She's coming from another city," Jay told us.

I was pretty certain there were no buses coming from out of town this late. Something wasn't right.

"Alright, well we can just wait here," Steph stated.

"That's probably not a good idea … just come for the ride."

"Shotgun!" yelled Steph excitedly.

Soon the spliff was finished and we piled out of the room, followed by a thick, humid cloud of smoke.

They directed us to go get our shoes on and said they would meet us downstairs in a few minutes. When we got to the bottom of the long staircase, I realized I forgot my drink on the table upstairs.

Struggling to make it up each step, I reached just a few stairs from the top, when I happened to glance in between the posts of the banister.

Jay tossed a small knife spiralling into the air, caught it and put it into his pocket.

He then turned to his friends with a grim smirk: "Let's take these girls to the bus station."

This is not happening! This is not real! I'm just trippin'! Wake up! Wake up! Wake up!

I quietly made my way back down the stairs, but before I could get to Steph to tell her what I had just seen, Tony, Jay and Malik were already coming down behind me.

Steph raced over to the truck and hopped into the front seat. The last thing I wanted to do was to get in, but we were in the middle of nowhere and I knew there was no place to run for help. Hell, I couldn't even run if I wanted to.

We drove and we drove and we drove. It was a long and tense ride. We pulled up into a dark alleyway and Jay parked the truck.

"Let's go."

My heart rate sped back up, thundering into my chest.

"It's cold! We'll just wait here," Steph told him.

"No one is waiting in the truck," he replied firmly.

We got out and followed them through the little alley and across the road. We actually were at the bus terminal!

Wow Sasha. You need to stop being so paranoid.

Jay and Malik went inside, and Tony asked us to stay out and have a smoke with him. When there were only a few puffs left, he told us we could finish it and went inside.

We each took another puff and went inside to meet them. There were only a few people in the station so late at night, and Jay, Malik and Tony were not one of them. We yelled into the men's washroom, but no reply. Then, we noticed another door leading to the back of the terminal. We looked outside. Nothing. We ran back to the truck and it was gone! They left us at a bus terminal in the middle of nowhere with no coats and no money!

"What the fuck do we do?" Steph panicked. "I have no fucking clue where we are!"

There were payphones on the wall, but our sorry asses had not even two quarters to make a phone call.

We spotted a security guard behind a glass window and pleaded with him to let us use a phone because we were lost and needed someone to come get us. He slammed the metal slider down in our faces.

Next, we saw a man wearing a nice suit carrying a briefcase and asked him if we could please use his phone to call for help. He ignored us and kept walking. My gaze remained on him as he passed us by, wondering how the hell anyone could be so cold toward a couple of lost, scared teenage girls.

Please wake up! This cannot be real!

We exited the terminal and stood outside in the crisp, eerie air, surrounded by some creepy looking homeless people and messed up crackheads. We begged every person we saw for fifty cents to make a phone call, and alas someone handed us two miraculous quarters.

"Steve! Where's my sister? I need to talk to her now!" Steph anxiously demanded to whoever was on the other end of the line she had called.

"Are you kidding me?" she continued, "this can't be happening!" She began to cry. "I don't even know where the hell I am! ... okay, thank you so much ... you're a life saver!" And she hung up the phone. "Let's go find a cab!"

We ran up the dark road until we found a cab driver who agreed to take us to where we needed to go. When we got to her sister's house, Steve met us outside with the money for the cab and the nightmare had come to an end. Turns out Steve was a good friend of Steph's sister who frequently stayed at the house and paid for the time of one specific girl named Marsha.

I was so drained, physically and mentally, that I crashed hard on the couch almost as soon as we got back. What seemed like moments later I was abruptly awakened by someone banging on the front door.

I opened my eyes. It was quiet and dark – everyone was obviously already asleep.

BANG! BANG! BANG! BANG!

Still disoriented, I got up and opened the front door.

"Who are you?!" they demanded. "and where is Marsha?!"

There were two women, one a little older than I was, and one who appeared to be her mother, and a man who was maybe in his mid-twenties.

"Sorry?" I replied, seeming confused by the question he was demanding from me.

"Do you live here?" he was prying.

"Yes ... I do." I may have become a lot of things, but a snitch was not one of them.

"Who is all here?!"

Just then Steph's sister's boyfriend joined us at the door and motioned for me to go back to bed.

"I know what goes on here you mother fucker! I know she's here! This is her mother and her sister, and I'm her boyfriend! She's only seventeen! You won't get away with this."

Only seventeen? Damn ... That's rough ... Come on Sash, this isn't any of your business. Go back to sleep.

I didn't get much sleep in what couple hours were left of the night. So much had happened in the last twelve hours, and my anxiety was not allowing me to get off so easily. I was just happy it was all over. No way I was ever sniffing that crap again.

You know, it's pretty insane reflecting on that night. I write from the perspective of how I experienced the events that happened, but of course now I see with a different set of eyes. I think it is so important for users to understand that when you're fucked up on drugs, you think the world is out to get you – everyone is conspiring against you. But, in reality, it is you who sets the tone for how the world responds to you. Looking back at it all now, those three guys probably genuinely wanted to hang out with us and have a good time, until they realized we were high on ketamine and were on a completely different level than they wanted to deal with. Their *conspiring* in the bathroom was probably just brainstorming how to get rid of us without stirring up drama or offending us. They brought us to a place where they knew there were resources for us to get home safely.

As for the knife, I presume it was merely a hallucination I had, since hallucinations are a key side effect of ketamine. What's more, is that when you look up the effects of Special K, the first thing that pops up is "being in a dream-like state," which explains my believing I was in a horror film/nightmare.

The security guard and the business man we asked for help probably saw two more teenage addicts all spun and tripping out. And really, minus the addict part, that's exactly what we were.

I share with you this story because it displays the main idea of this book in clear, extreme examples of how your perspective determines your reality. Every single occurrence, event, and situation is experienced differently by each person involved or spectating.

What do you tell yourself about your life or who you are? What do you think other people think of you from an outside perspective, based on the limited knowledge they have about you? What determines the difference? If you thought about yourself or about your life in other perspectives, in what ways would that open your eyes?

I'll leave you with that for now.

CHAPTER EIGHT

Falling Hard

"Take a lover who looks at you like maybe you are magic."
– Frida Kahlo

No one ever saw me for the wounded soul I was. I concealed that part of me far beneath. On the surface, I was popular, intelligent and outgoing. I was fun-loving and always down for anything – I loved a good adventure. I was confident, cocky, and wasn't afraid of anything. You could always find me in the presence of my friends, living my life like there would be no tomorrow – a free spirit.

I was out on my own, with no one to control me and no one to report to.

But a demon lived within me. A demon that possessed me the second I was alone with my own thoughts. I couldn't be by myself, so I almost never was. My distress became so dominant over me, that if I spent more than a few short minutes alone, I would be overtaken by anxiety attacks. The fear of my inner self only pushed me harder to find someone who'd love me and take all my pain away.

As we all know, *seek and ye shall find.* (Matthew 7:7).

I did find love. I was sixteen years old. It was passionate, exhilarating, and everything I imagined a relationship to be. For the first little while.

His name was D. I will never forget the first time I laid eyes on him. It was at the most massive house party I had ever attended, still to this day. Some rich kid who lived in a mansion on acres of property decided to host a triple-kegger while his parents were away travelling. There were over five hundred people in that house!

A group of my friends and I were hanging out in the six-car garage, which was the designated smoking area for the stoners. It was packed with people, everyone in their own little cliques. Except one guy. He sat alone at a workbench, wearing a vibrant, colorful hoodie with baggy jeans and his hat tilted slightly sideways. He wore a gold chain and fresh kicks. He also had a backpack on, which I found very strange considering we were at a party. It became obvious very quickly that he was some kind of dealer. Every so often, people would form around him and make cash exchanges for bags of one thing or another.

Something about his demeanor drew me to him, but I was too busy having fun to worry about anymore boy drama.

Shortly thereafter, I was at Brody's house with Tiffany and Leigha blazing a session at his kitchen table. There was another girl there hanging out whose name was Saidee. Saidee was a cute, sweet and meek girl about my age who I could tell was going through a bad state of depression. She was venting to us about her controlling boyfriend who she had been with since they were in elementary school. She explained how good everything was in the beginning, but that he had become a different person who treated her with constant disrespect, and she didn't know what to do anymore.

Just as soon as she had pulled herself together from her breakdown, the front door swung open, and that intriguing drug dealer from the triple kegger obnoxiously burst in.

Without taking much notice to who was around, he aggressively blurted out, "Saidee, what the fuck are you doing here? This is MY boy's house, get the fuck out. Go home!"

Without hesitation or trying to defend herself, she quickly gathered her belongings and left.

I was astonished.

What kind of power did he have over this sweet and beautiful girl for her to just bow down to his command like that?

"Yo, D, why you gotta be such a dick to her?" Leigha demanded. She had known D and Saidee since their childhood and was close friends with both of them.

"The bitch is wack man, she won't give me space. I've told her it's over a million fucking times and she keeps showing up everywhere I am like it's nothin."

I understood where he was coming from. Not that it was acceptable to be so disrespectful or demeaning, but I could imagine how frustrating that would be.

He stayed around and blazed with us a while, not paying any mind to me or questioning who I was. He said he had business to deal with and left a pile of weed for us to smoke. My fascination was heightened further.

Later that week, I stopped over at Tiffany's to see why she hadn't been at school all day. Her dad told me that she wasn't feeling too well, and that she had gone over to Brody's to smoke up. When I got there, no one was inside, so I went around to the backyard where I heard voices coming from a little tool shed.

I opened the door to a cloud of smoke emerging from inside.

"What's good Sash?!" Brody welcomed me as Tiff jumped up to hug me.

"Ah nothin, was just lookin for Tiff. Figured I'd find her here."

"This little bitch again eh?" commented an unfamiliar voice.

I looked down to my left side to see D sitting in a chair looking up at me.

"Excuse me?" I remarked sternly, getting up in his face, "who you callin bitch, bitch?" After all the bullshit I'd dealt with, I no longer took any shit from anyone.

"Woah, woah, she's a feisty one eh?" A huge smile spread across his face as he glared at me in admiration. "I'm just playin. What's up? I'm D."

"Sasha," I said unenthusiastically.

I didn't find him overly attractive, I mean, he was decent looking, but there was an immediate spark between us on a different kind of level – something surreal, and almost dark.

"Here, let me grab you a chair," insisted Brody, and he got up to go retrieve a chair from the deck.

"Or you can sit right here," D gestured me to sit on his lap, his face illuminated with hopefulness and curiosity.

I laughed, "I'll pass."

"Gunna play hard to get are you? That's okay, I like that."

His cockiness turned me on. I found it so sexy. We couldn't take our eyes off each other the entire time. The chemistry between us was so powerful that it made everyone else uncomfortable.

We spent the rest of the day razzing and teasing each other playfully. I wasn't looking for anything, but I genuinely enjoyed his company. His care-free confident energy was contagious, and it ignited a thrill within me.

I didn't try to contact him after that day because I didn't want anyone to know I was interested in him based on the reputation he had, and probably for fear of rejection. But I always liked the bad boys, and I could tell he was really, really bad.

A buddy of mine, Nick, grew and sold large quantities of ganja alongside his grandfather. Nick would pick me and my girlfriends up from school and bring us to his place to smoke us up every so often. He was a funny character, always making everyone laugh with his weird and uncensored sense of humor. I authentically loved hanging out with him. He put on this façade like he was a big baller, which I suppose, to an extent, he kind of was for a sixteen-year-old. He drove a nice new whip, always rocked name-brand clothes and shoes, and threw money around like it was nothing. I loved being spoiled by him, and he loved being surrounded by beautiful females, so it was a really compatible friendship. He provided the adventures, the weed, the booze, and I provided the girls.

One day, after picking Steph and I up like he usually did, he told us he had to make a drop on our way back to his place. We always tagged along with him on his drug runs.

When we arrived at a nice house in a newly-constructed, suburban neighborhood, he invited us to come in because "it would be heat" if we waited in the truck.

We followed him into a dark, unfinished basement, where loud music was bumping and a group of guys were hotboxing the room. Through the thick clouds of smoke, sitting on the edge of a bed, was D.

He noticed me right away, and I watched his face light right up in excitement. The chemistry was undeniable.

It turned out that Nick and D had been best friends for years. With that new knowledge, I began spending a lot more time with Nick . It was a way to indirectly keep in contact with D without letting him know

I was interested, and I was right. We stopped in there more and more frequently, and I got the vibe that D felt a little jealous that Nick and I spent so much time together. I was entertained by making him jealous and played it to my advantage. After all, guys always want what they can't have.

After a few visits, D invited us to all come back one weekend to party. Just to entice us, he said he'd provide the booze and weed, so we collectively decided to go. A night turned into a weekend, and a weekend turned into spending almost every day there. From entertaining ourselves by taking turns smoking salvia and laughing at each person's trip, to singing as loud as we could to Lil' Wayne songs at four in the morning, we had some pretty wild and memorable times.

Steph and I would stay over now and again, sharing a spare bed that was down there.

D and I grew really close really fast and formed a very open friendship. We fed off of each other's energy. We both acted like we weren't interested in each other, but there were months of undeniable tension built up between us that everyone could feel. We grew extremely comfortable with one another. So much so, I began staying after everyone left and hanging out just the two of us.

No one had ever made me enjoy life more than he did. He got excited about everything and made the absolute most of every single minute. He loved to entertain and was always the centre of attention. The way he saw life was magical, something so rare to witness.

One morning after drinking just a little too much, I woke up in a big, round wicker chair that had a giant cushion on top, in someone's arms. I lazily lifted my head and saw that I was asleep on D's shoulder.

How the fuck?... I remembered falling asleep, but I was sitting in the chair with Steph when I dozed off ...

As I tried to sneak away without waking him, he opened his eyes and smiled at me.

"I'm sorry," he said with embarrassment.

"Sorry for what?" I asked him, already knowing the answer but wanting to avoid the conversation.

"I told Steph to just let you sleep here when she was ready to go. You looked so peaceful and cozy passed out in the chair and I didn't want to wake you. When everyone left ... I don't know, you just looked so cute I couldn't help myself. I just wanted to cuddle with you. I hope you're not upset with me."

My heart skipped a beat. Or ten.

I think that was the moment I really started to fall for him.

"It's all good," I played it cool, like it didn't mean anything to me.

"No, it's really not. I have a girlfriend."

I was stunned. Why the hell was he acting like he was so amazed by every move I made when he had a damn girlfriend?! Whatever, it's not like I had expressed any kind of emotion for him so I had no reason to be upset.

"It's not a big deal. We were drunk. Nothing happened D. It didn't mean anything." With my back up against the wall, I lashed out, but I spoke from a place of disappointment.

"Well, that's the thing. It did mean something to me." I could tell he felt extremely perplexed.

"You shouldn't be tryna catch feelings for someone else when you have a girlfriend."

"I know you probably think I'm grimey, but to be honest, I started dating this girl at a party a few months ago, and I've only hung out with her twice. I wouldn't even call it a relationship. We barely even talk. I just don't really know how to go about breaking up with her when we never see each other. I'm not gunna do it over text, that's hurtin."

Oh. Okay. Well that's not so bad. I thought to myself.

"Do you care about her?" I asked, not wanting to know the answer.

"Yeah, I do, as a person. She's a nice girl, but she's not the one for me. To be completely honest, I've been trying to pursue this other girl, Star. She lives next door. I've had feelings for her for years, and she's been coming around a lot lately, but I think she's just using me to get high for free and for someone to boost her up when she's down on herself."

I respected how open and honest he was about everything. It's not like anything had happened between us, he really didn't owe me any answers. I also admired how vulnerable he made himself to me, sharing such deep, raw emotion. Not many guys were able to do that.

"I don't know what to tell you. If you're into someone else, then you gotta tell your girlfriend it's over. That's not fair to her."

"You're right."

Without even stopping to think about it, he picked up his phone, dialed a number and waited for someone to answer. I heard the faint voice of a girl answer.

"Hey Lana, it's D. Is there any way we can get together tonight? I wanna talk to you about something."

She must have known what was coming because I could vaguely make out her words, "You wanna break up, don't you?"

"Can we talk in person?" he pleaded.

"Just fucking tell me man. Don't make me come all the way there just to have to leave again." Her voice got louder. She was hurt. She sounded like she was beginning to cry.

"Alright. I'm really sorry Lana. I just don't think this is gunna work out."

With the cracking in her voice, I knew she was holding back her tears as she asked him if there was someone else.

He paused. He didn't want to hurt her so I didn't expect his honest admission.

"Yeah …" he said softly as he looked up at me, staring into the very depths of my soul, "there is."

I felt liberated. After spending my entire life feeling like a last option, here was this guy who I was in complete adoration of, breaking things off with someone he cared about for the mere hope of things going somewhere with me.

That night, a few of our friends came over, just like any other regular night. We had a quiet night in, just blazing and listening to music. Comfy and cozy in my pajamas, I lazily and peacefully drifted off in D's bed listening to the sounds of the surrounding music and people's laughter.

What seemed like moments later, I woke up to someone covering me up in a warm blanket. I squinted my face, and tiredly opened one eye to an empty, dimly lit room. I felt D lay beside me, close enough to feel the warmth of his body, but far enough to not be actually touching me. I opened my eyes to see him lying there with his head propped up, quietly watching me sleep. We stared deep into each other's eyes as he ran his fingers through my hair and leaned in to kiss me softly. When I kissed him back, he embraced me passionately, taking a moment between kisses to look at me in admiration.

We kissed for what seemed like forever, our hands caressing and exploring eachothers' bodies, and piece by piece, removing fragments of each other's clothing.

We made sweet, passionate love and fell asleep in one another's embrace.

When I awoke the next morning, as incredibly happy as I was, my insecurities took over. Unsure about how to think or feel, I quietly got up and put my clothes on without waking him. I sat on the edge of the bed and packed myself a bong. It was the first time I actually had consensual sex with someone, and I didn't know what exactly it meant. I didn't want him to know I was falling for him. That would make me too fragile, too vulnerable. So, when he woke up, I played it off as though nothing had happened between us and acted the same way I always did around him.

After hours of pretending, I needed to get away. I told him I had things to do and had to get going. He asked when I would be coming back and I told him I wasn't certain.

I went back to Kayne's house, where I had been living for some time now, and continued on with my regular life with the Dot kids. I told myself that all D probably wanted from me was a lay anyways, and now that he got it, he would lose interest and find someone else. That was what my experience with men told me, so that was how I perceived them.

I didn't have a cell phone, so there wasn't even any way for him to contact me, but D was persistent. When I didn't show up to see him over the next week or so, he had Nick bring him to where I was staying. He acted like it was a total fluke that he was running into me, as Nick and Kayne were good friends as well. We didn't have much of a chance to really talk in the crowded room, and plus, I wasn't really sure what to say anyways.

When Nick announced that it was time to get going, D quietly said to me in passing, "don't be such a stranger eh?"

Maybe he hadn't lost interest after all.

A few days afterward, I decided to pop in and go blaze with him. We avoided any uncomfortable conversation and just continued where we had left off, as flirtatious friends. As we sat on his bed, just listening to music, I saw him pull out a small white box, and from it, a beautiful white gold necklace with a heart shaped pendant made of diamonds.

"I bought this for Star a while ago, but something kept holding me back from giving it to her. Now I know why ... I want you to have it."

"Really? Why?" I couldn't believe it. Was I overthinking the meaning of this?

"I don't know ... You'd probably appreciate it more than she would."

I fell even harder.

Over the next few months, we spent almost all of our time together. Every day was a new adventure. D spent most of his time at Kayne's with me, informally moving in. It was kind of an open house that way - everyone stayed there for days and nights on end.

We were so ghetto that we made a bed out of a broken door that laid across two kitchen chairs and piled it with pillows and blankets for cushion. Surprisingly, it wasn't that uncomfortable.

Eventually D and our friend Stevo decided to rent out an apartment with Stevo's older brother just a few blocks away from Kayne's. It became the new party spot. I stayed there almost every night, as we carried on a purely sexual relationship (or at least that's what I convinced myself it was). I guess you could say we were "friends with benefits," and I was happy with that. He treated me like a Queen, catering to my every need and making me feel like I was the only girl in the world. I didn't need the label.

We would spend days at a time in bed, having wild sex all day and night, getting high and listening to music, and only ever getting up to make food, use the bathroom, or for quick deals. He cooked all my meals and served them to me in bed, making me feel like the luckiest girl in the world. There, we shared all of our deepest, darkest secrets, our hopes and dreams, and got to know each other on the deepest of levels.

I was fulfilled in every way possible.

We were always searching for new places to explore and let loose. We would often journey to other towns if there was nothing going on close by. Over that summer of 2008, we became good friends with some girls from the next town over, Sage, Lynn, and Krissy. Usually, they came to the Dot to party, but when they notified us that there was a big thing going down in their town one Friday night, we took the hour-long voyage on a paved trail through the woods that connected the two towns.

The walk there wasn't so bad because we were all jacked up and ready for a good time, taking shots, smoking bongs and blasting beats the whole way. Come four in the morning when we were all heading back, we were extremely sluggish and ready to crash. The walk seemed like it would never end.

I was a little pissed off with D, because I saw him flirting with another girl at the party right in front of me. Even though he wasn't technically my boyfriend, it hurt my pride because everyone knew there was something between us. So naturally, out of jealousy, the entire way back I walked with Steph and Bea, completely disregarding the fact that he was with us.

As we got closer to home, and I was ready to just lay down and sleep right there in the middle of the forest, I was startled when D drunkenly stumbled his way over to us. He dropped to his knees in front of Bea and Steph, loudly professing his feelings for me in front of everyone.

"You guys are her best friends! Tell me why the fuck she plays these games with me? Doesn't she see how much I care about her? How bad I just want her to be mine?!"

Despite his slurred words and corny approach, it felt like a fairy tale to me. That moment every little girl dreams of when the man of her dreams professes his love for her from the rooftops (with a few minor changes in details of course).

Bea was always very blunt, "I don't fucking know! Why don't you ask her? Why are you on your knees in front of us?!"

"Ya, idiot!" Steph chimed in like she always did.

He got up, shifted over, and stood inches away from me, flooded with raw, alcohol-induced emotion.

"I want you all to myself. I want you to be mine," he stated with intensity in his voice.

"What are you trying to say?" I just wanted to hear the words.

"I want to be your man."

I was still pissed about him flirting with another girl. But I realized in that moment, it was all part of one of his little games to see if I would react to let him know if I had feelings for him. What I didn't realize in that moment, was that subconsciously, I was playing the same kinds of games.

"Say yes!" the girls shouted in approval.

I grabbed his face and kissed him hard. He picked me up and spun me around as everyone yelled "AWWWW!"

It was my fairy tale moment I had been waiting for all my life.

CHAPTER NINE

The Man Behind
the Mask

*"Sometimes you just have to dance with the devil. You know
exactly what's gonna happen, but you have to."*

– Anonymous

The summer of 2008 was the first time I bragged about having the best summer of my life. It was perfect in every single way. I had the most fun I'd ever had with the most incredible people. The friendships I formed became my family. No matter what kinds of trouble we got ourselves into, we always had each other's backs – through thick and thin. From sharing our money and our meals to lending a hand or word of advice, we protected each other, and no one could interfere with that. Or, so I had thought.

The best part of all was that I was madly in love with someone who loved me just as much as I did him. Though I had no stable home, and often wondered where my next meal would come from, that summer I worried for nothing. The missing love I'd longed for since I was a little girl was entirely fulfilled.

D took good care of me. He did everything in his power to make sure I was happy. I never asked him for anything, but he took it upon himself to hustle enough to be able to provide for the both of us. I was so grateful to him. He made sure I had food in my stomach, a roof over my head, and even went the extra mile in attaining new clothes and accessories for me once in a while. I use the word attain because he made a living on hustling, not ethics. It wasn't only the drugs, he saw money to be made everywhere. He'd go to reserves and purchase cheap cartons of smokes and sell them by the pack at higher prices. He stole clothes, shoes, and electronics from different stores – anything that would sell in the streets. He participated in robberies and other similar jobs. It was his living. It didn't bother me. I grew up in poor and unfavorable circumstances, so that type of lifestyle wasn't a crime to me – it was a means for survival. In my eyes, all I saw was someone determined to make it through each day and who put himself at constant risk to provide for me. He jumped on every opportunity he could to make us money.

In return for his taking care of me, I provided unconditional love and emotional support in every way I could. I was there through his darkest of times, caring for him physically, mentally, and emotionally, and always put his needs before my own. He'd never had that in his life. Never having met his real father, and having a mother who was borderline delusional, he had a very psychologically damaging upbringing. He spent most of his pre-teen and teenage years in juvenile detention, or on house arrest and probation. He suffered through some extremely traumatic things in his life, and my mission became healing him.

We became extremely, and dangerously codependent.

The level of connection we shared was something so rare in this world. To know what someone was thinking before they expressed it in words, to know how that person felt by the mere look in their eyes, and understanding their pleasures and pains without ever saying the words – that was what we shared.

As our relationship became more serious, D admitted that he had warrants out for his arrest for skipping out on his meetings with his probation officer. I reluctantly tried swaying him to turn himself in, but he knew he would be seeing jail time with the record he already had. He said he just wasn't ready to do that. He had been locked up for so much of his youth that he wasn't ready to give up his freedom. But I understood that running would mean a worse sentence when the time finally came. It was a hard pill for me to swallow, always on eggshells worrying about when the cops would catch up with him and take him from me.

The excitement of summer soon faded and fall approached. The nights became shorter and the parties became fewer. I returned to school, and with that, had less time to spend with D. I couldn't bear that while I was stuck in school, I had no idea where he was, what he was getting himself into, or if he would be coming back home to me. He lived on the edge in everything that he did, without any fear of consequences. To make it worse, he refused to have a cell phone because it was just another way for the law to find him. My insecurities ate at me from the inside out. My worries followed me to school, and my once nearly-perfect grades steadily declined.

I took my frustration out on others; starting fights with people over nothing and lashing out on everyone around me over any little thing. Unable to control the fate of my relationship and terrified of losing the only person I felt actually loved me, I needed the control of everything else around me.

Day after day I returned from school and D was nowhere to be found. Not a note, not a call, nothing. Anxiety and fear became my prominent state. He always came home with pockets full of cash and told me every little detail about what he had done that day, and only in those moments was everything bearable. I hated waking up in the mornings because I knew each day would be just like the one before. I spent most of my time sitting around waiting on his return (or a call to let me know he was in jail). After endless sleepless nights, I'd had enough, and decided to stop living my life around his.

One Friday night, after I hadn't heard from D all evening, some friends talked me into accompanying them to a party at a friend's house. After only a few short hours, there was a sinking feeling in the pit of my stomach that I just couldn't shake. Something told me to call Kayne.

"Hey Kayne. It's just me. I'm wondering if you've heard anything from D tonight?"

"Yeah …"he said with a certain transparency in his voice, "he's here right now…"

"Oh really?! Can you put him on the phone please?"

"Uhm …" he was hesitant. "Yeah, okay …"

"Is everything ok?" I asked, sensing the turmoil within him.

"I'll just let him talk to you."

"Okay…"

What was going on? I wondered. Kayne was always happy and cheerful. I could tell something wasn't right.

"Sup babe?"

D seemed perfectly fine, though I could barely hear him over the loud voices and music in the background.

"Ugh, nothing? At a party right now." I tried to play it cool, but I was no longer any good at holding back my feelings. "Where have you been all day? You know I hate when you do this to me."

"Chill the fuck out, yo. You know what I'm doing all day."

Why was he being so rude? It was a simple question.

"K well stay there. I'm gunna call a cab and head back."

Just as I was about to say goodbye, I heard some unfamiliar female voices giggling close by him.

"Who's all there tonight?" I continued.

"Don't freak out ok?" he started.

"Uhm k? What do you mean by that?" Now I was freaking out.

"We were just chillin outside when we saw Lana and her girls walking by. They asked us to buy some weed so we invited them up for drinks. Kayne's tryna hit 'em up.

I hung up the phone. A jealous monster inside me was raging. I called on a group of my girls and told them I wanted her dealt with. They had my back, no questions asked.

Who the hell was she to come parading around my neighborhood where she had no right to be?

I knew she was looking for him. My thoughts just snowballed and the anger built within me while we waited for our cab. We all piled into the van and headed for the Dot.

I powered through the front door in a rage, yelling, "Where the fuck is she?!" my army close behind.

As I got further down the hall, I could see her in the room sitting next to D. She looked petrified. D knew what was going to happen and felt responsible for keeping her safe. He knew the damage we'd have done – hell, the damage I would have done on my own with the fury I had within.

"Sash, stop! Think about what you're doing," Kayne intervened as he tried holding me back. "There's nothing going on here, trust me."

That feeling of betrayal I'd experienced so many times took over. I didn't process anything that anyone was saying, all I saw was a threat to my security.

"Get the fuck out, now! You have two fucking seconds before I tear you apart!" I was furious!

D pushed Lana behind him and told me to stop being so jealous, and to grow up.

Why was he taking her side?

I felt myself shrinking, like I was nothing. As a defense, I lunged to attack her. Arms reached out at me to hold me back.

She was scared shitless.

D escorted Lana and her friend out of the apartment. When he didn't return, I knew he had taken them to his place just up the street.

I downed some shots.

Screw this. There was no way in hell I was giving him up so easily.

We made our way up the street. My girls told me to wait outside while they handled it. They proceeded to kick his door in.

I heard screaming and crashing from outside as he fought them off with a broomstick. At that point, I knew there was nothing I could do and insisted we all leave. I wouldn't be made the fool, fighting for someone who clearly had chosen another girl.

The next morning D showed up at Kayne's to assure me I was overreacting and that he was just trying to protect an innocent girl from being potentially seriously injured; that he could not reason with me being in the intoxicated rage I was in. With Kayne confirming validity in what he was saying – that he didn't seem to have ill intentions, I put my emotions aside and put that night behind me, but my gut still told me it was another one of his manipulative games to see what lengths I would go for him.

Later that week, I came home from school to find that D was gone, as per usual. I asked Kayne's mom if she knew where he had gone, and she explained that he had left only an hour prior to my arrival, with all of his belongings, not saying where he was headed.

I stayed awake all night waiting by the window, watching the lights pass by as each car came and left, hoping he would emerge from one of them. But he didn't.

Every time I heard the splash of tires rolling through puddles on the road below, I caught a glimpse of faith. I was let down over and over. Those feelings of unworthiness and abandonment consumed me once again.

All that night, and into the next day, I still hadn't heard from him, and came to the conclusion that he had left me, without the balls to say goodbye. For the next two days, I waited by that window, exhausting myself with sleepless nights and endless tears – feeling like that lost little girl my mom had left behind.

Three nights later, downing shots with swollen, red eyes, I could hear the voices of some girls just outside. I leaned out of the window to see Lana and a few of her girlfriends walking up our street.

I raced outside – feeling used by D and ashamed of my actions toward Lana – to confront her and tell her that I was sorry for coming at her the way I did; to acknowledge that I had behaved totally unreasonable.

Low and behold, guess who pulled up at that exact moment? Jumping out of an old beaten-up car with an older man I had never seen before, D stumbled over to where Lana and I were. Having no idea what the hell was going on, my adrenaline kicked in and my thoughts raced wildly.

Was this a set up? Did he leave me for her? Did they come to rub it in my face?

With a glowing, conniving smirk, no "hello" or anything of the sort, he immediately grabbed me and kissed me like the past few days hadn't happened. I was utterly mind-fucked and relieved all at the same time.

He turned next to Lana, "What the fuck are you doing here? You have no business being in my town. Get it through your head: this is my girl. I love her. Not you. You've caused enough drama for us. Now BOUNCE!"

She ran away crying. I couldn't believe he was being so heartless. I chased her up the road and apologized on his behalf, insisting that she deserved way better.

She turned around and said the last three words I'd ever hear from her: "So do you."

At that point in time, those words meant nothing to me. I had what I wanted – him back.

Disillusioned by his condescending behavior, I went back to face him.

"What the fuck is wrong with you? Where have you been? Why haven't you called? You could have left a note or SOMETHING! You think you can just come back after three days and act like nothing happened? What the fuck D?!"

He was acting very odd, like he was a completely different person. His eyes were very wide and his pupils dilated. He kissed me hard to shut me up.

"Chill out baby, I'm back now. Sorry I worried you, I had to work for a few days," he replied nonchalantly, almost with a sense of gratification for the turmoil he had caused. "And as far as Lana, I was just tryna prove to you that it's only you. I don't care about that girl."

I fell into his manipulative trap.

I had so many questions, but relief outweighed my concerns, so I brushed it all off and appreciated the fact that he had come back to me.

He wrapped his arm around me and led me up to Kayne's apartment.

We continued on with life as we knew it, but I recognized something different in D's overall demeanor.

I was oblivious at the time to the effects of hard drugs, until one day it hit me square in the face.

It was Halloween.

D, Kayne, and another friend of ours, Dale, rented out a little house in a nearby town. It was a three-bedroom, two-storey house in a nice suburban neighborhood, with a big backyard. I loved it ... it was finally our own space!

I returned to the house that evening already in my costume (which of course was a concoction of sleezy clothes that I used Halloween as an excuse to wear), with booze and decorations, thrilled that it was one of my favorite days of the year (I've always been a sucker for holidays)!

I was surprised upon entering the house to see a couple of shady guys standing around our dining room table with D. The energy completely shifted as I approached them, like they didn't want me to know what was going on.

"Hey baby, give me a minute ok?" D said to me as I started walking toward him.

Right away I knew something was up. He always dropped whatever he was doing when I entered the room to greet me.

I walked closer, and noticed piles and lines of white powder on a mirror on the table.

"What the fuck are you doing? Are you fucking kidding me?" I demanded in outrage! D knew how I felt about cocaine, and here he was sniffing it in our own home with some low life losers!

Before he had a chance to answer, I pushed the two guys out of the way and blew the coke into clouds of dust.

I'd never seen D infuriated with me like he was in that instant.

"You fucking little cunt! Do you know how much fucking money you just blew away?! You wanna come up in here and embarrass me like that in front of my boys?!"

Is he seriously talking to me like this? He's the one going behind my back doing this shit, and I'm the bad guy? I couldn't believe it.

He ran toward me with a look of vengeance on his face, pinning me against the wall by my throat.

"You fucking piece of shit! You can't control what I do! This is MY house! That was MY money! Who the fuck do you think you are you little bitch?!"

He went on and on, screaming in my face as I squeezed my eyes shut, unable to look this monster in the eyes. I didn't catch most of what he was saying because I was in such disbelief that this was happening. I don't know what hurt more, the fact that he had been hiding this from me, or the pain of his hands clenched around my neck.

Macy intervened and I ran downstairs in tears. I heard him chasing behind me. He pushed me into our room, locking the door behind him. Throwing me on the bed, he pinned me down and put me into a choke hold, restraining me with one hand behind my back and continuing to scream in my face.

The door burst in and Macy ran to my aid.

"Get off of her!" she screamed as she somehow pried him off of me. She was tiny but damn was the girl mighty when it came to the people she cared about.

She pushed me toward the door and I dashed back upstairs. Again, he chased me. He caught up as I reached the top of the stairwell. The next thing I remember was him holding me over the railing at the top of the stairs, threatening to throw me over. Macy ripped him off of me, and in turn, he grabbed her by the throat the same way he did me.

I'm not sure if it was something she said, but he seemed to snap into reality and realized what he was doing.

"Holy shit, I'm so sorry ..."

He panicked and left the house in a hurry.

Dale got home from work and Macy told him what happened. Some time later, D returned with two of his friends. Dale met them at the door, and without warning punched D in the face.

"Don't you ever lay your hands on a female in my house again! You fucking coward!"

D took the hit and did not try to fight him back. I thought maybe he accepted his faults. He left with his boys for a little while, but was still heated when he returned.

"Get out! Now!" D yelled at me when he finally got back. "We're done! Get the fuck out now!"

"D ..." I started.

"Nah bitch, I have nothing to say to you! Get the fuck out!"

"You should go, Sash," Dale insisted regretfully. Afterall, it was technically D's place. I just stayed there.

Feeling lower than life, like my world was crashing down all around me, I made my way up the stairs. As I stepped outside, D ran up the stairs behind me, yelled "PEACE BITCH!" and slammed the door and locked it.

The air was crisp and frigid. My body collapsed onto the cold patio stones. With no money and no place to go, I laid there crying in despair. Through the walls were the muffled sounds of Dale and D yelling back and forth at one another. I couldn't quite make out what was being said, but it was apparent that Dale was defending me.

Kayne and Macy called a cab and the three of us left to Macy's grandparents house. Her grandparents were pissed that we came in so late and woke them up. Being the dedicated friends they were, they refused to leave me alone and told me I could come back to the house with them and stay in their room for the night.

Thankfully, when we got back to the house, D was already gone to bed.

I attempted to drown my sorrows by drinking the night away, but the memory of what had just happened kept playing on repeat in my mind. With no control left of myself, I gave into the over consumption of alcohol and passed out on the couch.

It must have been 5:00 a.m. The sun was beginning to rise and the house was quiet. Someone was gently picking me up off the couch. Still intoxicated and struggling to open my eyes, I saw the faint outline of D's face. He was cradling me in his arms and holding me close to his chest.

I asked what he was doing.

"Shhh. Close your eyes baby, I'm bringing you to bed."

I relaxed into his arms.

He carried me down the stairs and tenderly laid me on our double-sized mattress that sat on the floor of our small room, placing the blanket overtop of me and snuggling in to hold me close.

Though my eyes were closed, I could feel him staring upon my face.

"I'm so sorry," he whispered softly.

Tears began to fall softly from my swollen eyes and rolled down the sides of my face. We stared deeply into each other's eyes, speaking volumes without saying a single word.

How could I possibly give up on someone with whom I shared such a soul-binding connection?

CHAPTER TEN

The Eye of the Barrell

"Worst nightmares can also appear with your eyes open."

– Mark Twain

Have you ever heard that saying about how near-death experiences miraculously cause a person to change the course of their life? I'm not entirely sure how valid that theory really is. It took me facing death more than once to realize how brutally I was destroying myself, and even still, it wasn't like fireworks went off and it was an *aha* moment where everything just made sense. You hear all these stories about people coming face to face with death where their life flashes before their eyes and they are instantaneously transformed into a new person. I must be pretty thick headed – because it certainly didn't happen like that for me. Even in those brief moments of paralyzing fear, I still felt untouchable. It didn't seem to affect me beyond the discomfort in that moment, or so I thought. That is, until years later when floods of torturous memories began to haunt me in the form of traumatic night terrors and undefeatable insomnia.

One of those memories was a night that started out like any other. A close friend of ours named Ezeikiel was having a party at his house. Same story, different day. I was out of the Dot that evening visiting friends in town when D called me to inform me that the party had started and to hurry up. I could hear the sounds of music and laughter echoing in the room beyond his voice. It sounded like I was missing out on what was going to be a pretty epic night!

Little did I know just how unforgettable it was going to be.

I expected to show up to a yard full of friends welcoming me enthusiastically, but instead, I recognized that something was very wrong the moment I got there.

People were flocking away from the house in panic. As I approached the front door, Lynn bombarded me hysterically – hair a mess, makeup running down her face from crying, and a look of horror-stricken panic in her eyes that I will never forget.

"Sash! I think someone slipped something in his drink! He's going crazy! Help me! Please, help me!!"

Having no idea the terror that I was about to walk in on, I stepped inside as people pushed past me, running out the door screaming frantically. I stopped dead in my tracks, peering around the room in absolute shock.

The house was trashed beyond recognition. Almost everything in sight was destroyed. There was blood all over the walls, cupboards, doors, furniture ... everything.

The piercing sounds of my people yelling, screaming, and fighting echoed through the house. I followed the screams into a small sitting room where I saw D holding Zeik on the floor in a restraint as Zeik struggled ferociously to get out of his hold.

He wasn't the Zeik I knew. I'd seen people totally obliterated on all sorts of drugs, but nothing compared to what I was witnessing in that moment.

"What is going on?!" I demanded Lynn and Sage to tell me.

"We don't know! Everything was fine and then all of a sudden he just started going crazy, smashing everything and chasing people around trying to stab them! He cut himself up pretty bad smashing the windows and he's bleeding everywhere! There were some random guys here for a little while and right after they took off, he lost it. We think they might have slipped something in his drink!"

"Sash, get everyone the fuck out now!" D demanded, struggling to keep Zeik contained. "We need to calm him down!"

I did as I was told and cleared everyone except a few of our close friends from the house. The only people (to my recollection) that were left in the house were: D, Lynn (who was seeing Ezeikiel at the time), Sage, Carl (Zeiks best friend), and myself.

We all remained quiet as D optimistically and persistently attempted to get through to him.

"Zeik! It's okay bud! We're all here for you … you're going to be okay! We love you bro, just chill out ok? Everything is okay … Relax … that's it bro, calm down …"

It was as if he had just come to reality at that moment. He stopped struggling and his body relaxed.

"Guys?" Zeik looked around at each of us, whimpering in fear and desperation. "What is happening to me …? I'm scared … I'm sorry… I'm so sorry!"

This kid, who was a hard ass and dare devil in every sense of the term sat there on the floor sobbing and shaking, petrified, with no control over his thoughts, emotions, or actions. Assuming you've never had a bad trip, let me be the first to tell you that drugs can really take control of you like that.

We had handled enough bad trips to feel confident in dealing with the situation ourselves (not that police were even an option to any of us) and grasp control of the situation. D slowly released him. With deep empathy, we all sat huddled around Zeik trying to keep his mind in a better place.

"Sasha, D, I love you guys so much! I don't know what I would do without you. You guys are my best friends! My brother, my sister! I love you guys," he kept repeating himself, pouring his heart out of his great love for D and I.

The three of us sat there on the dirty, blood-soaked carpet hugging and crying, cracking jokes, and riding the trip out.

Just as we let our guards down and everyone felt at ease, Carl harmlessly walked past the doorway, and that insignificant minor change in the environment altered his trip once again.

Like Dr. Jekyl and Mr. Hyde, Zeik lunged up off of the floor, grabbing a kitchen knife and chased his best friend in a rage trying to kill him!

He pursued Carl throughout the house, roaring and destroying what little was still intact, including his grandmother's glass china cabinet!

D and Lynn intervened and fought tirelessly to restrain him once again as the rest of us safely removed Carl from the house. Carl was devastated, knowing he had to leave and could do nothing to help his friend.

Trying once more to stabilize Zeik's trip, we informed him over and over that Carl was gone and that everything was going to be okay. That only infuriated him even more. He was convinced that Carl was a demon who needed to be slaughtered.

He picked up tables and smashed them through the walls. The soil from houseplants scattered across the entire house. He grabbed every last dish he could get his hands on from the cupboards, throwing them at us and screaming with the superior rage of an untamed beast. He put his head through walls and ripped the doors off of their hinges, leaving every room turned upside down and inside out.

Remembering that his powerful love for D and I had been the trigger in calming the last storm, I told everyone to leave and insisted that we needed to be the ones to handle it.

Lynn was the most resistant, not wanting to leave her boyfriend in a situation where all of our lives were in danger. She did her best to control him, jumping on his back, wrapping her legs around his torso, and putting him into a choke hold. He lashed around with super-human strength, whipping her from side to side and finally body-slamming her into the ground! She cried out in great pain as Sage grabbed her and dragged her out of the house, realizing that D and I were his last hope.

With everyone now out of the house, D and I both wrapped our arms around Zeik, bear-hugging him and forcing him to the ground into another restraint.

We showered him with love, telling him how much he meant to us and that everything was okay. To the best of our sober abilities, we embraced the mind state that dominated him and tried to explain the situation in a way that made sense to him in that state. We professed that the demons were gone and he was now safe. He started to come back.

I felt his unfathomable pain and sincere confusion as his persona changed yet again into the Zeik we knew. He laid on the floor weeping, succumbing to the power of his uncontrollable, dictating thoughts. We held him in relief and consoled him the best we could. For a few moments, everything seemed like it was going to be alright.

Only moments later, Zeik raised his head and looked around frantically. Without warning, he escaped our embrace and began rushing around looking for something.

D calmly asked, "Zeik ... What's up man? What are you looking for?"

"WHERE THE FUCK'S MY TWENTY-TWO?!" he furiously demanded.

I prayed to God he didn't know what he was talking about.

We followed close behind him, trying to keep control of the situation.

Zeik dropped to his knees and rummaged around, grabbing something out from under a bed. It was his grandfather's hunting rifle! Blocking the only way in and out of the room, he stood dominantly in front of the doorway. I quickly scanned the room. D was standing to my left, about six feet away from me, a look of pure dread painted across his face. I felt helpless, wanting to run to him, but not wanting to make any sudden movements to set Zeik off.

With a blood-curdling grin, Zeik looked me dead in the eye.

I met the Devil that night, for there was no soul in the depths of the eyes I stared back into. It was just blackness; cold-hearted evil. I crouched down submissively as he aimed the barrel of the rifle at my face, standing a mere five feet away from me.

Slowly and sadistically, he maliciously recited these words as though it were some kind of game: "Eenie ... meenie ... miney ... moe," and he pointed the gun back and forth from my head to D's.

On *moe* he stopped at me.

"Bye bye," he spoke with the placid voice of a deranged psychopath, as he cocked the gun preparing to pull the trigger.

I stared at him in shock, having absolutely no capacity to process any thoughts. I hoped his soul would connect with mine and bring him back.

Before I had time to even comprehend the severity of what was happening, D jumped onto Zeik in one swift move, deterring the gun from being pointed toward me. Zeik fired the gun. I'm not sure exactly what happened next because it all happened so fast, but by the end of the struggle Zeik was unconscious. D dragged him outside and laid him on the front yard, demanding that I run home as fast as I could.

Adrenaline taking over my body, I started up the street as the sounds of sirens nearby approached. I turned back to see D climbing up onto the roof of the house so that he could inconspicuously make sure that Zeik was taken into good hands by the police where he could be properly cared for.

****

The next morning, Zeik came down to Kayne's. He appeared to be back to his normal self, although was very quiet and seemed very traumatized. He had no recollection as to what happened, but informed us that he had spent the night in the drunk tank. His trip must have come to an abrupt end when he was knocked unconscious, and fortunately for him, the cops thought it was just a case of extreme intoxication by alcohol.

I thought about not telling him what had happened, but I saw in his eyes that he was really struggling with unfinished pieces to a complicated puzzle in his mind. I debriefed him on the events of the night before. He broke down in shame, guilt, and self-hatred. I couldn't bear to see him in such pain, so I buried my traumatic memories in order to assure him that everything was okay.

Lynn swore that there was no way that rifle was loaded, being the defensive and loyal girlfriend that she was, but we know what we experienced that night. The post traumatic stress eventually seeped in and I couldn't so much as have a fake gun pointed at me without falling into anxiety-ridden flash-backs.

But here's the thing, in that instant when that gun was pointed at my head, it was like time stood still. There was no *life-flashing-before-my-eyes* moment. It was only paralyzing fear. Even when realizing that dreary night could have been the end for me if it weren't for D, my life didn't change. I didn't stray one increment from the life I was living. In fact, it excited me – I felt more invincible than ever.

CHAPTER ELEVEN

The Surrender

"Courage is resistance to fear, mastery of fear, not absence of fear."
– Mark Twain

"I'm turning myself in."

I never thought I'd hear those words come from the mouth of the stubborn fool I loved so much.

"I can't live like this anymore," D continued. "You're right, I don't want to hide my whole life. It's not fair to you. I love you and I want to build a life and a family with you, and that's never going to happen if I keep running. I have to just get it done with. When I was hiding on that roof waiting for the cops to show up for Zeik, all I kept thinking was, *what if they find me? What if they think this was my fault? Who knows how much more time I'll face?* But I couldn't leave him there. That was one of the worst moments of my life. Do you know why?"

Still baffled by his statement and trying to determine whether he was being serious or not, a blank look painted my face.

"Because I never got the chance to ask you if you would wait for me. I would never make it in there without knowing I'd be coming home to you one day."

Only he could turn a crisis into a romance.

Butterflies flapped vigorously throughout my stomach, my heart feeling so full with the intensity of his statement. I'd tried to convince him time after time that turning himself in was the right thing to do (because it was), but now that it was real, I wanted to eat my words. I couldn't possibly bear to go through my days without him, but in understanding how difficult a decision it was for him to make, I swallowed my pride, and with that, my uncertainty.

"Of course I'll wait for you," I smiled as the scorching acidity of tears built up in my eyes.

We held each other like we'd never let go and wiped each other's tears as we cried in each other's arms. When the emotions simmered down and the moment of acceptance was over, he put his gentle, warm hands firmly on the sides of my face and held his forehead to mine. Looking into my eyes, lips softly planted onto mine, he whispered, "I have to go now."

"What? Now?!"

My head was spinning! It was all happening too fast!

"You can't just fucking spring this on me all at once D!"

More tears filled his eyes, and I saw his heart breaking just as mine was.

"Sash, I'm so sorry baby. This shit's just eating at me! I've been thinking about it for weeks, trying to avoid it, but it's driving me crazy! I have to go and get it done with! The sooner I do, the sooner we will be together again."

He always knew just what to say. No matter how terrified I was of not knowing what was going to happen, I understood exactly how he felt. I knew he was right.

He promised me he would call me every chance he got and write me every single day. He asked me to take care of his belongings and gave me all the money and weed he had. Anxiously, he sat down and smoked bong after bong, trying to get as high as he possibly could to avoid the reality of what was about to happen.

He emptied his pockets, making sure he had nothing else to incriminate him, and no property to be lost during his incarceration.

Ready to say his goodbyes, he appeared to be a little confused when I grabbed my shoes and purse.

"Where are you going?"

"I'm coming with you. You're not doing this alone."

He smiled from ear to ear, firmly embracing me in a passionate kiss.

With his arm around me, we walked more slowly than ever before to that station, trying to savor each of our last seconds together – not having a clue as to how long it would be before we would see each other again.

My stomach in knots, nauseous in the sickliest way, we stood in front of the police station and introvertedly said our prayers. After a few moments, hand in hand, we walked through the front doors.

"How can I help you?" asked the police woman behind the glass.

"My name is D Manson. I have warrants out for my arrest and I'm here to turn myself in."

She searched his file on the computer, wrote something on a piece of paper, and then routinely stated, "Please have a seat. An officer will be out to arrest you shortly."

As D turned back around, I saw the overwhelming emotion within him. There was no turning back. He paced the room back and forth, barely making eye contact with me, palms sweating and knees shaking. As the minutes went by, his agitation grew stronger.

"Is someone fucking coming or what?" he demanded to the woman behind the glass.

"We're busy today, please be patient," she responded, not even looking up from her computer.

"Are you fucking kidding me?! A criminal comes to turn himself in and you tell him to sit and wait?! What a fucking joke this system is! You realize nothing is stopping me from leaving right now, right? Then I bet you'll have your men on me in a fucking heartbeat wont you?!"

He was losing it.

"Sir, I need you to calm down," she blatantly stated, almost robotically.

I tried to calm him down by hugging him and whispering, "Shhhh, relax baby, it's okay. Come sit with me a minute, chill out," but there was no calming him. I had never seen him like this.

Just then, the door leading into the back of the department swung open, and a large, stern-looking policeman appeared.

"D Manson?"

"That's me."

The officer cuffed his hands behind his back as he placed him under arrest and read him his rights. It was so surreal. There I was losing the only sense of love I had felt in as long as I could remember. I tried to show strength, but I could not stop the tears from falling or the pain from escaping my voice as I told him I loved him.

"Please let me kiss her good-bye," D pleaded with the officer when it was time to take him away.

"Five seconds," he responded flatly.

I wrapped my arms around his neck and squeezed him with every ounce of might within me, kissing him hard and assuring him that I would be there every step of the way.

And just like that, he was gone.

Tears clouded my vision, turning everything around me into one big blur. Somehow, I found the door to exit. The instant that door closed behind me, I broke down, sobbing and crying harder than ever before. My heart was completely shattered.

When would I get to see him again? How long until I would hear from him and know what was going on? When would his trial be held? What would his sentence be? What would I do to pass the time?

The old feelings of loneliness I knew so well devoured me. I was back to being on my own.

The hours slowly passed and turned into days that seemed to never end, until at last, I received the call.

"Hello," began an automated voice, "an inmate at PTG Correctional Facility by the name of D Manson is attempting to contact you. Please press one to accept the call."

I pressed one.

"D?!"

"Hey sweetie ..." spoke a weak and insecure voice I barely recognized.

"I miss you so much! Are you okay? What's going on?"

I had so many questions, but before I could get everything off my chest, he cut me off.

"I can't talk long. I only have a couple of minutes on here. They're looking for eighteen months ..."

I couldn't help it. I cracked. The strength I held onto suddenly was gone and I began to ball uncontrollably. Eighteen months was a really long time for a couple of teenage kids. It was longer than we'd even been together.

"My trial is on Monday. I really hope I see you there ..."

"I'll be there D, you know I will."

"I have to go babe. I'm so sorry for all of this ... I love you."

Again, just like that, I was alone once more.

Monday rolled around and I made sure I was dressed my very best. I stepped way out of my comfort zone and put on some nice dress pants and a cute blouse. If the judge saw that he had a nice, respectful girlfriend, maybe they wouldn't think he was such a low life and be a little easier on him.

I got to the courthouse half an hour before it was open to the public. As soon as they unlocked the doors, I sat in that courtroom without so much as leaving for a smoke or to use the bathroom. Hours passed and still he had not been dealt with. It was nearing the end of the day when finally I heard those magic words.

"Next case. Please bring out Defendant D Manson."

Hand-cuffed and escorted by a police officer, he was led into the *penalty box* where the accused are contained while the trial is in order.

There he was, only twenty feet away from me, yet so far from my reach. The pain of having someone you love so dearly right there in front of you, and being denied the ability to talk to them or hold them, not knowing when you will see them again, is a torture I do not wish upon anyone.

We locked eyes and mouthed, "I love you," and "I miss you" back and forth to each other, like we were the only two people in the room.

"Communication with the Defendant is not permitted. Mr. Manson, please keep your eyes toward me," the judge commanded with a zero-tolerance attitude and instructed the counsel to proceed.

I couldn't believe it.

How inhumane can you be?

I sat in silence staring at him, my face soaked in tears. The only thing worse than being kept away from him was knowing that he had to return to a cold, lonely jail cell where only God knows what would happen. It tore me apart.

After some deliberation, the judge ordered a remand, which meant that there was no resolution being made that day. The case was adjourned to a couple of weeks later.

As the police officer unlocked the box to escort him back to his holding cell, D glanced up at me for a fraction of a second with pure sorrow in his eyes. Then, he was gone.

I returned promptly to the remanded trial a few weeks later, hoping that the information they gathered over that time would lead to his release. Instead, I was in for quite the surprise.

The process occurred in the same manner it did the time before. Only this time, during the speech his lawyer gave defending him, some new and unknown information was disclosed. The lawyer said, "Mr. Manson plans to return to work full time upon his release in a construction job that is waiting for him at that time. He plans on being a productive member of society in order to provide for the child that he and his girlfriend are expecting."

I gasped. *What the fuck?!*

Everyone in the courtroom turned to look at me. I felt my face go flush, hoping they would not ask me whether I was actually pregnant, because I hated lying and was incredibly horrible at it.

The lawyer continued, "We ask that you take this information into consideration while making your decision. Mr. Manson sees this as his opportunity to focus on something good and make a powerful transformation in his life."

He was sentenced to three months.

Three months at that time seemed like forever.

The hearing ended and the courtroom began to clear out. I sat there choked, lost in a whirlwind of thought – devastated that it would be three long months before I got to see D again, and afraid of the potential consequences of him lying in a court of law.

I began to collect my belongings when a woman I had never met before, but immediately recognized as D's mother, approached me confrontationally.

"Are you guys seriously having a baby?!" She was furious.

I just stared at her blankly, taken aback, pondering how to respond. I couldn't sell him out, but I didn't want to lie to this woman either.

As if I were on autopilot, my loyalty to D took precedence and I felt myself slowly nod.

"You've got to be fucking kidding me," she hissed as she stormed away.

Completely beside myself, naturally, I wanted my mom for the first time in forever. She tried to be supportive and agreed to give me staying with her another shot, but of course, that didn't last very long.

I threw a party in her house that got completely out of control – people came from everywhere to be there. With loud music blaring into the quiet night, and dozens of people getting high on the rooftop, it was bound to get busted.

Come the end of the night the house was totally trashed, five cruisers showed up and Kayne was arrested when he defended a chaotic disturbance that I was involved in outside.

My mom was not happy about it. I blew my shot at redemption.

I couch surfed for a little while, bouncing around from place to place, feeling like a lost soul wandering around in search of herself. I tried to keep myself busy to make the time go by faster and spent most of my nights getting intoxicated trying to drown out the pain, but that only made it worse.

D wrote me a couple letters and called me a few times in the beginning, but as time went by, there were fewer and fewer attempts to contact me. He said he didn't want me to visit him during his incarceration because it was too much to put on me, even though I wanted nothing more than to be able to see him, no matter the circumstances.

After a few weeks, he insisted that I go on with my life without him and we could reconnect upon his release. I begged him not to say that, that I wanted to be with him no matter the circumstance, but he was adamant.

How can you just cut someone off that you love? He must've never loved me at all.

My thoughts snowballed until I convinced myself that he would be released and move on with someone else, so I began to detach myself from him all together.

Weeks went by and I had zero contact with D. I slipped into depression that I knew so well. The only thing that kept me sane was knowing that he had to see me again, because I had all of his belongings. No matter how many people I surrounded myself with, there was a gaping void that could not be filled. I stopped going to class and thought about dropping out, but something within me wouldn't allow me to do so.

I was losing control of myself, and fast. The first indication of my loss of self was the first time I tagged along in a robbery. I mean, I had gone car hopping with the Dot kids here and there, and I stole during odd times from stores – but that was more a rebellious teenage delinquent thing. I was arrested when I was fifteen for stealing from a Wal-Mart, and the embarrassment of being dragged out in handcuffs was enough to make me not want to do that again!

This time was different. I connected more with other angry people – people who felt alone in the world and believed that anything was theirs to take since the world didn't ever help them. Most of the conversation that took place in my life was of judgement and hatred of others. I didn't realize it at the time, but it was because I envied happy people.

Why did all of these people have families and people to love and take care of them, when I had done nothing to deserve being abandoned and unloved?

One morning at school I was hanging out with some new friends. They were like a little gang, all from impoverished circumstances and all hustled in whatever way possible to get by – usually jumping and robbing people (the first time I hung out with them outside of school, I witnessed them lure in an ecstasy dealer, beat the shit out of him and rob him for hundreds of pills). They weren't an actual labelled gang, but their morals and ethics reflected that of a typical street gang.

I liked being part of something so powerful.

"Yo, that kid Ken had a couple ounces of weed on him eh?" Dre, one of them started up this particular morning. "Dude thinks he can come around here and start choppin? Little punk. Let's see what he's got."

I still don't know why exactly I wanted to be a part of it. Maybe to feel powerful. Maybe to release some anger. I really don't know for sure.

We conspired to wait until lunch and ask him to buy some weed. Spliff, a big girl that looked like a dude and could knock most dudes out, would restrain him while Dre would take his backpack, and the rest of us would strip him down, search all his pockets, and take everything he had.

That's exactly what we did.

I'll never forget the look of fear and sadness he wore as we left him on the ground in the forest. He didn't come back to school for quite a while, and when he did, he was no longer selling.

I didn't like the person I was becoming. I went into the office and asked to speak with the Vice Principal (VP). I told her a little bit about what was going on – that I was having a really hard time with life and had no support from my parents. Breaking down into tears, I explained that I was really struggling to find a reason to not give up on myself completely. By the grace of God, she took me under her wing and paid me the special attention I desperately sought.

First thing in the mornings I would go to each of my classes to collect my workload for the day, then spend my school hours sitting in the VP's office working at my own pace. She allowed me to come and go as I pleased, giving me the freedom to make the choice for myself. If she saw me start to show weakness, she would talk me through what was going on and help me to push through.

Until this very moment – I never recognized just how much her great act of kindness impacted me. She even went as far as to acquire a key to the gym for me so that I could work out whenever I needed to blow off steam. Some days I would sit in the gym all day long, splitting my time between working out and doing homework, only leaving for the duration of classes that were in there.

More and more frequently during lunch hour, a very handsome and sweet boy by the name of Sly would come into the gym to get in a workout on his break. He had these huge brown eyes with the longest, thickest eyelashes you've ever seen on a male, and an enormous smile and quirky laugh that could make anyone see light on their darkest day. Sometimes it would be only the two of us in there, so we became relatively comfortable in each other's presence.

From time to time I would catch him watching me while I worked out, glancing at me through the mirror and shyly looking away when I noticed. It was never in a creepy or demeaning way. In fact, it was the complete opposite. The way he looked at me was like no other guy had ever looked at me before – like he was truly in fascination of me for all the right reasons. He was one of those people whose emotion you could read so clearly through their eyes, and the more intensely he looked at me, the more uplifted and empowered I felt. It wasn't long before we started making small talk, which led to joking around and having fun together. He made me feel like a little kid again, always teasing me innocently and playing jokes on me.

Our bond grew stronger, and we formed an incredible friendship. As our connection grew, he gathered that I was in pain and started asking deep questions about my life. When I would share even small increments of what I was dealing with, the sadness exposed in his eyes gave me comfort because I knew he genuinely cared. I fell in love with him for that – and for many other reasons.

I finally looked forward to waking up in the mornings and going to school just so I could see him. Every time I laid eyes on him I got butterflies and couldn't help but to smile any time he was around. I know he felt the same because the moment he'd spot me his eyes lit up like the sun, he would stop whatever he was doing and come to wherever I was just to be in my presence.

This is what love is supposed to feel like!

He knew about my messed up relationship with D, and did not want to cross any line that would confuse me or hurt me in any way, so he never tried to pursue anything beyond my friendship, but everyone knew he was totally in awe of me.

I opened up to the possibility that I needed a healthier relationship – hell, I needed a reason to get through my days – and moving on from D was the right choice. After contemplating for quite some time, I decided to ask Sly to hang out after school one Friday. I wrote him a note on a small piece of paper because I was too much of a chicken shit to ask him in person.

The note read something like:

Hey Sly,

I think you can tell that I really like you …

I'm just wondering if you wanna maybe hang out sometime? I'm free this weekend …

Text me if you do :)

Sash

All day long I anticipated how to smoothly give him the note without seeming awkward, and wondered what his reaction would be. I'd never done something like this before, and the fear of rejection ate away at me.

What if I was reading the signs wrong? Maybe he just enjoys our friendship? How awkward will it be between us if I tell him how I feel and the feeling isn't mutual?

But what I felt for him was so undeniably amazing that I couldn't risk not knowing if he felt the same.

At the end of the day as we stood behind the school waiting for our buses, I waited for the right moment to do it. All of our friends were standing with us, and I just wanted to give it to him in private. Then my chance slipped away:

"K peace out guys! Gotta go catch my bus," Sly declared as he high-fived everyone and proceeded toward the front of the school where his bus picked him up.

I watched in slow motion as he walked further and further away.

It's now or never! Just do it!

Something took over me as I ran after him yelling his name. He stopped as soon as he heard me and turned around smiling happily to see why I was chasing him. I cheekily ran right up to him, handed him the note, turned around and ran away. A few seconds later I heard him yell after me, trying to hold back his laughter.

"Sash!"

Embarrassed and vulnerable, I turned to face him.

"Wanna hang out tonight?"

"Yeah," I hollered back with a playful smirk across my face.

"Alright," he was smiling even harder, "I'll call you when I get home."

Sure enough, I was barely in the door when I heard my phone ringing. I picked it up right away.

"So you like me huh?" asked a flirtatious voice on the other end.

"Hahahaha," I laughed, "like you didn't know."

"I like you too. A lot."

My heart just fluttered, skipping beat after beat. I'd become such a dominant person, and yet here was this guy making me submissive like a giddy little school girl.

He picked me up about an hour later. We spent most of the weekend together, and he asked me to be his girlfriend. Instantly I thought of D and felt resistance toward Sly. Then I reminded myself that D was the one who had broken it off with me, and of all the chaos he caused in my life.

I told Sly I'd give it a shot.

Over the next few weeks, we did everything together. We loved being with each other so much that we spent almost all of our time – at school and afterwards – together. With his support and unconditional love, I became well enough mentally to return to class.

Everyone told me how much they admired what we shared together. He walked me to all of my classes and kissed me goodbye. At the end of my classes, he would be waiting for me and insisted on carrying my books. He piggybacked me through the halls and complimented my beauty no matter how large the crowd. He was so proud that I was his. He'd play for me on his guitar, serenading me to sleep when my anxiety got the worst of me. At parties, he would dance me around and sing to me, and made sure I was always having fun. If I had too much to drink, he would take care of me – hydrating me with water and making sure to bring me somewhere safe to sleep, never leaving my side for a moment. He brought out a sensitive side of me – but I wasn't sure I wanted to be that nice girl anymore.

As incredible as he was to me, a distrusting, damaged and insecure demon resided within the cage of my soul.

CHAPTER TWELVE

Deeper into the Rabbit Hole

"It's not the bruises on the body that hurt. It is the wounds of the heart and the scars on the mind."

– Aisha Mirza

Jaxon and I were like brother and sister. We always had each other's backs and I loved him to death, but I could not stand the way he treated women. He was always on and off with different girls – usually my friends. One of those girls was little Fay from the Dot. She was such a beautiful soul, that girl. We became very close, likely since I was the only female she could trust to talk to about her problems with my cousin. Maybe my being there for her is what compelled her to help me.

Fay knew that I had been bouncing around from place to place and invited me to come live with her, her mother, and brother. They treated me like part of their family. Her mom prepared meals every night that I was welcome to join in on, and I even had my very own room. Fay became like a sister to me.

One evening we were hanging out at home (secretly smoking some bongs in Fay's room) when we heard a knock at the front door.

"Shit!" Fay scrambled around putting away all of the paraphernalia and spraying air freshener around her room. No one ever knocked at the front door ...

She ran to answer it, and after a few seconds summoned me to come out.

I walked into the living room, and emerging from behind her was none other than D.

How the hell did he find me?

I didn't know he was even being released!

"I'll leave you two alone ..." whispered Fay as she glared at me with wide eyes of shock and a look of discomfort. She went into her room and closed the door behind her.

Time stood still. I stared blankly at him, not knowing whether to hug him or hit him. So much love, hate, happiness, anger, bitterness, joy, pain, fear ... confusion.

"I'm back," he penetrated the moment with his snarky remark.

"I see that ..."

He slowly approached me with open arms. I backed away.

"What is it?" he asked, not understanding my hesitation.

My eyes swelled in tears. I was not expecting this and had no idea how to handle it. No matter what I did, someone would end up hurt.

"Aaaaaah ... I get it," D said acceptingly, knowing me so profoundly that he could read me in an instant. "Who is it?"

"Sly."

"Really?" he began to taunt me. "Sly? Damn baby I thought you wanted a man? He's a little punk!"

"Fuck you! You left me high and dry and just cut me out like it was nothing! This is what you wanted wasn't it?! At least I found someone who loves me and takes care of me! You think you can just come back and claim me like a fucking possession?"

"I told you to find someone to take care of you while I was in and that we would be together when I was released. I'm back now. You. Are. Mine."

That manipulative act of possessiveness appeared in my eyes and my heart as passionate and powerful love. I was reminded of our soul-binding connection and was torn between what was right for me. The love Sly had for me was so foreign, almost uncomfortable to think about, and the love that D and I shared was what I knew love to be – an unstable rollercoaster of intense passion and rock bottom sadness.

We yelled back and forth at each other for hours. I expressed every raw emotion I had about his abandonment and betrayal. When he forcefully wrapped his arms around me in a powerful embrace to comfort my despair, I felt myself melt into him and all of my problems disappear. What I see now as pure control, I saw then as true love.

"I can't do this," I resisted. "I love Sly. He makes me happy."

"He doesn't love you like I love you, Sasha. No one does and no one ever will."

Just then the phone rang. D grabbed it, looking at the call display.

"This is him, ain't it?"

"D, don't. I'm not ready for this!"

Against my plea, he answered the phone: "Yo bro what's good!?"

I heard Sly's voice lower and felt his energy weaken. I wept even harder. I knew what was about to happen.

"Thanks for taking care of my girl, but I'm out now. She belongs to me."

"Let me talk to her," demanded Sly as his voice cracked.

D handed me the phone.

"Tell him," he commanded me.

I took the phone and cried as I could not find any words. I was under his complete power and I didn't even see it.

"I'm so sorry ..." I cried softly into the phone, and Sly hung up.

D looked at me in satisfaction and took me firmly into his arms.

"I'm here now and I'll never leave you again. I promise."

His promise gave me absolute comfort and a strong sense of security; I trusted him with my life. Being reunited put all my worries to rest because I believed I was safe and that he would always take care of me. We fell in love all over again, and I buried the feelings I had for Sly.

D was released early on house arrest. He got a job with a family friend and was living with an elderly lady that his mother knew, who agreed to be his assurity and house him throughout his terms of probation. I stayed there with him most of the time, as we became inseparable and co-dependent once again after being away from each other so long.

Of course, he did not follow his house arrest for very long.

Within a few days, we were out running the streets, developing that Bonnie & Clyde mentality – *catch me if you can!* I was caught up in the adventurous love we shared, being fuelled once again by rushes of adrenaline rather than by logic. He lost his job shortly after his release and went back to making money the best way he knew how – hustling. This time, it was more than just weed and cocaine.

He expanded his supply to a larger variety to appeal to a greater market. Now in the mix were different types of pharmaceuticals like perks, Xanax, morphine and oxies. It wasn't long before he started dabbling in them himself, assuring me that he just needed to test his product.

I guess I'd become too accustomed to being around users, because it didn't bother me as much as it had in the past. I didn't want to cause another rift between us, so I chose to not challenge his decision and allow him to be free.

New Year's Eve rolled around.

D, Faye, and I celebrated just the three of us. Late into the night, D pulled out some blow and two containers that he kept all of his pills in. Each container had seven little compartments, labelled Sunday through Saturday. He opened them up and I saw that each compartment held a different type of pill, a mixture of uppers and downers.

He thought it would be fun to snort "rainbow-coloured lines" in celebration of the new year. Faye enjoyed doing coke so the two of them took turns sniffing whatever was on the table. It was around then I decided to go to bed; I wasn't into that, and didn't really want to see the effects it would have on him.

When I woke up in the morning, they were still awake – flying higher than birds, laughing and yelling, appearing to be on top of the world. They both seemed to be in good spirits, and I was well rested, so we decided to head back to Faye's so we could shower and change, then we'd find some other parties to hit up later that day.

Upon arriving at Faye's, we all went into her room to smoke some bongs before we showered up and got ready.

As Faye and I sat on her bed joking around with each other, I noticed D's attention toward the bedroom door, making kissing noises with his lips and rubbing his fingers together like he was summoning an animal.

"Heeeeere kitty kitty," he said sweetly.

We did not have any cats…

Faye burst into laughter, "Holy shit D, how high are you? You're trippin' out man!"

"I think I need to lay down," he slurred in response, although it sounded more like, "Ah link a needa lah dun."

I immediately grabbed him and helped him to stand, leading him out of Faye's room, across the hall into mine. He could barely walk. His feet would not take proper steps, like he was a baby trying to learn how for the first time. He fell repeatedly, bumping into walls every step he took.

"Is he okay?" Faye asked me, concerned, "he mixed a lot of shit all night."

"Yeah, I'm sure he's fine. Give us about an hour so he can sleep it off," and I closed the door behind me.

No sooner than he collapsed into my bed, I saw his eyes start to roll back into his head. His skin was white as snow, and dark shadows encompassed his eyes.

"No cops," he mumbled. I had no idea what he was talking about.

I ran to get him some water, and as I re-entered the room, he began to convulse uncontrollably, soap-like liquid foaming from his mouth. He was overdosing!

That's why he said no cops!

He knew what was happening and knew that if I called the cops he would be thrown back in jail. He made it very clear to me upon his release that he would rather die than end up back in the system.

On the inside I was screaming, adrenaline raging through my entire body, petrified beyond any fear I'd ever had! I wanted to call an ambulance, but I was too loyal to him to go against his orders.

Think, think, think! What the hell do I do?!

I knew my freaking out would not help the situation – I had to remain focused! I turned him on his side to allow the foam to pour out of his mouth so he would not choke on it. Uneducated at the time about how to handle seizures, I tried to restrain him to prevent any further injury. He was lashing around violently and uncontrollably, thrashing into the walls and headboard with every jolt; I just wanted to protect him.

Then, all at once, he stopped dead.

Literally.

He went limp and showed no signs of responsiveness. His skin was gray. I checked for a pulse ... nothing. Heartbeat ... nothing. Breath ... nothing!

A bone-chilling, blood-curdling scream escaped from my mouth: "FAYE!"

She raced through the door as I hovered over top of him, giving him CPR the best I remembered in the craziness of what was happening. I couldn't concentrate long enough to hold count of my pumps, so I breathed into his mouth every time I felt he was ready, praying with every ounce of faith within me.

Please God, don't take him from me! Please be with me!

It was no use.

"Call an ambulance!" I screamed to Faye.

No sooner than those words had escaped my mouth did he choke up some fluid and catch his breath. He was breathing!

I tried to communicate with him but he was non-responsive – body weak and limp. However, he was snoring, which indicated that he was taking in oxygen, and had a steady pulse. I sat beside him all evening and late into the night, keeping my hand lightly rested on his chest in order to monitor his heartbeat.

Sometime early in the morning, he regained consciousness.

He looked at me in embarrassment and shame.

I grabbed him and squeezed him as tightly as I could. He gathered what strength he had to comfort me.

"Thank you, God," I muttered.

"Sash, don't overreact ..." Suddenly there was a tone in his voice that told me he knew exactly what happened, but didn't want me to be further traumatized, "I remember everything. It wasn't what you thought. Chill out. I'm okay ..."

"D, you fucking died! I know it sounds crazy, but I brought you back to life!"

"Don't be such a drama queen," he said like it was supposed to reassure me of something.

I think he knew I had already suffered symptoms of PTSD and didn't want to be the reason for any more of my pain, but I remembered every moment crystal clear; one more memory to add to my list of *suppressed, unresolved emotions, to come back and haunt me.*

CHAPTER THIRTEEN

Coming Undone

"You are free to choose, but you are not free from the consequences of your choice."

— Ezra Taft Benson

This time around, we were going to do things right ... or at least better than before. After the near-death encounters and being ripped away from each other for so long, D and I wanted to lay low for a while.

He promised me no more hard drugs. It was all about the two of us from there-on-out. That didn't last long either.

Weeks had passed since I had been to school. I was on cloud nine with D being free – I didn't want to miss a moment. We hadn't left each other's side since he showed up on my doorstep.

D recognized what was happening and told me that I needed to go back to school and graduate – that I wasn't going to fuck up my life on his account.

"You're so intelligent," he would tell me, "don't you want to get married and have kids and have a nice life together? You need to focus on yourself so that we have our best shot at those things."

I knew he was right.

Going back to school was the easy part. Knowing that I had to face Sly was what tore me apart.

I was ecstatic to see everyone. I had isolated myself in a little bubble with D since he returned, and it was nice to be surrounded by friendly faces who cared about what I was going through.

As tradition went, when lunch approached, we all went out to the Greens, catching up in clouds of smoke, sharing in contagious laughter. The bliss of the moment ended when I saw Sly walking toward us.

"What's up gangstas!?" He announced cheerfully, trying to pretend like he didn't see me. Everyone greeted him and went back to their conversations.

He attempted to hide the sadness in his heart as he playfully nudged me and said, "Welcome back, loser. We missed you."

What a relief!

My anxiety dissipated. My heartbeat eased. What an incredible person he was to treat me kindly after what I had done to him. Talk about guilt trip! Nonetheless, everything seemed back to normal. I could finally breathe again!

I went to all of my classes and made it clear to my teachers that I was determined to catch up on all my work. Unfortunately, because I had been absent so much of the semester due to all of my mental health issues, and had technically informally dropped out, there was only so much they could do to help me. I would be one credit short of graduating with my class.

They said I could still attend the ceremony and accept my diploma, but it would not be legitimate until I completed that credit. I decided not to go. I did attend prom, with Sage as my date. D refused to go since he didn't exactly fit into such a formal event.

The school year ended and the security I had living with Faye came to an end as well. She found out she was expecting Jaxon's baby and would need my room for a nursery.

D and I found a cute little house on the outskirts of the next town over that we rented out with a couple I knew from school, James and Starr. Things were perfect for the first little while. I got to fall asleep in the arms of my favorite person, and to wake up each morning excited for a new day, having no obligation to go to school – or be anywhere for that matter.

We finally had nothing to fear. Nothing could go wrong. The next couple of months were filled with innocent playfulness, endless laughter, spontaneous date nights and adventures, and pure, unconditional love.

Keeping true to his word, D steered clear of the harder drugs, and diversified his inventory for his weed customers instead with options like hash and oil. We spent every day producing them in our living room. Other than the house smelling of butane and chemicals all the time, I loved the processes. Cooking the substances was a new hobby we indulged in together. He was so smart, so focused, so creative, and resourceful in his methods, and I admired his multitude of knowledge and skills.

We were making good money, smoking good shit, worrying about nothing and living present in every single moment.

Of course, nothing lasts forever.

Starr and James split up, and we collectively decided to move. Since we already spent much of our time at Nicks, he invited D and I to stay with him until we figured out what we were going to do.

Nick lived with his grandparents, Dave and Agnus, in a desolate area in an old log-cabin style house surrounded by forest. It was beautiful and serene. They tried to help us in whatever ways they could and made us feel welcome and at home. They provided us with blankets and pillows, toiletries and anything else we needed. They even invited us to eat the meals they prepared.

D and I set up a blow-up mattress upstairs in the loft, just off of Nick's room. Dave and Agnus's room was on the other side of the stairwell. We had no door for privacy, but who were we to complain?

The only downfall to being there: Nick loved drugs. He loved getting high out of his mind – mushrooms, pills, cocaine … it didn't matter. He created a persona like he was a big shot who had no limits. He lived his life like it was something out of a rap video. He used drugs and money as a way to get females to like him … only he was too naïve to realize that they didn't actually like him, they were using him. D admired his attitude toward life: making stacks of money and blowing it like it was nothing, not giving a shit what anyone thought about him. The two of them together became an issue. As soon as we were officially living under Nick's roof, things went downhill fast.

Nick wasn't shy about doing his drugs. He was a very open recreational user, and since we were living in his house, there wasn't much I could say about it. At one point not so long before, I would refuse to be anywhere around hard drugs, but constantly being around users and addicts caused me to grow more comfortable around them.

Nick offered lines to D, and out of respect for me, D always declined the never-ending offers. But Nick was tenacious, and D was weak when it came to avoiding bad decisions.

"You're so fuckin pussy whipped man," Nick finally unleashed one night. "That's why I stay solo, don't need no bitch telling me what to do."

"Don't call her a bitch man," D defended me.

"I didn't mean *her* bro!" he said apologetically, "She knows I love her, right babe?"

Sometimes I couldn't stand him.

He continued ... "I just mean I wanna do my own thing, and not have to answer to anyone, you know? Free like a bird!"

He had this snarky little annoying laugh that was nauseating sometimes. Life was a complete joke to him.

Nick was a great friend in the grand scheme of things, but he was not the best influence. He wanted everyone to live life according to his terms and exist in some fantasy world all the time. He was very lonely, and deep down he envied the relationship that D and I had. He projected his insecurities onto us and began using petty attempts to try and sabotage us. He eventually got under D's skin, and D started to dabble in oxies and blow with him. He justified it by telling me that I knew his lifestyle when I got with him and I needed to respect the choices he made – that I wasn't his mother and had no right to tell him what to do. He insisted that I worried way too much – that it really wasn't a big deal and nothing bad would come of it.

I felt so betrayed, like he cared more about what Nick thought of him than about his promises to me. My sorrow turned to anger, and I decided to get back at him and show him what it felt like.

Nick teased me now and again, asking me if I wanted a little line. I always told him where to go, so you can imagine the surprise when I changed my mind.

"What is that? Oxy or blow?" I asked him one night, pointing at a tray of white powder on his table.

"Why do you ask princess, you want some?" he joked.

"Yeah, I do."

"Real fuckin funny," D remarked.

"I'm not joking."

He looked so angry that I thought he was going to hit me.

"What are you doing? Trying to get back at me or something? Don't be fucking stupid Sasha."

"Oh what? You can do whatever the fuck you want and then turn around and be a hypocrite?"

He could tell I was serious. The regret in his face said it all. He knew that I was impulsive and had a history of being self-destructive.

"Bust me a rail."

"Okay!" Nick was always humored by our fights. I swore he got off on watching me challenge D's control tactics. "That's what I'm talkin' about! Let's have some fun baby!"

D watched silently, vibrating with hostility as I grabbed a rolled-up bill from Nick and sniffed the small line of oxy he busted for me.

I was satisfied in knowing I got under D's skin the same way he did mine. Karma's a bitch, right?

I sat there for the rest of the night in la la land, my body light like I was floating on clouds. I could hear the words that were being spoken around me, but was completely oblivious to what was going on. I eventually nodded off and passed out on Nick's futon. D called it a night and carried me to bed.

Late into the night, I awoke to D breathing down my neck, kissing me softly and sliding my pants off slowly. I tiredly smiled and let out a sigh of pleasure.

"Be quiet, you," he teased as he pushed himself inside of me.

I tried my best to remain quiet, but faint moans escaped. He covered my mouth with his hand and held me down firmly to keep me silent. Out of the corner of my eye, I saw a dark figure in the stairwell, but with a second glimpse, it was gone. I brushed it off as nothing and we continued having very passionate, but very quiet sex.

Just as we finished, I noticed the silhouette of Nick's grandfather peering at us from the stairway. The stairs creaked as he slowly backed down them.

I told myself I was overthinking it all – that he probably just got up to use the bathroom and happened to glance over as he passed with no bad intention, and awkwardly tried to pretend he didn't see anything. After all, he was like a grandfather to us.

· I didn't say anything to D because I knew he wouldn't take it lightly and I didn't want to stir the pot.

The next morning was extremely unpleasant. I noticed that Dave was looking at me differently than before. He has this sort of predatorial look I'd never noticed, almost as if he saw me in a way he never had before.

Before I had time to analyze the situation thoroughly, Nick had gone up to his room and D hopped into the shower. Agnus was also gone, presumably for her nap she usually took around that time, and I was left alone in awkward silence with Dave in the living room.

He leaned forward in his seat and remarked: "We just love having you here Sash. Anything you need, just ask, okay?"

"Thanks Dave," I said kindly. "I appreciate that."

"D is such a lucky guy to have such a sweet and beautiful girl like you."

A certain tone in his statement made me cringe. I knew I didn't like where this conversation was headed. Out of respect for the (now) deceased, I will not quote the words he said next, as I do not accurately remember the exact wording that was used. He said something to the effect of envying D based on what D had told him about our sex life.

I was speechless. I could not see D sharing such detail with an old man, however we were both very open about our sex life, so I wasn't sure what to think.

Regardless, I was a minor, and that type of explicitness was totally unacceptable.

A few nights later, I got up in the middle of the night to use the washroom that was downstairs. I crept down the creaky stairs and quietly closed the bathroom door to not wake anyone. A few moments later, the door burst open and Dave observantly glared at me sitting on the toilet for a few seconds before anxiously apologizing and closing the door behind him.

As I exited the restroom, I saw his silhouette sitting on the couch in the darkness of the room.

"I'm sorry, Sash," he tried to sound genuine. "I didn't know anyone was in there."

Yeah right. I thought. *It's 3am. The bathroom light is on and the door's shut. Even an idiot would know it was occupied ...*

I ignored my gut instinct and told myself that I was overreacting. However, I became a little more cautious of him.

From that point on, I made as minimal contact with Dave as possible. I told D it was time to get serious about looking for a place of our own, and did whatever I could to ensure we spent as much time as possible away from Nick's house. Living in that house caused enough grief in my life, and I wasn't willing to allow it to cause more.

CHAPTER FOURTEEN

Miracle

*"For God commands the angels over you to
guard you in all your ways."*

– Psalm 91:11

"His name is Keiran."

"Who? What are you talking about," I asked D, having absolutely no idea what he was talking about when he randomly stated this fact.

"My dad. His name is Keiran. He lives a couple of hours away. My mom gave me his information and I got a hold of him. He offered me to come stay with him and hook me up with a job … get to know him n shit …" I could tell he wasn't sure how to feel about that.

"Wow baby, that's so amazing! I'm so happy for you!" I tried to be supportive. I mean I really was happy for him but the selfish part of me wanted him all to myself. He needed to make that connection to make sense of his life and figure himself out, but I couldn't help but to wonder where that left me.

"So … what does this mean for us?" I didn't want to know the answer.

"I know I just got out and it's so hard being away from each other, but I need this Sash. I don't know who the fuck I am. I'm gunna go out there and work, save every penny I make, and get us a place of our own." He looked at me lovingly waiting for my approval.

I'd just gotten him back, *again,* how could I just let him leave again? Every second that he was away was torture. I went through every day as a zombie, like an empty vessel of nothingness.

The thought of being alone again made me start to cry.

"I'm sorry sweetie. I know the timing is shit, but this could be the start of something good for us. Get us the fuck away from this shithole …" He held me close to his chest, running his fingers through my hair.

"I'm nothing without you," he continued as he used his index finger and thumb to guide my chin upward to face him, "I love you more than anything. We were made for each other, you know that right? Nothing will ever keep us apart. I am yours and you are mine."

That weekend, Nick drove him out to his dads with all of his belongings. Just as every time he'd left before, a piece of me went with him.

Nothing will ever keep us apart. Those words rang over and over in my mind, keeping me sane in the midst of all of the self-destructive thoughts that devoured me.

We talked every single day, and he kept me updated on every interaction he had with his father. He told me how cool Keiran was, and how alike they were. He rode a Harley, smoked a lot of weed, and was a truck driver for a living. He also said he was very intelligent and that they'd had some pretty intense conversations. It sounded like they were really bonding.

Without any warning or asking my approval, D sent Nick to pick me up to come visit him one weekend. That's kind of how our relationship was – he called the shots and I did as he told me. I didn't mind because he aimed to make me happy in almost everything he did. I found a sense of security being able to put my life in his hands and always be taken care of (to the very low standards I had).

After a two-hour drive, we pulled up to an old ratty building alongside a large stretch of highway. Transport trucks filled the unmaintained, loosely-gravelled parking lot. It was eerily quiet. There was not a soul in sight … until D came out smiling ear to ear, almost as thrilled as I was to see him. We raced to each other's arms, and he spun me around as we locked our lips together.

I was home.

Home was wherever he was.

He led me inside and down a long, jail-looking corridor that had metal doors lining each side of the hall. We went up to the second floor, and he unlocked one of the doors about halfway down the hall. Behind the door was a tiny room that consisted only of a bed, a dresser with a TV and DVD player on top, an end table that held an alarm clock, and a mini fridge.

"I really need to pee! Where's the washroom?" I asked, confused. There was no other door other than the main one to get in.

"It's up the hall," he said with a smirk.

"Huh …?"

"It's a rooming house for truckers Sash. We have shared washrooms."

Great! I thought. *Oh well, at least we're together!*

We spent the entire weekend laying in bed watching movies and having lots of sex, which was basically all there was to do.

We didn't have much to eat since we were in the middle of nowhere with no vehicle and no place around for miles, so Keiran would have us over for dinner when he got off work in the evenings. He lived just downstairs in an actual apartment that had a bathroom and kitchen.

I wasn't sure what to think of him – he kind of creeped me out! He had a ritual of shaving his entire body head to toe every morning, and had a glow in the dark tattoo of satan's face on the back of his skin head.

Sunday came quickly, and D begged me to stay. He worked all day throughout the week, so I'd be there alone, but to me it was worth being able to fall asleep in his arms each night. So I stayed.

I didn't bring enough clothes to last the week, so I wore his. He brought me home dinner every night, as well as extra food to last me the next day. I used my free time to write songs and poetry, which was always a therapeutic outlet for me. It kind of felt like a nice little vacation where I could unwind and have nobody to please but myself.

The week dragged on and Friday rolled back around. D told me that Keiran was going away for the weekend on a bike trip, and had left the keys to his old-school 1990 Range Rover, which basically looked like a box on wheels. D convinced me that his dad let him take it out a few times, so he wouldn't mind if we went out for a drive to get something to eat.

D didn't have a license, but his dad didn't seem like he was a by-the-books kind of guy anyways. I usually tried to be a good influence on him, but I was always down for a little risky adventure. Still, something in my gut told me it was a bad idea.

"There's a strawberry field a few miles up the highway. You need some food in you, so let's go! Don't be a pussy on me now," he joked as he tickled me to loosen me up.

He was right, I was famished.

"Fine," I agreed. "Straight there and straight back."

"Deal!"

He ran downstairs to grab the keys and met me outside. He demanded that I sit in the back in case we got pulled over so I could easily hide under the seat.

I got into the back seat of the old tin-box looking truck, and D instructed me to put on my seatbelt. I did as I was told.

"Good girl." He leaned over the back seat to kiss me in approval for not challenging him.

"Shut up asshole," I teased. "Put yours on too."

"Don't you worry your pretty little face about me baby."

And we were off. All I could think about was how delicious and fulfilling those strawberries were going to be! I was beyond hungry.

We drove for about fifteen minutes or so when, without warning, he made a last minute sharp left turn onto an old dirt road that lined a huge hill into the forest.

"What are you doing?" I asked mischievously.

"Having some fun!" He looked back at me with a devilish look of wonder.

He fish-tailed the truck from side to side, peeling up the dusty road behind us. I always loved off roading, but the last time he took me drifting was in the middle of the winter and we slid on black ice and missed a pole by only inches!

"Hold on!" He yelled enthusiastically. I clenched the back of the passenger seat as we drifted from side to side up the winding road. As we reached the peak of the hill, he turned the wheel hard to clear the sharp bend ahead.

The tires lost traction! D fought to regain control of the vehicle as we smashed into a tree! The force of the impact sent us barrelling into a larger tree. In a swift motion, the truck flipped over! I extended my arms to hold the roof in order to brace myself from the impact as we rolled over and over down the steep wooded hill. My focus was on D, who wasn't wearing a seatbelt. He was thrown all around as we bounced and flipped, smashing his face off the wheel and head off the roof repeatedly. My peripheral vision caught glimpses of the world going sideways and upside down outside of my broken window.

Alas, the truck came to an abrupt stop. The trees were upside down beside me. Horror-stricken, D turned to face me.

"Sasha! Are you okay?!"

"I'm fine," I replied in utter shock. "Are you okay?"

"Stay there! Don't move! I'm coming to get you!"

He struggled to exit through his window and ran around the truck to help me out. Gently, he pulled me out of the window, holding me close and checking me for wounds. To both of our surprise, I had merely a few scratches from being pulled through the broken glass in the window frame.

D had tears pouring down his face: "I'm so sorry Sash! Holy fuck! You could have been killed! I'm so, so, so sorry!"

"I'm okay D, really. Are you?"

He assured me that he was fine but I could tell he was in a lot of pain. His nose was bleeding and he was full of cuts and bruises.

We stood there blankly looking at the mangled truck. It was upside down and the roof was completely caved in. It was a miracle that we weren't crushed.

"I'm so fucked. My dad is going to kill me."

"D, I'm sure he'll just be happy that you're okay!"

"No. You don't understand. He will literally murder me ..."

I stood there terrified, running through every possible scenario in my head and unable to come up with any reassuring solution. I knew he was doing the same. Moments passed as we stared back and forth from the wreckage to each other.

I broke the silence, "Where are we?"

"It's a long walk back. It'll give me some time to figure out what the fuck to do." He looked down at my feet, "Where are your shoes?"

"I don't know..." I said, only just then realizing I was barefoot.

He looked in the truck to see if he could find my shoes, but it was no use. There was no way to get back in. How we even got out was mind-boggling.

"Holy shit..." he suddenly gasped. "Look..."

I walked to the other side of the wreckage and almost threw up. A large boulder is what had caused the truck to stop rolling. On the other side of that boulder was approximately fifteen feet between it and a thirty-foot drop off a cliff to the highway!

Thank you, God! Thank you, thank you, thank you!

That was the second time I stared death in the face and escaped. Still, nothing in me changed, and subconsciously I became even more invincible.

We trekked down the highway, barefoot and battered up. A short-ways up the road, a car pulled over to see if we were okay. D explained to the man what happened, and he suggested that we return to the scene, remove the key and replace it to where we got it from, and set it up as though it were hotwired and stolen.

At first it seemed like a good idea. We went back and the man followed us down to the truck. He was in more shock than we were.

"Holy fuck!" he said wide eyed. "You two are seriously lucky to be alive! Someone must be watching over you!"

D decided that he owed his dad the truth. He needed to own up and take responsibility for what he'd done.

The man drove us back to the complex and wished us luck.

D first called the police to turn himself in, then called his dad to apologize (hoping the police would get there first). As we sat in the blistering heat waiting for the situation to be dealt with, D told me that he would be thrown back in jail and that I needed to call Nick to come get me immediately. He made it very clear that it was not a safe place for me to be alone.

When the police arrived, they separated us to get each side of the story. D instructed me to tell them the truth, so I did. I told them I was just as much to blame as he was since I knew we shouldn't have taken the truck and that he didn't have a license. The officer scribbled down some notes, and then spoke in private with the officers who had interviewed D. I assumed we would both be arrested and charged for theft.

One of the officers cuffed D and put him in the back of the cruiser. Another approached me and told me I was off the hook.

"What are you talking about?," I wasn't letting him take the wrap. "I'm just as guilty as he is!"

"Well then he must really love you because he made it firm that he is taking sole responsibility. Let this be your lesson."

"Can I please have a minute with him?" I pleaded.

"No," he replied sternly.

They all returned to their cars and drove off, taking D with them.

I dropped to my knees on the ground, crying hysterically. He was gone again! And I was stuck in the middle of nowhere with no phone, no money, and no clue of what the hell to do!

I returned to D's room and collapsed into his bed completely distraught. All of a sudden, I heard a knock at the door. I quietly tiptoed over to the door and looked out the peephole. It was a man named Rick. I met him earlier in the week when he came up to lend D and I a few movies to watch. He was a trucker who also stayed there. He was probably in his late thirties or early forties, and seemed friendly.

I opened the door.

"I saw what happened … you wanna talk?" He pulled out a joint and handed it to me.

"What's there to say?" I remarked coldly as I lit the joint. As cool as he might have seemed, I wasn't about to trust a random guy to know that I was alone and stranded without any form of communication with anyone.

"Are you alright?" He seemed sincere.

"I'll be fine. My dad is coming to get me first thing in the morning," I lied.

"Well I totally get if you're not comfortable with this but I'm going to a club meet tonight a few towns over. It's just in a Tim Horton's parking lot – lots of people. You're welcome to join me if you don't want to be stuck here all alone with a bunch of weird old men."

I remembered Rick telling D about his prized possession – his Camaro. He was part of a car club, which consisted of a bunch of other people who also had Camaros, and they would meet up weekly with other car clubs to compare and admire each other's cars and the customizations they had done to them.

I hesitated to answer. I was stuck between a rock and a hard place. Which was the lesser of two dangers? Going on a trip late at night with some guy I barely knew or being stuck in a building with twenty other men who knew I was alone in there?

"Sure," I decided.

A couple of hours later we met up and headed off to the meet. We drove for about an hour through long, dark roads that had no street lights or signs anywhere. If anything happened, I had no idea where the hell I was, and surely there was no place to run or hide. Fear began to set in and the severity of the whole situation became clear.

Just as I started planning my escape, there it was! Tim Horton's!

Hallelujah!

Rick really did his best to cheer me up. He bought me something to eat (although I couldn't stomach it), smoked me up, and hooked me up with cigarettes to keep me sane. He tried to distract me by introducing me to everyone and showing me some beautiful exotic and expensive cars. But it was no use. My mind would not stop racing.

He could tell that I had lost interest after about an hour, and selflessly offered to take me back. He returned me safely and I thanked him for being so compassionate.

I threw on some of D's pajamas and snuck out to the bathroom to brush my teeth. As I approached the bathroom door, out came an old, fat, hairy man with a dirty, smoke-stained, untrimmed beard and faded tattoos, wearing nothing but underwear. He walked past me with no shame.

I locked myself in the bathroom and began to cry once again.

When I could no longer hear anyone in the corridor, I ran back to the room and locked the door behind me. I stayed awake all night, heartbroken and petrified, cringing every time I heard footsteps outside the door. When the sun began to rise, I felt safe enough to drift off.

I awoke a few hours later to the sound of a motorcycle. I looked out the window, and sure enough, it was Keiran. He looked absolutely livid!

Some time later, I heard someone walking down the hall toward my room. The footsteps stopped outside my door and a little piece of paper slid underneath it.

I waited until the footsteps walked away, then picked up the note. It read:

Come down for dinner at 5. We need to talk. -Keiran.

As instructed, I went down to his apartment at five. I owed him that much ...

He opened the door and without a word, summoned me to come in. There was a movie playing on his projector, so I sat down and watched it. He fixed me a plate of food, and when I was finished, he started to speak:

"What the fuck were you two thinking?

His demeanor was intimidating.

"I don't know ..." I replied quietly, unable to look him in the eye.

"He could have killed you!"

Then a long, awkward silence where those words should have seeped into my thick skull ... but did not.

"I'll take you home in the morning. Be ready for eleven. Don't worry about D's stuff, I'll have it sent to his mother."

"Thank you," I whispered, and I looked up at him for the first time since I got there. I was beyond happy to be going back home, wherever that was ...

Disgust and disappointment radiated from him as he looked back at me.

"Go. Get some sleep."

The next morning I rode the most awkward two and a half hours pressed against his back as I clung on for dear life on the back of his bike. He dropped me off and said goodbye by telling me that I deserved someone better – that D would only fuck up my life even more if I stayed with him.

Defensive and loyal as I was to D, I reminded Keiran that maybe D would have had a better shot at becoming a man if he grew up with his father in his life.

"Probably not," he said. And I never saw him again.

I escaped death for the second time, but was too blind sighted to realize just what that meant in the grander scheme of things. How was it that I made it out of what should have been a fatal crash without so much as a bruise? Was there a reason my life had been spared on more than one occasion? At the time, I believed it to be a result of good luck. But I see now that it was because my time was not yet over – my purpose here on Earth had not yet been served.

CHAPTER FIFTEEN

Crack Fiend

"Addiction doesn't kill the addict, it kills the family, kids, and people who tried to help."

– Abhishek Tiwari

This is the part of my life where I'd exhausted most of my resources. I was nearly eighteen and had bounced around from place to place for three years. I was tired of ending up homeless, wondering whether I'd be able to find somewhere to sleep at night. I was very fortunate to have had plenty of friends to turn to, but I couldn't help but feel like I was nothing but a burden. I had not taken responsibility for myself because I was still angry at my parents for leaving me to fend for myself. The truth is, I felt sorry for myself.

With D back in jail, I realized that the only way I was going to survive was to get a job to support myself. So I did what I had to do. And it was about damn time.

I started working at a local buffet as a hostess. It was my second real job aside from babysitting (my first one at McDonald's lasted a whole three months before I was fired for skipping work to attend that triple kegger where I first saw D – foreshadowing at it's finest).

It wasn't the best job, but I was given enough shifts to keep myself from starving and provide a roof over my head. This time I was much more dedicated. I knew I needed an income if I wanted to eat. I was tired of depending on other people to make sure I had food. It had gotten to the point where when offered something, I would decline, and say that I wasn't hungry. I had grown so used to eating very minimal in a day that my body was constantly weak and shaky. My stomach didn't even grumble anymore because my body was so used to starving. I felt sick most of the time but the weed and alcohol helped to numb it.

I know, I know. How the hell could I afford to be drunk and high all the time, but could not afford to eat? Well, all we did was party. Whoever had the bottles and weed shared amongst everyone, so I felt no way about indulging. Sometimes I would rob bottles from liquor stores so that I could contribute once in a while too. Somehow, I made it work.

D made Nick promise to take care of me while he was locked up – which meant making sure I was safe on the outside. Their word to each other was their bond.

Nick had a customer named Chad who was forty-two and had two beautiful daughters named Destiny and Hope, who were two and three years old. They lived in a decent sized (although run-down) house that he wasn't able to maintain, so Nick suggested that I move in as a live-in nanny. Chad was all for it.

The only downfall … he was a crack addict and alcoholic.

I agreed to stay there because I saw two amazing little girls who had a fall-down father and no mother in their lives. The only purpose I had in my life had been helping others to never experience the pain I endured. They needed a role model – someone to influence them in a better way and keep them from the insanity of their environment. I was far from perfect, but I knew I could be a better influence to them than what they had.

I fell in love with them, and they with me.

My days consisted of working at the buffet and then coming home to make dinner, catch up on housework, entertain the girls, then bath them and get them to bed. On my days off, I spent my free time with the girls, doing my best to stimulate them the ways that they needed to be at that stage in their development.

Meals were supposed to be provided for my services, but Chad never had any food in the house. I spent any extra money I had on food for me and the girls, and on activities to keep them away from the house as much as possible.

I learned very quickly that the house was merely a place for Chad and his buddies to party and get high. They sat in the backyard from morning until night every single day getting messed up, disturbing the neighbors and causing chaos. The guys who hung out there, who were much older than I was, would gawk at me and make comments to Chad as I passed by. They made no effort to hide their remarks:

"Who's the little hottie?"

"Damn bro, that your new girl or something?"

"Where can I get me one of those?"

…only some of the things I would hear them say.

I would just strut on by paying no mind to them, acting as if I didn't even notice them sitting there. Eventually, the indirect comments became more direct. They would holler at me and hit on me whenever I came around, some of them even tried to make moves on me.

To any normal young girl, that would be uncomfortable, maybe even threatening, but I can admit now that I enjoyed the attention. It made me feel recognized. The only form of affection I had in my life was locked away rotting in a jail cell, and only provided me a glimpse of hope each time I received one of his letters in the mail.

D wrote me love notes and drew me pictures every single day. At the end of the week, he sent them out in a bundle, and I would return every single one. I'd stay up late each night writing to him about my days or how I was feeling or how much I missed him. I also sent him a number of provocative photos of myself, at his request, to ensure he wouldn't lose interest in me.

Even with all of the exchanging of letters, I was still very much alone in the world. Not knowing how to properly deal with my emotions, I sought approval from the wrong people in the wrong kinds of ways. I'd been conditioned to think that having men want you, and fight for your time and attention made you worth something, even if you had no interest in them. I genuinely believed that if men were not attracted to you, you were worthless. My mind had been programmed as such.

As much as I enjoyed the attention Chad and his friends paid me, I had no intention of ever being with any of those men in any way, shape, or form. Yet, it gave me power to know that I could have them wrapped around my finger the way I did; they did anything I asked and gave me whatever I wanted.

But the façade wore off when I opened my eyes to the extreme lengths they were willing to go. Their petty remarks became harassment, and their interests in me became obsessions.

I awoke in the middle of a hot summer night to rocks being thrown into my broken window. I peered out to see a shirtless, tattooed man – maybe thirty years old, drunkenly trying to balance on one knee holding flowers in the air yelling at me:

"Where art thou my princess?"

What the fuck...

I closed the curtain and went back to bed as his voice echoed into the silent night.

It sounds silly, sure. However, I was young and defenseless, in an unlocked house with not so much as a door for my room. I'd be lying if I said I wasn't a little scared of how far he might take it … people are unpredictable when they're drunk and high on crack.

Then there was Ronnie. Ronnie was a coke fiend who thought he was God's gift to women. He would hit on me right in front of his pregnant girlfriend, asking me to dance with him or sit on his lap, always trying to get one up on the other guys. Naturally, it would start a war between him and his girlfriend, one which I did not like being a part of.

But the worst of them all was a man named Dan. Dan was an attractive guy. He was smart and well-mannered, and often very quiet. I never really understood why he hung out with the rest of the crowd. I kind of liked when he gave me special attention, but I did not reciprocate the affection. As lonely and lost as I was, I loved D, and I was committed to waiting for his release.

One evening after I put the girls to bed, I went downstairs to make some food when Chad called for me to come smoke a joint and watch a movie (I tried to take time here and there to hang out with him to stay on his good side, which was sometimes difficult because he was a ticking time bomb, as most addicts are). I went into the living room, where he, his girlfriend Lidia, and Dan were sitting. We smoked a joint and harmlessly hung out together, enjoying a nice relaxing end to another busy day.

I got so into the movie that I didn't realize Chad and Lidia had passed out.

Suddenly, I felt a set of strong hands begin to massage my shoulders. It was Dan. Unsure of how to handle the situation, I stood up and told him he should probably go home since Chad was sleeping, and that I had to go get some sleep for work in the morning.

I went upstairs to my room, which had only a blanket hanging from the frame as a door, and got into bed, which was a small, dirty, piss-stained mattress that laid on the floor with no box spring or sheets.

A few minutes passed when I got a strange feeling that someone was watching me, and turned over to check out my surroundings in hopes it was just paranoia as usual.

A man's silhouette contrasted against the light in the hallway was peeking in through the blanket in my doorway.

"What the fuck are you doing Dan?"

"What are *you* doing?" he replied, in a low and seductive tone.

"Going to sleep ... can you please leave?"

"Is there any room for me in there?" He was persistent.

"No. Now get the fuck out of here before I call for Chad."

"Holy, you don't have to be such a little bitch," he said angrily before he closed the blanket-door and left.

But he did not give up.

Over the next few weeks, he came around almost every day. When he knew I was alone in the house, he'd come inside and try to be affectionate with me by grabbing my hand softly or sneaking up behind me and massaging my neck. One afternoon he cornered me in the kitchen trying to kiss me. Chad caught on to what was happening and could see that I wasn't okay with it. He told Dan he should stay away and try to find a girl his own age: thirty-two – almost twice my age.

Chad became very protective of me. He developed a strong appreciation (at least temporarily) for my taking such good care of his girls and his home. He would playfully flirt with me or compliment me from time to time, but it was always in fun. However, he saw how aggressive and invasive his friends became in trying to pursue me, and told them to back off or they wouldn't be welcome anymore (not so nicely, of course). Nobody wanted to mess with him because, as I failed to see at the time, he was a psychopath.

Days passed and Dan still hadn't been back. We didn't put the pieces together when the phone would ring from time to time, and as soon as Chad would answer, the person on the other line would hang up. Until the time that Chad was outside playing with the girls and I answered the phone when it rang:

"Yeah?"

"Saaashaaa," said a low and seductive voice.

"...Dan?"

"Mmm. You sound so sexy. What's up sugar?"

"Chad is busy right now, I'll get him to call you back."

I didn't want to give him any sign of interest.

"I'm not calling for Chad," he continued in an eerie, wanna-be-phone-sex-operator voice.

"Okay? Who are you looking for?" *Please don't say me you fucking creep.*

"What are you doin' tonight?"

"Dan. What do you want? I'm not trying to be rude but this needs to stop."

"I'm lonely over here. Why don't you let me pay for you to cab over and we can snuggle and watch a movie or something?"

He spoke like he was beating himself off on the other end of the line. It was disturbing on so many levels.

"Dan. I have a boyfriend. Just stop, k? I'm not interested."

"Oh yeah? Haven't seen him around …I want you so bad baby…"

I hung up the phone.

I told Chad about the call. He immediately stormed inside in fury, picked up the phone and dialed a number, then started screaming into the phone.

"Stay the fuck away from her you sick fuck! She's a little girl! And stay the fuck away from here too!" He slammed the phone down and came back outside, wrapping his arms around me and apologized for putting me in such a horrible position.

"I'm so sorry my angel! Don't you worry! That fucking scum bag will stay far away from here if he knows what's good for him! You tell me if he ever bothers you again! Fuckin piece of shit…" He rambled on and on in a tantrum and he stormed back outside.

I felt safe.

The novelty of the attention from all those men wore off, and I realized it wasn't serving me in any way. It was dangerous to entice such wild beasts.

From that point on, Chad became extremely protective of me. He would snap on any guy he saw look twice at me, declaring that I was his adopted daughter and he was done with them treating me like an object. Lidia didn't seem too fond of the special attention he was giving me.

I grew closer with Chad, and with Destiny and Hope. They became my family. I bonded with the girls so deeply that people often asked me if they were my children when I took them out.

One evening I was tucking them in and reading them their bed-time stories, when Hope (the younger of the two), looked at me with a twinkle in her eyes and said, "Are you my mommy?"

It took everything in me to not burst into tears. The pain I felt for them was tormenting. The abandonment and confusion brought me back to the childhood I buried in the past, and I knew in that moment that whatever my response was would affect them in ways I couldn't begin to fathom.

"No, honey, I'm not. But I love you both very much and I am always here for you, okay?" I spoke softly and looked back and forth from Hope to Destiny as I told them I loved them. Then I sang their poor little souls to sleep.

As sure as a tree grows from the earth, the good would end and my life would crash down beneath me yet again.

Chad had started showing his true colors. Every other day he was on a rampage because he was losing control of things. He owed everybody money and was struggling to get his fixes of dope. I did my best to help keep him sane, and to keep the girls away from him while he figured his shit out. Trying to balance all that plus keep a clean house with the amount of traffic he had in and out of there was nearly impossible.

He reached his breaking point and cried on my shoulder about how he wanted to get clean and get his life together for his kids. I helped him to map out a plan and told him I would take care of the girls in the meantime. The very next morning I woke up to the smell of burning rubber throughout the house. I knew exactly what that was.

I ran down the stairs and saw Chad leaning over the kitchen sink smoking a hit of crack.

"What the fuck are you doing?! The girls are in the house!"

I was infuriated! Despite him being an addict, he never put the girls at risk like that before. I retrieved the girls and kept them away so he could think about what he was doing.

We returned later that night, and I put them straight to bed. I went downstairs to confront Chad. He was standing in the kitchen with Lidia. I could tell they were both as high as kites.

"Thank you, my angel. Thank you for protecting my babies when I was weak." He hugged me and kissed my forehead as he cried real tears.

I felt so sorry for him. I watched many people suffer with addiction and knew how destructive it was. He really wasn't a bad guy. He had good intentions, but he was a lost soul, caught in a cycle of fear and no self-control.

The crowd that hung around changed from a group of wild party animals, to a group of gang members, whose identity I will not mention for my own safety. I'm still unsure of what Chad's ties were to the gang, but I figured he must've been doing some work for them to fuel his drug habit.

I got off work late one evening, and the girls were already in bed. I brought Chad back a container of food from the buffet as I usually did, hoping it would put him in a good mood, and more so, to make my life a little easier. I sat down at the kitchen table with him and another man who I knew was a part of said gang.

He was the scariest looking seventy-two-year-old you could dream into fabrication; three hundred pounds of lean muscle, with a long, dirty, wiry beard and beady eyes that had so evidently witnessed things I couldn't imagine. People called him *Little*.

The three of us sat at the kitchen table having a few drinks and casually talking about nothing in particular. Little started to shift his focus onto me, first complimenting me, and eventually asking me to go on a date with him to the drive in. I thought he was joking – I mean really, he was seventy-two! But I picked up on Chad's nervous energy.

"She's not going anywhere with you, Little," he said respectfully, throwing in a bit of a chuckle to lighten the way he was coming across to this man.

"Oh come on sweetie, I won't hurt you."

I laughed it off, again underestimating the intent of an old man.

I couldn't believe what I heard come out of his disgusting mouth. He went on to explain in detail, with no sign of shame, how he had raped and murdered countless young women, his own daughter being one of his rape victims.

This is the part where you're watching that predictable horror movie yelling, "RUN YOU IDIOT!" Nope, not this idiot. What was I supposed to do? Call the police on an ambassador of a well-known gang? I knew better than that!

I sat in terror listening to his dreadful stories, not wanting to run away and appear to be an easy target. I stayed seated beside the mass murderer until he was ready to leave. There was no way in hell I was going to trap myself in a room that had no escape, nor was I letting him out of my sight and endangering the babies upstairs.

I started conspiring a plan. I would find somewhere else to go, and when I was safely out of the house, I would call Child Protective Services (who had been called on Chad on multiple occasions and never had enough hard evidence to remove the girls) to have the children placed into a safer environment.

Not feeling safe anymore, I brought Macy over after work the next evening to keep me company. As we entered the front door, I heard the familiar sounds of some of the gang members who had been hanging around. I told Macy to go upstairs and wait for me while I checked out what was going on.

I walked into the kitchen where a crowd of rough-looking outlaws were sitting around the table. A huge pile of dishes were stacked on the counter. The kitchen was clean before I left for work earlier in the day, so I decided they could wait till the morning. It was already late and I had held true to my end of the bargain the whole time I was there, even when Chad did not.

I brought Chad his container of food from the Buffet, and he thanked me kindly for thinking of him.

"You two faced piece of shit!" Lidia yelled angrily at Chad.

What now you bat-shit crazy lunatic?

She went on, "You bitch all fucking day about how she does nothing, is a leech and should be paying you rent, and then she comes home and you're gunna kiss her little fucking ass cause she brings you food? I do everything for you and you still treat me like shit!"

I couldn't believe it! I had gone above and beyond for him and his children! There he was talking trash about me behind my back! I glared at him, furious and unappreciated.

"I didn't say that!" Chad defended himself.

"Are you fucking kidding me?!" She was so worked up that she was literally screeching! "You just finished saying how she hasn't washed these dishes in a week!"

I was vexed! "I do these fucking dishes every day, Chad! And buy the food! And do the laundry! And even pick up the empty fucking beer bottles that your friends leave laying around every day! What the fuck! You want me to do the dishes after working and taking care of your kids all day?! FINE! Move!"

I nudged my way aggressively in between him and Lidia, who were standing in front of the kitchen sink, and filled up the sink to do the dishes.

I was vibrating!

Standing on either side of me, they yelled back and forth at each other like crazy people. Chad was defending himself, denying the accusations Lidia was making.

"Why do you like her better than me!?" She screamed at the top of her lungs, crying and breathing heavily in what appeared to be the start of an anxiety attack.

In a sudden movement, she grabbed a dirty kitchen knife off the counter and held it inches away from my throat.

Chad tried to deter his crack addicted girlfriend who was wasted out of her mind.

"Lidia, baby! I love you! What are you talking about?"

He tried to console her as she stood there in tears, still threatening me with the knife.

Then he turned to me, "See what you did? Get the fuck out of here!"

I held back tears as I stormed up to my room. The moment I saw Macy, I broke into quiet sobs, making sure they didn't hear my weakness.

"What the hell am I supposed to do?" I asked her, my voice drowned out by the ongoing commotion downstairs.

I had nowhere to go.

"Let's get the fuck out of here!"

"I can't leave the girls here alone when everyone's fucked up like this!"

"Sash, you know he would never let anyone hurt those girls!"

She was right. They were his world. But I couldn't bring myself to do it.

Before I had a chance to answer her, she shushed me.

"Shhh! ... Listen ..."

I'd never seen her look afraid until that moment.

In their mental instability and raging, amplified emotions, drug addicts have a tendency of blowing things up to the ultimate extreme. That's precisely what happened. We eavesdropped as Chad, Lidia, and the gang bangers conspired to strip me down and hang me by a telephone wire by my ears amidst the overwhelming smell of crack smoke.

In that moment, I experienced my first real panic attack.

My heart hammered into my chest so rapidly that I was sure I was having a heart attack. The pressure in my head so intense it felt like it was going to explode, and ultimate fear paralyzed my body. Tears flooded down my face uncontrollably, and I stared blankly at Mazy, praying she had a solution.

This is it. They're going to kill me.

"We need to leave! Now! I'm getting you the fuck out of here! Don't worry about the girls, they're safe!"

Without hesitation, she grabbed my hand and rushed me out of the house. We ran as fast as we could and did not stop until we knew we were in the clear. With no place to go, we walked around aimlessly for hours, then returned to Chad's. Macy snuck in the front door to make sure it was safe to enter, then summoned for me to come in.

The house was empty, so I presumed they were out back. We snuck up to my room quickly, turned out the lights and crawled into my bed, hoping no one came to see if I'd returned.

It was a long, dreary, sleepless night.

The next day, Chad didn't seem to remember anything that happened and acted as though everything were normal. I did my best to act the same way.

I knew that D's time was almost fully served, so I decided to wait it out, having nowhere else to go. I went through the remainder of the time keeping to myself and making sure everything was taken care of. I did my best to stay on Chad's good side.

Finally, one sunny afternoon, I was inside preparing lunch for the girls when I heard some excitement between the guys outside. I didn't pay too much attention to it because they were always going on about one thing or another.

Then I heard D's voice.

"Where is she," I heard him ask.

"She's inside," Chad told him.

Before he made it to the door, I had already run through the house and out the door, jumping on him and bombarding him with a thousand kisses.

I wept tears of joy.

I was finally complete again.

CHAPTER SIXTEEN

What Lessons?

"Sometimes painful things can teach us lessons that we didn't think we needed to know."

– Amy Poehler

That summer was full of drama, and full of lessons – lessons that I blatantly disregarded. I *should* have learned not to seek approval from strange men. I *should* have learned not to trust people so openly without knowing their character. I *should* have learned not to place my fate in someone else's hands. And I *should* have learned to stop putting myself in positions that made me vulnerable to attack.

That summer marked a new era that didn't involve accepting any valuable lessons at all. It marked one more step toward a world of darkness.

Theoretically, when someone is exposed to crime for the first time, it is frightening and overwhelming. If the exposure continues, one adapts to the lifestyle, and it rapidly becomes normal. The longer that person remains witness to ongoing criminal behavior, the more likely he or she is to indulge in those same actions themselves.

It is one thing to come from a sheltered home and be taught about crime and the severity of the risks and consequences involved, and to then witness it with that awareness and see the truth in what you've been taught. But it is a completely different angle to grow up surrounded by criminal activity and be taught that it is bad without seeing what the alternative is. In that reality, an alternative is non-existent.

People are wired very differently and thus, react to things in different ways. Everyone has their own outlook, their own perception, their own beliefs – constructed by past experiences. Some people learn by watching other people make the mistakes. Some make one poor decision down a bad path, recognize it right away and stray from that road all together. For others – the hard-headed – it takes many mistakes and years of pain to finally take control. And the rest of us? We get so lost in a condition of suffering that we see no possibility of anything different. We lower our standards and settle for what we know to be real. We become a product of our environment.

Somewhere within the concoction of pride and denial, I did passively learn two very important lessons that summer.

The first thing I learned is to always trust your instincts! If somebody gives you an unsettling feeling in the pit of your stomach, do NOT give them the benefit of the doubt! Energies don't lie.

I wish I let that lesson penetrate my brain when I figured it out, but again, my hard-headedness has been the leading factor in my having to learn the same lessons multiple times. It is said that God, or the Universe (or however you choose to refer to the divine infinite power), will send us the same trials and tribulations until we consciously overcome them, and each time we fail the same test, it will come back more drastically each time until we pass it.

I didn't trust my intuition when it came to Kyler, Gage, or Chad. And even after those experiences, I still didn't trust it when it came to Nick's grandfather.

One gorgeous, sunny day just during that summer of trials and tribulations, I was visiting a friend when I received a call on my cell phone from Nick's house. I thought it was a little odd because Nick always called me from his cell phone.

"Yoooooo!"

"Hey Sash, sorry to bother you. This is actually Dave calling."

Weird ... in the past couple of years that I'd known him, he's never had a reason to call me.

"Oh ... hey Dave ... everything alright?"

"Oh yes. Everything is fine. Happy belated birthday! Eighteen, huh?"

"Thank you! Yep, the big one-eight ..."

"So Nick told me about D going back to jail. I've been a little worried about you. How are you doing sweetheart?"

"Oh. I'm doing okay. It's hard, but I'm surviving." I had a feeling he was calling for more than just a quick check-up.

"Listen. There's something I want to talk with you about. I think I might have a way that I can help you and D get back on your feet."

"What do you mean?" I was curious now.

"I can't really talk about it over the phone. But I may be able to help you ... financially. Are you free this afternoon? I can send a cab over to get you if you don't mind coming here and talking."

I figured he would have me start dealing some weed for him since he grew a ton of it. A few times D and I helped trim it and he paid us for our time. He and Agnus always tried to help us in whatever ways they could.

"Thanks Dave. That sounds great! I'll just call Nick and see if he can give me a lift over!"

"No!" he exclaimed with a rather nervous tonality. "Nick and Agnus are away for the evening. This has to stay between the two of us."

RED FLAG!

My intuition was screaming at me to decline his offer, but the devil inside needed to know what financial gains he was referring to. I was not in a position to pass up a good opportunity.

"Uhm ... okay. Sure. I'll call a cab and head over then."

"Okay dear. I'll see you shortly. Just run in and grab the money when you get here."

As I waited for my cab, my friend's mom came outside and asked where I was headed. I told her about the conversation and her reaction should have been my next red flag.

"Sash. My arm hair is standing up, look."

Sure enough, every single long, black hair on her arm was standing straight up. I'll never forget the disturbed look on her face.

"This has only ever happened one other time in my life," she said concerningly, "and it did not end well. Please. Don't go."

"Don't worry. I trust him. He's a bit weird but I know he would never hurt me." I'm not sure I entirely believed the words coming out of my own mouth.

She couldn't shake the feeling, "If you say so ... but something is really telling me not to let you go."

Just then the cab pulled up. I looked at her reassuringly and said I'd be back in an hour or two. She informed me that if I had not returned within two hours, she was sending police to his house. I told her that wouldn't be necessary.

As I arrived at the house, I saw that Dave was standing outside on the porch in a nice button-down collared t-shirt and some casual shorts. Barely saying hello, I ran over to grab the money to pay the cab driver.

Right away the vibe felt off. We talked outside for a few moments, breaking the ice in the weirdness of my being there without Nick. He invited me in and, as he typically did, asked if I wanted anything to eat or drink. We then proceeded to the living room and right away I knew something wasn't quite right. The lights were all off and the stillness within the empty house was almost sinister.

During the first ten or fifteen minutes, he rambled on about nothing as we smoked a joint. He was acting very peculiar. None of what he was saying made any sense and I had no clue as to where his point lied in any of it.

When the joint was finished, I excused myself to use the washroom, and when I returned, I observed that he had undone two of the buttons on his shirt.

He's probably just hot …

He started to tell me about different businesses he'd run throughout his life, and how much he loved helping people. He talked about how he and his wife had raised Nick as their own, and how they have always done everything in their power to give him the world. I got the impression that he was trying to sell himself in some way.

"Sash," he leaned forward, "I'd really like to help you. It must be so hard to go through life on your own, not having anyone there for support, and having your boyfriend locked away. It must be so lonely."

I started to tear up.

Why is he trying to break me down?

"If I told you I knew a way that I could help you make enough money to get you and D set up in a nice apartment when he is released, so that you have a full stomach every day, maybe a car if you want ... so that you wouldn't have to worry about going hungry ever again, would you be interested?"

I became very emotional, doing everything in my power to hold back the tears, but it was no use. I had so much bottled up. I felt so alone in the world and just needed a break to get me set up on the right track so that I could have a chance in life to find happiness.

"Of course I would be," I replied, full of so much gratitude for the mere fact that he acknowledged what I was going through and cared enough to want to help me. Doing some quick math in my head, I wondered how I would make that much money off selling his weed. He did grow a lot, but that paid for all of his expenses and for Nick's high-maintenance lifestyle as well.

In that instant, it was like he could read my mind.

"I could front you a couple pounds for a really good deal if you can turn it, and we'll see how that goes."

I'd have to crunch some numbers and see how it would all be possible, but I was just thankful for the help.

"Thank you so much, Dave. Really. You have no idea how much this means to me."

"But you probably won't make as much money off of that as you think."

I was so confused.

Where are you going with this? Didn't you just run a big game about an apartment and a car and not worrying about starving again?

"I have another idea that would make you much more money than that." He was uneasy about what he was saying, and I could tell that he was selecting his words very carefully.

The pieces started to fall together.

He changed the topic, recanting the history of his relationship with his wife – how things had been hard on them since she developed medical issues and how he felt the same loneliness that I did.

He was all over the place with his story, changing from topic to topic, and nothing flowing or having any predetermined point to it.

"You know, the first time I saw you, I knew you were an angel. You were just glowing – so beautiful, so full of life. You make everyone around you happy, you know that? You bring a certain joy wherever you go."

From that point forward, I knew exactly where he was aiming. I just wanted to see if he had the audacity, and the balls, to take it that far.

"That's so sweet," I smiled and played it off like I was clueless.

"I mean it. D is so lucky. And God, I love him, but he doesn't deserve you after all the things he's done."

Since I was a very young girl, I've been fascinated by deranged minds and how they work – maybe trying to bring myself closure in understanding the reasons all the men I'd been exposed to were so warped. I've studied tirelessly how predators manipulate their victims and different tactics they use to control someone. I saw right through what he was doing – breaking me down to a vulnerable state so that he could play hero and gain my trust in order for me to be coaxed more easily into whatever proposal he had in mind. I surveyed our interaction from a third-person point-of-view, anticipating each move and each tactic before it even came.

As much as I wanted to leave in that instant, I needed to know what his intentions were.

"What do you mean by that?"

"Well, it's no secret that the boy doesn't treat you the way you deserve. He's always running his mouth behind your back and lying to you."

"I'm not sure what you're talking about ..."

Even with the awareness that I had, part of me was slipping into his trap. He struck my weakness – D.

Were there things going on that I didn't know about?

"Well, you know, since he doesn't tell you everything, you have the right to not tell him everything."

His hand moved up his lap and rested in between his legs. He appeared to be getting a thrill out of the whole situation.

"I'll be right back, I need to use the washroom again." Things were getting to be very uncomfortable.

I went into the washroom and looked in the mirror, deep into my own eyes.

Get out of here. Find an excuse and get the fuck out.

When I returned to the living room, Dave's shirt was completely unbuttoned, and he was sitting slouched into the couch smoking another joint.

Uneasy about how to approach the situation, I casually stated that I had people waiting on me so I should probably call my cab. Pretending he didn't hear me, he changed the topic to something lighter and passed me the joint.

I questioned my intuition and persuaded myself that I could've just been paranoid from being so high, going over the conversation and trying to reason with myself. I fell lost into my own thoughts, no longer hearing the words that he was saying.

Then, catching the bizarreness of his words, my attention was reverted to him just as he said: "I mean, you and I could go upstairs right now for twenty minutes – hell, who am I kidding, I probably wouldn't last five – then you could come down, shower and leave with a pocket full of cash to go visit D and buy yourself something nice, and no one would ever even know."

Did he really just fucking say that? Please tell me that was not what it sounded like. I must've missed something there ...

I didn't know what to say or how to react. Here was this man who had been like a grandfather to me and D, asking me to have sex with him, and even worse, to PAY me like I was a damn prostitute! Not only that, but he was an old man and I was barely legal!

"Honey, we're both adults," he proceeded, "You're eighteen now. There's nothing wrong with two adults engaging in some consensual sex. I have needs and you need money, right? We could help each other out. You can give an old man the time of his life. I'll make sure you're well taken care of. What do you say?"

I spoke sternly and furiously, "First of all, I have a boyfriend, and second of all, I'm not a prostitute." I stood up to leave.

"I didn't mean to offend you! I wasn't implying that at all ... I just thought ..."

"No," I cut him off, "you didn't think. I'm leaving now, goodbye."

As I passed him to exit through the doorway, he reached up and grabbed my arm. I turned back and looked down on him sitting there on the couch, with absolute horror in his face.

"Please don't tell Nick."

I turned around and left, feeling proud that for the first time in my life, I stood up to a scumbag and took away the power he thought he had over me. With that, I took back the power I'd given away so many times before.

****

The second thing I learned that summer was to not take anyone you love for granted, because in a split second, everything can change. No one is promised tomorrow. We never know when it is our time, or the time of the people close to us.

Macy spent the summer working at a marina out in the middle of nowhere, where she boarded in a house with the other employees. She and Kayne invited me to come up one weekend and do some mushrooms. I called them as I was leaving to let them know I was on my way, and everything at that point was nothing short of normal. They were already pretty drunk off the Absinthe Nick brought out and they'd gotten into the mushrooms without me.

For your information, Absinthe plus Mushrooms is an obvious recipe for disaster.

After driving down never-ending winding roads through the woods, far away from any sign of civilization, we pulled up to a large, white house that sat on top of a small hill overlooking the water.

Right away I saw commotion out front of the house. I scanned the surroundings to try and figure out what was happening, and as I glanced upward, I noticed that a big, bay window three stories up was shattered.

What the hell happened?

Macy ran toward the cab in a high-speed wobble. She had blood all over her hands and clothes, and black makeup smeared all over her face.

"HELP!" She shrieked, "HELP! HELP! HE'S DYING! I DON'T KNOW WHAT TO DO!"

"Slow down!" I tried to remain calm as adrenaline pulsed through my veins. "What's going on Macy?"

"Kayne got way too fucked up off of the mushrooms and we got into a huge fight. He locked Nick out of my room while he was screaming at me, so Nick thought I was in danger and kicked in the door to defend me. Then he and Kayne got into a fight and Kayne ended up going through the window! It cut his throat really deep. They kept fighting through the house and the entire house is covered in blood. I'm going to get fired, and Kayne is laying right over there (she pointed to the top of the small hill near the house) bleeding out so fast and I don't know what to do! The ambulance is going to be another half an hour and he's losing so much blood I don't know if he's gunna make it that long!"

BAM! The information overload hit me at full impact! My mind raced a million miles a minute as I followed her to where Kayne was laying in the grass.

There he was, drenched in a river of blood. My heart shattered. *Please God be with him, I can't lose him! Please!*

"I'm so sorry," Nick was crying. "I didn't mean to … it was an accident." He stood there, his own arm sliced from the glass, pacing back and forth looking petrified.

I hadn't paid much attention in my first aid course, but I did know that it was in Kayne's best interest that I remain calm and not add any extra stress to the situation. Though anxiety and fear coursed through my entire body, I spoke to him softly and calmly, trying to play off that it wasn't a big deal.

"What the hell happened to you?" I tried to joke with him.

"Hi Sash," he chuckled, "I'm so glad to see you."

"I'm glad to see you too! But I wish it wasn't like this!" I tried to be comical. He was a sucker for witty humor.

He smiled and began to reply.

"Shhh ... Don't talk Kayne. You need to save your energy."

"I'm so scared." He looked deep into my eyes waiting for some reassurance that he would be okay. I was always the one running to him with my problems, and he was always the one helping me. I had to be strong and to put my emotions aside to be there for him this time.

Macy was still running around hysterically, not that I blamed her.

"Macy," I put my hands on her shoulders, "I know this is fucking terrifying, but you need to relax. He needs us to be calm babe. Why don't you go inside and breathe for a few minutes, I've got this, k?" She did as I suggested.

I sat beside Kayne, pressing a sweater against his sliced throat to slow down the bleeding until the paramedics arrived. I couldn't take my eyes off him. His eyes were blobs of blackness, and his skin was pale and cold. He was shivering on the warm summer night from having lost so much blood. I didn't know what to say to him, so I kept blabbering on just trying to keep him awake and focused on what I was saying.

Suddenly, his eyes started to roll back in his head.

"Sash ...I'm gunna die in 3...2...1" He closed his eyes and his body went limp.

"Kayne?" I cried, waiting for a response. "Kayne?"

"GOTCHYA!" He yelled, opening his eyes and laughed at me for believing that he was dead.

"You asshole! Why would you do that to me? I fucking hate you! This is not the time to play a joke like that on me!"

I didn't know whether to laugh or cry, in fact, I was doing a bit of both. Even as his time was ticking, it was in his DNA to be a smart ass and mess with me! As much as it almost gave me a heart attack having thought I just watched my best friend take his last breath, it made everything a little lighter – a little easier to handle. He was still … him.

He was shaking like crazy, and still trying to talk like the stubborn bugger he was. I took off my sweater and covered him up to maintain some of his body heat.

Alas, faint sirens grew louder and louder. Ambulances and police cars made their dramatic entrance. Paramedics jumped out and bolted over to us with a stretcher.

Thank you, God! Everything is going to be okay.

They strategically bandaged the wound and placed Kayne on a stretcher, ensuring that his head was held firmly in place. He screamed and resisted in a hallucination from the mushrooms, believing that they were trying to put him in a coffin and bury him alive.

Macy, Nick and I went into the house where the police interviewed us about what happened. I had never seen so much blood in my entire life! No horror movie I'd ever seen could even compare to the scene before my very eyes. It looked as though someone had been brutally tortured and murdered.

Kayne was released from the hospital with an enormous gash of stitched flesh on his throat. Turns out that if he was sliced a mere eighth of an inch deeper, he would have bled out in minutes!

Never in a million years did I think I would be faced with a circumstance where I would be sitting beside my best friend, watching blood surge from his neck, praying that God spare him from death. We planned to have a fun night, get fucked up, and let go of all the stress we'd been carrying. Instead, we experienced something nobody should ever have to endure.

Life is so precious, yet so often we wander aimlessly through it, showing no gratitude for the gift we've been given. We take the people we love for granted, assuming they'll always be there. But they will not. Life may be unpredictable, but death is certain – it is a matter of whose time is when. Be grateful for each day you are blessed with, and make sure the people you love know that you love them, because in an instant, without any time for preparation, they could be gone – just like that.

Almost losing Kayne opened my eyes for an instant: an instant where I would never take anyone for granted again; an instant where I would be forever grateful; an instant where I would make the most of my own life, knowing I was not promised tomorrow.

As it usually happens, the intensity of those realizations wore off, and things went back to *normal*. I got caught up in the every day drama and insignificant issues in my life, and over time lost sight of that very important lesson I almost learned.

I believe that it is so important to reflect on the lessons we learn in life, and to practice them often so that we embed them deep into our subconscious in order to understand them thoroughly, and avoid making the same mistakes again.

To learn a lesson doesn't necessarily mean we will never make that mistake again. Knowledge is not always power – contrary to popular belief; it is potential power. Knowledge opens our minds, but implementation of appropriate action is where all of the change occurs.

How do we progress in life if we keep falling back into old habits?

In order to break old habits, we have to create new ones. New habits that align with the person we want to be - a higher version of ourselves.

It took me years of making the same mistakes again and again to understand this concept – but it makes all the difference in life.

If we are not growing and progressing, we are dying. There is no such thing as stagnancy in life or in time.

CHAPTER SEVENTEEN

Mind Fucked

"To love an addict is to run out of tears."
— Sandy Swenson

All I wanted was for D and I to live in peace in a place we could call our own – I didn't care where it was or how small it was, just that it was ours. He stayed with me at Chads while we figured out our next step.

We knew that there was no way we could afford a place in the situation we were in – him just having been released from jail, and me having spent all my earnings helping Chad out with the girls (as well as my own bad habits), so we agreed to go on government assistance – better known as welfare.

We left Chads and found a little two-bedroom apartment in what was known as the *Red Zone* that we split with Kayne and Macy. The area was called the *Red Zone* because it consisted mainly of low-income housing, drug dealers and addicts.

[For peace of mind: soon after we left, authorities finally intervened and Destiny and Hope were sent to live with Chad's mother, in a much safer and more stable environment. Unfortunately, that is all I know. It pains me to say that I was unable to remain involved in their lives, and maybe for the sake of the person I became, it was better that I wasn't around much longer].

The apartment was very tiny – maybe 600 square feet – but we loved it!

I returned to school for a victory lap to obtain the credit I was missing. I was so close to being done with school, and I couldn't wait to start a fresh chapter. I could go anywhere and become anything! I really thought I had life figured out.

After a late night partying, D and I roamed the streets in the brisk of dawn, wearing off the remainder of our intoxication.

We laughed, and played, and danced in the rain, when a police car unexpectedly pulled up beside us.

"D Manson?" the officer asked through the rolled down window.

My stomach twisted into knots as D looked with guilt written all over him.

What now?

"Fuck," he whispered under his breath.

He hadn't been attending his weekly probation meetings and his probation officer issued a warrant for his arrest.

The officer stepped out of the vehicle. He looked like a marine: over six feet of hard body mass with a buzz cut and a seriously smug look on his face. He grabbed D and threw him aggressively onto the hood of the car, not taking the time to read him his rights or explain why he was under arrest.

"What the fuck dude, I'm not resisting, take it easy!" D snarled at him.

The officer did not like his attitude. He pressed his face into the car and roughed him up as he patted him down. Then, instead of searching his pockets, he ripped D's pants down to his ankles.

"What the hell are you doing?" I intervened, stepping toward him and being stern. I knew that the way he was treating D was a clear violation of his rights.

"BACK UP!" the officer yelled at me, pushing even more of his body weight onto D, who let out a groan from the force.

"You can't do this! He's complying with everything you're telling him!"

In a swift motion, the officer pushed me back into a telephone pole. He was a very large man and I was no more than one hundred pounds soaking wet. I'd like to say I couldn't believe he would do that, but everyone knew that the cops in our small town were as crooked as they came. I couldn't tell you the number of times my friends and I got busted with drugs and the drugs would be confiscated, yet reports were never filed … hmm … I wonder where all those drugs went?

"Alright, that's how you wanna play? Just fucking wait bud!"

I grabbed D's bike and jumped onto it.

"Don't worry babe, I got you!" I yelled back as I raced to the police station.

I pedalled as fast as humanly possible as fury surged through every bone in my body.

I arrived at the station and asked the police woman at the front desk who to talk to about an officer abusing his powers toward a civilian. She looked up at me, and I could tell by the look on her face what the outcome was going to be.

I explained in detail exactly what happened.

"Get out," she said, looking at me like *what-are-you-going-to-do-about-it?*

"Excuse me?"

"Leave," she demanded, "and do not come back!"

I lost it! I felt completely helpless.

"You're all fucking scumbags and I cannot wait until you get your karma, bitch!"

(Ironically enough, a few years later the whole department was shut down, I'm sure I could take a few guesses as to why that might have been).

Knowing there was nothing more I was able to do, I made my peace with the fact that D was gone again, for God knows how long.

As usual, the calls kept coming and the letters were consistent, but I felt differently this time. I was fed up with him making stupid choices and jeopardizing our livelihood time and time again. I began to shut down and resist his love, not wanting to hear anymore of his bullshit excuses. I needed him to step up and stay true to his word. I told him that it was the last time I would have his back while he was in jail – there would be no more of my waiting for him if he kept choosing to make the same mistakes. He begged for my forgiveness and promised me that he learned his lesson. For whatever reason, I trusted him. Again.

During his incarceration, Kayne, Macy and I had moved into another apartment in the building right beside our old one. A couple who D was close with, Jaycee and Dom moved in next door, and Lynn and Zeik moved into the apartment across the hall from us, along with my best friend from elementary school, Brie. Brie and I were very close when we were young, and had drifted apart in high school, so it was nice to have her so close and be able to reconnect.

Being surrounded by my friends made life easier to deal with, but in those moments when I saw couples express their love for one another, and at the end of each day when we said goodnight and Kayne and Macy went into their room, and I into mine, the loneliness set in. I spent many of those nights sobbing into my pillow, wishing for consistency, love, and stability in life.

In the back of my mind, I wished that my prince charming would come to my rescue and take me away from it all...

About a month passed when I was partying at Jaycee and Dom's apartment. Jaycee was like a big sister to D, and Dom was his best friend. It made me feel more connected with D to spend time with them, because none of the people I was close with were fond of my being with him. They swore I deserved better, but I swore they were too hard on him. I knew he was just damaged, like me, and needed someone to love him, just as I did.

Time went by and as usual, I dealt with the pain by remaining drunk and high all of the time.

Finally, one evening, as summer faded away, I noticed a car pull up in the driveway in the midst of our partying. I was immediately drawn to it. It was like I knew it was him; like our souls were so connected that I felt his presence before I even knew he was around.

My attention shifted to what was going on outside. I heard voices full of enthusiasm welcoming someone as they stepped out of the car. The force pulled me toward it.

I opened the front door and there he was, his eyes locked on mine through the midst of the crowd the moment I was in his line of sight. We were always the only two people no matter how many people were around.

I ran to him and lunged into his embrace. He squeezed me with all of his might and lifted me up to spin me around and kiss me. We both cried tears of joy – our hearts were full again.

But something didn't feel the same. I couldn't help but shake the feeling when I looked into his eyes that something happened on the inside that he didn't want me to know about; something that brought out a certain bitterness within his soul.

Almost as soon as he got there, he told me he had to go.

"What do you mean, you have to go? You just got here … I haven't seen you in over a month!"

It was like he ripped my heart right back out. I had desperately yearned for his love, numbing myself through each passing day, getting too high to feel anything, and wasting the nights away with endless amounts of liquor awaiting his return.

"I'm sorry babe. Dale bailed me out and I have to go stay with him till everything's straight." (Dale was his mom's ex boyfriend, who had been like a father to him during his childhood).

"Okay … can't I come with you?" I pleaded, hoping he would pick up on the overwhelming sadness within me.

"Sorry babe. I can't ask that of him. He's doing me such a solid right now."

Part of me understood what he was saying, but the D I knew and loved would have done whatever he needed to do to be with me. Our whole relationship, we were two delinquents without families who relied on each other for our sanity, and now without warning, he had a new life that I wasn't going to be a part of.

I wanted him to make the right choices, but I wasn't ready to be left in the dust in order for him to do so. I got into such a habit of waiting for him each time he was in jail, that my mindset became fixed on craving him. He was like a bad drug. The only thing I looked forward to in life was being with him. When he was with me, I felt on top of the world. I had no fear. And the moment he was gone, I felt broken and lost, like I was incomplete without him.

"I'll call you soon ok, I love you." He kissed me goodbye, got back into the car, and drove away with Dale. A piece of me stayed with him.

As per his usual patterns, him complying with his conditions did not last long. When he was finally ready to come home, things just weren't what I thought they would be. It was supposed to feel right – after all of the moving around and him in and out of jail and always living by other people's standards, I thought I would be at peace. But he was different ... colder than I knew him to be. Each time he went to jail, he came back a little different ... more trapped in the mentality of a criminal and more resistant to my love.

It wasn't long before he was hustling harder drugs again – perks, oxies, coke, valiums ... whatever he could get his hands on. I challenged him, trying to force him to remain true to his word, but that only caused chaos between us. Soon, he was putting the shit up his nose again, and became unpredictable in everything he said and did.

The person I once knew down to the very core became a complete stranger to me.

The more drugs he did, the more we fought about stupid things. Something so insignificant could happen and it would turn into a war. Neighbors up the road heard us fighting on a daily basis. The fights became so intense that it would sometimes escalate to him being physical. Naturally, I would defend myself, and things would get extremely out of hand. Every other day we broke up over one thing or another, and then make up after some hardcore, anger-releasing sex. It became our normal. I still loved him with all of my heart. I just could not accept that the person he became was who he truly was, because it wasn't. He was trapped in the mind and body of an addict.

I fought tirelessly and desperately to get him back, but it was no use. He got worse and worse. First, it was the disrespect and the constant lies, then came the control and manipulation. It became the back and forth between treating me like I was nothing to him for no reason at all, and crying on his knees apologizing and professing his love for me.

You want to talk about mind-fucked?

I didn't understand the cycle of abuse, because abuse was something I had become accustomed to. I lived for the rare moments where we were happy together, and forgave him over and over for the same things.

The severity of the physical altercations in the beginning weren't anything more than two angry teenagers smashing each other's belongings and pushing each other around. But the deeper into addiction he slipped, the more dangerous he became. There were so many times throughout our relationship that I should have called it quits, but instead I chose to give him a million second chances. His apologies always seemed so sincere. He would cry real tears and beg for my forgiveness on his knees in the presence of our friends. He would involve them and make them feel bad for him so that they would convince me to give him another chance. But the day that he hit me in the throat with all of his strength, taking the wind out of me, and then bragging to his boys about how he "clotheslined that bitch" a piece of my soul was destroyed.

I cried so many tears that I ran out of tears to cry - no exaggeration. I prayed that in one of those glimpses where he was truly sorry, he would remain there and love me the way he did before. But the thing about drug addicts is that they have no control over how they feel or how they treat others. Being an addict means being one person before a hit, and a completely different person after. It means endless lies and broken promises. It means delusions and bipolar swings. It means psychotic breakdowns when they don't have a fix, and blaming the people they love for everything wrong that happens to them.

After months of physical, mental, and emotional abuse, and the persistence of my close friends, I ended things for good. I believed in him so much, that I trusted in my heart he would realize how bad he'd hurt me and get clean. Instead, he moved in with Jaycee and Dom next door, and started dating someone who enjoyed doing the drugs with him.

It killed me knowing that he was only yards away, sniffing blow, and popping pills with his new junkie girlfriend, kissing her and touching her after all we had been through together. I couldn't leave my house without bursting into tears and wanting to puke. There was no escaping it – he lived right next door.

Ironically, the only thing that held me together at that time was Sly. Since things had gone sour between D and I, he was there for me every day to lift my spirits, with no ill intentions. Through the duration of the steadily worsening events, he would approach me at school every day to ask how I was doing. He would hold me as I cried on his shoulder, affirming how amazing I was and how I deserved so much better. And each time D and I worked through our issues, Sly would lie to me and tell me he was happy that things were good.

I remembered how genuine he was and realized how unconditionally he loved me.

My whole heart belonged to D, but he had moved on, and I deserved to find happiness as well. I had so much love and respect for Sly in a way that I could never comprehend, because I had never experienced an authentic love quite like that. Opening up to the idea that maybe I didn't know what real love was, I pursued a relationship with Sly again, only without a label.

I smiled every time I saw his face, then thought of how D had someone making him smile the way I used to. I found comfort in his embrace, then thought of how D was where I felt home. And when he did everything in his power to make me happy, I thought of how hard D and I fought to be together, and how it was all for nothing.

He completely ruined me for the chance of falling in love with someone else. I believed that our connection was just too powerful, but the truth is, my mind was conditioned through abuse and manipulation. Being a victim for so long, I became an extremist. If there weren't extreme highs and lows, I felt uncomfortable and bored, like something was missing. I needed the adrenaline, the chase, the drama. It reminded me that I was still alive when inside, I was dead.

I didn't understand at the time what probably seems obvious to all of you reading this now: I became dependent on external validation and found worth only in the approval and acceptance of men. All of my value came from a man. I wanted to feel loved more than anything else in the world, and I would lower my standards to nothing to experience it even in the slightest way. I felt truly worthless.

CHAPTER EIGHTEEN

A Fool's Revenge

"Holding onto anger is like drinking poison and expecting the other person to die."

– Buddha

Everyone experiences it at some point – that emptiness and unworthiness that comes with heartbreak. It can nearly destroy you. It breaks you down into the dark abyss and can change the way you view the world forever. Some people find ways to cope with the heartache through their support systems, through music, dance, art, and through other constructive manners. Others fill that hole and numb themselves with a number of different things that aren't so constructive.

I filled mine with revenge.

I could not wrap my head around how you could give your entire heart to someone, do everything in your power to make them happy, stick by their side through hell and high water, and they could just forget about you like all of that meant nothing to them.

It was a hit to my ego, embarrassment to my pride, a knife in my heart and a captor of my soul.

I've found in life that so many people become cold hearted. They grow to care about only themselves and are unable to empathize with other people. They think the world owes them something because they feel disadvantaged, and don't realize how their actions and decisions affect others. They are afraid to love because of the risk of being hurt. The minute they are betrayed, they build walls of steel around them that are nearly impossible to break through, causing them to shut down emotionally and not trust other people – especially when it comes to falling in love. They play games, lie and cheat, because they don't take love and commitment seriously anymore. That, or because if that other person hurts them, they can justify it and don't feel like a fool for opening up. For some reason that makes the situation more bearable. But that cycle is what creates even more pained souls. It is a ripple effect that continues to darken souls. Strong and healthy relationships are so rare to see in this generation, because everyone is so broken and afraid to connect with other people. In fear of being betrayed or hurt after experiencing that pain before.

I really tried to love Sly the way he loved me, and somewhere deep down I really did love him. I just did not have it in me to express my feelings anymore. Subconsciously, I told myself the story that there is no point in giving someone your all, because you'll only be hurt in the end. I couldn't bear to ever feel the unbearable pain I felt, again.

Managing my emotions and dealing with my issues properly were concepts completely foreign to me. I wasn't taught proper coping techniques, so my strategies only ever consisted of self-harm, shutting down, getting too high to function, and drinking away my problems. I told myself that I was so strong that I was able to just move on and forget about the pain. But I was lying to myself.

I let go of any trace of self-love that remained in me.

Nobody else loved me, so how could I love me? My life wasn't worth anything to anyone, so what did it matter if I died anyways?

The pretending I was strong, the black-out drinking, and the getting-too-high-to-function methods were no longer enough. I needed something much stronger to numb myself.

The thrill of sniffing that first line of cocaine empowered me.

I knew how much D hated the idea of me doing hard drugs, and I wanted him to know that he had no power over me anymore (how counterproductive).

Spitefulness led me to dabble in cocaine and a variety of pills.

It was instant gratification.

The more I dabbled, the more the drugs affected me. It was like nothing mattered – none of the pain, none of the heartbreak, nothing. I didn't care what anyone thought. When the chemicals took over, I was free, careless, powerful, unstoppable. I came to the conclusion that life was better while high, no matter what drug it was. Some nights it was coke, others it was oxies. Some nights it was crushed up perks, valiums, morphine or whatever other pills were kicking around. And damn, did I ever love mushrooms for a long trip into another dimension. Why deal with life when I could just forget about it?

As I mentioned before, drugs have a tendency of amplifying emotions.

My anger became rage.

My pain became torture.

And my desire to be loved consumed me.

I liked spending my time with Sly, but I never felt whole. How could I when I was relying on someone else for that feeling of completion?

I still longed for attention and affection from other guys.

I know now it is because my walls were too high to let someone else in, but back then I believed that it was because I was meant to be with

D. He had instilled it deep into my brain: I belonged to him and no one would ever love me the way that he did. I believed that to my very core. So, when I lost him, it became my mission to prove him wrong – that someone could and would love me in the ways I deserved. It wasn't about love anymore, it was all my ego trying to win some game.

All along, I had what my heart desired from Sly, but I did not know what love really was to recognize it. I played with his heart and took advantage of his love for me – believing that it couldn't be real.

I behaved even more promiscuously, seeking attention and leading guys on when I knew I was not interested, just to see what lengths they would go for me. Cold and bitter as I was toward men, I treated them all in ways that made me feel superior. I dominated them and did everything in my power to play them for fools. I wanted them to feel the same embarrassment and shame that they had inflicted upon me. After all, I'd concluded that all men functioned the same way.

The drugs only further disillusioned me; I met a twisted and deranged version of myself. But Karma extinguished my out of control, man-eating days very quickly.

I spent a lot of my time at Jaxon's house. His hate for D made me connect with him even further – not that he was any better. He was always messing around with different girls, telling them he loved them, and manipulating them to always be there for him. I can't even tell you how many girls ended up in mental institutions and put on medication because of how much he messed them up.

One of those girls was Amy. She must have really had a thirst for vengeance, because when I received a message from a girl I went to school with asking if I wanted to make some good money dancing, Amy convinced me to go for it, and that she wanted to join in – obviously trying to get back at Jaxon.

The girl assured us that it was a classy style of dancing where we would be fully clothed and at zero risk. I had nothing to lose.

That weekend, two pimped-out Jamaican men came to pick us up. They took us out shopping for new shoes and skimpy little outfits, which were similar to bathing suits, only with a lot less material. Then they took us back to a hotel where we drank a bottle of rum and sniffed a bunch of blow.

I was naïve when it came to the world of stripping and how pimps worked. I thought they were just trying to be nice to us. I guess that's how they reel you in.

I thought it would be some kind of a go-go dancing gig, where we would be entertainment at some kind of event. Nope. We ended up at a sleezy strip club.

When we entered the club, all eyes were on us as the two men led us to a back room. Looking back now, it must have been apparent that I was underage and being taken advantage of – but nobody seemed to mind.

The two men told us to choose stage names and when we heard those names called to enter onto the stage. Without any more information, they led us backstage and told us to change into the outfits they had bought us. I had no idea what I was in for.

We entered a dressing room that was packed with topless and fully nude women doing their hair and make up. One by one, when their names were called, they exited onto the stage and returned a few songs later without any clothes on.

Amy was called before me. She confidently went out onto the stage. When her time was up, she returned without her top on, looking very uneasy and ashamed.

I didn't want to go out. This was not what I signed up for! But I didn't want to know what would happen if I refused. I put myself in the situation, so I had to man up and deal with it. Amy played her part, I had to play mine.

"Ladies and gentlemen, next up is a cute little number we like to call Miss Sassy!" the announcer's voice introduced me. There was no turning back.

I walked on to the stage, nearly blinded by the bright lights. I noticed right away the silhouettes of a huge crowd of people. I swallowed hard and took a deep breath as my legs began to tremble beneath me.

Thank God for the drugs, because that was the only way I was able to shut myself off and become someone else.

I danced sensually on the poles as whistles and cheers came from the crowd below, praying for it to come to an end quickly.

Half-way into the second song, I had not removed any clothing. The announcer took it upon himself to come up on stage and undo my top so that it would fall off. The crowd went wild, banging on the stage and yelling for more. That song seemed to last forever.

Just hurry up and be over already ...

Finally, the second song started.

"Who wants to see more?!" enticed the DJ, and again the crowd roared with applause and whistles.

The announcer summoned me over to the side of the stage where he was standing. I hesitantly made my way over, blind to what was about to happen.

He reached up, and pulled my g string to my feet! Chants and cheers overpowered the loud music.

I was humiliated!

I froze, completely exposed, watching as hundreds of people stared at my naked body.

When the song came to an end I pretty well ran off stage, my entire body shaking from the embarrassment.

The worst part of it all was having to go back into the club amongst all of the people who had just seen me onstage, to wait for the two pimps to come back and pick us up. We were miles away from home. I kept my head down and avoided making eye contact with anyone at all costs. Different men approached me for private dances, but I was not about it.

After being further degraded when the pimps learned I earned no money from doing private dances, I returned home, and back into my lonely shell I went.

****

A few weeks later I was visiting Jaycee and Dom, unaware that D was in his room.

It was the first time I'd seen him in what felt like months. Catching me off guard, he came out of his room, right away noticing me. He looked deep into my soul for only an instant as we exchanged energies of mutual despair. He grabbed a drink of water, and walked back to his room, closing the door behind him.

A few moments later, the door opened again.

"Sash …?" He said my name like it tormented him.

I looked at him in disgust.

"Come smoke a bong with me?"

"I'm good," I laughed. I needed him to fight for me.

"Please … I don't want anything from you, I just wanna talk … that's all."

I didn't respond because I didn't know how. I wanted nothing more than to run into his arms, but my gut told me to stay strong and resist.

He took the hint and returned to his room.

"Just go talk to him babe," Jaycee finally stated as she saw me struggling with the angel and devil on either shoulder. "You guys both need closure. He's been so messed up without you."

Ya right. I thought to myself. *That's why he moved on like I never meant anything.*

Apparently, I was transparent.

"I can tell he's not even into that girl," Jaycee assured me. "He talks about you to her all the time. She's a rebound and she knows it."

Hearing those words from someone who knew him so well drew me back to him. Maybe I did mean something to him after all.

I got up slowly and knocked on his door – my heart pounding right out of my chest. He opened the door and lit up like a kid on Christmas.

I sat down on the edge of his bed, and all I could think was: *he's been fucking her on this bed, and here I am sitting on it.* I wanted to puke.

I sat in silence, unsure of what to feel, watching as he busted up a pile of weed for us to smoke.

Alas, he broke the tension.

"I miss you," he said shyly, unable to turn to face me.

"I'm sure your girlfriend wouldn't appreciate you saying that."

"I know ... and I should care, but I don't ... She's not you Sash. No one can compare to you. It's driving me insane that I fucked up such an amazing thing. I'm so sorry for hurting you."

It took everything in me not to cry.

"I need you," he went on. "I'm so lost without you … and I know you're lost too. Everyone keeps telling me you're fucking around with different dudes and putting shit up your nose. What the fuck man? How could you let me do that to you? Let me make it right … please. You know we belong together."

I knew right away I would take him back. He was my everything. He could have done anything to me and I would always forgive him just to have him in my life. My sanity was dependent on his love.

Of course, I made him fight much harder than that before I gave in.

We jumped back in, really deep, really fast. He moved back in with me, trying to pick up where we left off, but the damage had already been done. Our fights worsened, yet our co-dependence was indestructible.

I couldn't handle the constant battles – they literally drained the life out of me. I was constantly walking on eggshells waiting for him to explode like a ticking time bomb.

Realizing I really was better off without him, I tried ending things with him again.

He said he couldn't live without me and tried slitting his throat right in front of me. Luckily the knife he grabbed was a butter knife and barely pierced his skin.

Instead of leaving him, I came to the *understanding* that he loved me so deeply that he did not want to go on without me. It made me love him even more.

The toxicity of our relationship led to our home becoming a warzone. Our fights created fights between other people – particularly people who tried to intervene, as well as between Kayne and Macy who became affected by all the negativity we emitted. It caused our friends to choose sides, and to turn on each other as a result.

We all started robbing each other and fighting each other. Things eventually escalated to our neighbors having their door kicked in by an angry mob of people, because of the accelerating series of events.

I can't say that our relationship was to blame for all of that, because it wasn't. But the law of attraction holds no bounds when it comes to its principles. We created a circle of chaos all around us, and chaos generates more chaos.

That January, a little more than a month after we got back together, the physical abuse had gone to new extremes. Every argument escalated to a wrestling match, and I always lost. With no place else to go, I showed up on the doorstep of an abused women's shelter one rainy day.

They took me in and provided a room for me to stay. There was a "no-men-allowed-on-the-property" rule that gave me a sense of security that D would not be able to get to me to manipulate me any further. There were finally glimpses where I saw the reality of the power and control cycle I was trapped in with him. I felt understood being able to connect with other women who were going through the same issues. There was constant support around the clock from on-site counselors, and we had plenty of food to keep us nourished. But it was very depressing.

Being surrounded by depressed women with black eyes and bruises was a constant reminder of my struggles. A young woman in a full body cast caused by the abuse from her husband was a harsh realization of what could be in store for me if I didn't get out of my relationship with D. I recognized the pain in her eyes all too well.

Every night I would cry myself asleep, feeling like scum that I had nobody to be there for me in such a hard time. Normally, my go-to would be Kayne, but he had enough going on in his own relationship and had done more than enough for me. I couldn't impose on his life anymore than I already did.

One sleepless night, needing someone to talk to and someone to comfort me, I called Sly.

"Hello …?" spoke the soft tone of a familiar and soothing voice.

"Hi …." I said softly, weeping into the phone.

"Sasha?! Are you okay? Where are you?" His sincere worry was a beautiful reminder that someone cared.

"I'm okay … I just needed to hear your voice." I didn't want him to know where I was. I was embarrassed and ashamed.

"Sasha. Where are you? What did he do to you?"

I broke into tears.

How could he always see right through me? How could I have hurt him so many times and given up such unconditional love, for someone who left me heartbroken time and time again?

"Don't worry about me Sly," I tried to console his panic. "I'm okay, really …"

"Sasha. Where the fuck are you? I'm coming to get you right now!"

I'd never heard him get angry before. I knew he wasn't playing around with me.

"I'm at the shelter …"

"That fucking piece of shit! What did he do to you?" It sounded like he was going to cry. "Never mind, I'm leaving now. I'll see you soon!"

He was outraged. I did not even try to challenge him.

About forty minutes passed, and he still was nowhere in sight. That was totally unlike him. It was only a twenty-five minute drive, and I knew he was leaving right away. I started to worry.

He showed up about an hour after I talked to him in his sister's vehicle. I thought it was strange but did not think too much into it.

I found out the next day that he had raced so sporadically to come to my aid that he crashed his van, left it in the snowy ditch, and called his sister to use her car to get to me.

We spent the entire night sitting in the park with our seats reclined, enjoying each other's company. His light-heartedness and quirkiness had me laughing like nothing was wrong. Every so often I caught him with stars in his eyes, falling harder for me. In turn, I fell harder for him.

I forgot all about my problems any time he was around.

We spent many nights over the next few weeks in that park.

He was an angel sent from heaven. I knew how badly he wanted us to be together, and deep down I wanted that too, but I was way too damaged to love him the way he deserved. He looked at me like he was amazed by every word I spoke, every move I made, and yet my loyalty was to someone else. Even with the peacefulness and serenity he bestowed upon me, a piece of me was still missing. My head was way too fucked up.

When word went around that D wanted to see me and apologize, I fought the urge for as long as I could.

One evening I made up the excuse to myself that I needed to get some more of my things from the house, hoping D would be there.

When I showed up, I felt like I was suffocating.

There was D sitting in my living room with a bunch of my friends, joking and laughing like nothing was wrong.

Did no one give a shit that I was alone in a shelter feeling lower than ever before?

There they were going on through life without me, not so much as calling to see how I was doing - another fact to store away for later.

I pushed my quarrels deep down and sat down to smoke a show. It felt great to be away from the shelter and back in a familiar place. I stayed a while and hung out, reminiscing on life before the shelter – missing my bed … my privacy… my friends … and even D.

When it was time for me to go, D asked me not to leave. His eyes apologized with the pain and shame within them. It felt good knowing he was pained by his actions. I took back my power for a brief moment and returned to the shelter anyways.

I continued going back home day after day, and D and I began to reconnect again against my better judgement. I'm sure you can guess what happened next. Yup. We got back together, and right back into the same cycle.

By this point in the story I know exactly what you're thinking: *What a friggen idiot! How stupid can you be to keep going back to such a toxic relationship? You're asking for trouble!* You're absolutely right, and I agree 100% from the viewpoint I have now. It is easy to judge from the outside. It's easy to say, *"I would never do that!"* But the mind is such a complex thing. Especially when it comes to manipulation and years of repeat trauma conditioning it.

Our brains are wired to fight for survival and to attain our basic needs – love and belonging being third on the list after physiological (air, food, water, etc.) and safety (security, resources, health, etc.).

Because I believed that nobody in the world truly loved me (which was not true whatsoever), I kept desperately fighting for the only love I knew to be true by my naïve experience. I didn't know how to find value in myself. I lost sight of everything I stood for, and forgot who I was deep down in order to fulfill a desperate need to be loved and needed.

Figure 18.1: Maslow's Hierarchy of Needs

When two tormented souls fall in love and thrive off of each other with no other guidance, there is very rarely a good outcome. That being said, that is no justification for the abuse that took place.

The way I see it, I can view myself as a victim and hold onto the pain of being beat up again and again by someone who claimed to love me, constantly reliving the events and carrying the weight on my shoulders, or I can open my mind and observe the relationship from a different point of view that accepts that no human is perfect – we all have our own demons.

Let me be clear: I do not encourage anyone to stay in an abusive relationship! It has taken me a decade to overcome all of the anguish and underlying issues that stemmed from what I went through. There are still side effects that surprise me here and there. But to anyone who is struggling with overcoming past abuse, I encourage you to try to view what happened from another perspective, to help yourself heal.

Some people spend their entire lives trying to make sense of their victimization or torment, when it is much more effective to see it from a higher standpoint. That is, anyone who can inflict such pain on another human being has got to have some serious issues. It is never personal and it is NOT the fault of the victim! No matter what you think you might have done to *deserve* it or to *instigate* that person, those theories are not justified.

Maybe the predator suffers from a number of different mental health issues. Maybe they're bipolar. Maybe they're an addict with no self-control over their emotions. Or maybe they're broken from trauma in their past and have not dealt with anger or confusion. It could be a number of different things. I'm sure with some digging and strategically putting pieces together, those reasons will become obvious.

That doesn't mean you should go back to them or try to fix them – that's where my fault has always lied. My empathy and caring heart, paired with my insatiable desire to be loved, minus the ability to set boundaries in self respect, kept me vulnerable and susceptible to being abused. I disregarded my own needs, and honestly believed that every apology meant it was going to be different next time.

But accepting truth can make the process of forgiveness much more effective. I might add that forgiveness is essential to attain inner peace. As the quote in the beginning of the chapter suggests, "Holding onto anger is like drinking poison and expecting the other person to die" (Buddha). Forgiveness, however, does not necessarily mean having a conversation with the person who inflicted the pain onto you, but rather to accept that you cannot go back and change things, and that it was not personal to you. Hurt people hurt people. Nothing that anyone says to you or does to you is personal. The ways that people act and react are direct reflections of their experiences and perspectives on life.

D was not a horrible person, and to this day I've found in my heart forgiveness for the misery inflicted upon me through his actions. He was a damaged soul just as I was. We both played a role in the toxicity and we both had needs being met from one another.

Where I used promiscuity to seek the things I wanted, he used manipulation. Where I resorted to self-wallowing to deal with my pain, he resorted to violence. I watched as he expressed his emotions through anger, and I found that to be more effective than crying about it. It made me angry too. At least with yelling and screaming, I felt heard. And the more we fought, the more I learned to fight back.

I guess in an ironic twist, it made me stronger in the long run.

Everything happens for a reason, and God really does have a plan for us all. I didn't see it in the midst of all the chaos and torment, but there really was a reason for it all. God doesn't give you what you want, but instead, what you need - to grow and flourish as an individual and to align you with your purpose here on Earth.

As Albert Einstein said, "Adversity introduces a man to himself." It is in those painful and dark times that we have to sit with ourselves and sort through our thoughts and emotions in a way we wouldn't in easy times. It is in those dark places where we discover our strength and develop our courage, and where we understand just how truly resilient we are.

Like I said before, God will send the same lessons over and over until we pass them, each time more abrupt and painful until we finally get it.

CHAPTER NINETEEN

Spiraling Out
of Control

"Sometimes following your heart means losing your mind."
– Michelle Monet

I liked living on the edge – the constant risk and adrenaline acted as a certain fuel for me. But I knew I didn't want to live a life of crime forever. It was never my plan to end up on such a path; it was my conditioning and programming that influenced my course. I was a product of my environment.

Deep down I always had a good heart and good intentions, and saw more for my future than where I was. I just wasn't sure what or how to get there.

After risking my own freedom covering for D to the police numerous times, hiding him when he robbed a laundromat with my cousin Bo, having to mediate between many of his fights – often times jumping in to protect him and getting hit myself, watching him draw a knife on someone who owed him money right in the middle of a shopping mall, and acting as an accessory by allowing him to store stolen dirt bikes and snowmobiles at our house, I had very few morals that remained.

I stooped lower and lower until I lost sight of the values I once stood so strongly for.

The stress started to catch up with me.

Everything spiraled out of control – even to our low standards.

D recognized it just as I did. He knew that despite the reckless wannabe-gangster I became, that wasn't who I wanted to be – it was who I felt I needed to be to survive, and it was draining.

He tried to convince me that I was better off without him, but he already had my heart and there was no going back. To me, love was forever.

Starting to understand the influence and impact he had on me, and trying to do the right thing, he slowly began detaching himself from me, trying to *save* me from the monster I was becoming. It was far too late – I was way past being saved.

He told me he wished he could give me the best day of my life to remember him by and then set me free. He explained that his only problem in setting me free was that he couldn't bear to live without me, or to see me love someone else, but that he knew how selfish that was. There was sincerity in what he was saying, and it did not sit well with me. Yet, as usual, I ignored my gut instinct.

One glorious day (or so it seemed), we spent the most incredible day together at the beach drinking with friends. The day was absolutely perfect! It was full of laughter and love, affection and fun, and not so much as one argument arose all day. I caught a ray of hope that we could make it together. We found love again!

Oh wait, nope … it was just the drugs in effect …

His entire demeanor changed when we got home.

He asked me to join him for a bath.

I was joyful to do so.

He filled the tub right to the rim and sat across from me staring blankly into my eyes. His mind was very clearly rattled with something very concerning.

In all seriousness, he spoke purposefully: "I love you so much Sasha, but I will never make you happy, and you deserve to be happy." Tears built up in his eyes. "You deserve better than me, but I know you'll never leave me. And I can't bear to live without you …"

He was crying as he spoke to me.

He kissed me intensely, lips quivering like it was the last time our lips would ever meet, then plunged himself under the water and held himself down so that I couldn't pull him up.

"D!! What the fuck are you doing?!" I thought it had to be some kind of joke.

I used all of my strength to try and pry him out of the water, but he held himself down, gagging and choking on the water trying to drown himself.

"Help!! Someone help!!!" I screamed at the top of my lungs, but no one was around to hear me.

I pulled the plug, praying for the water to drain faster. Still immersed, he began to vomit mass amounts of black substance into the water. The tub emptied more and more slowly as the chunks of puke clogged the drain. When it lowered to a level where he was not at risk of drowning, I wrapped myself in a towel and ran across the hall, pleading for Zeik to help me.

Zeik raced to our apartment and pulled D out of the tub and carried him into the living room where he laid him on the floor. Embracing him with comfort, though radiating confusion and anger, he demanded answers. But D was lost in an alternate universe, as though he were unsure of whether to be relieved or devastated that he was still alive.

I blamed myself for what happened, disillusioned that I was putting too much pressure on him to change, and that I needed to put my feelings aside and be more supportive of whatever he was going through.

I gave up all my power and submitted to his controlling ways entirely.

My naïve realization permitted him to be even more dominant over me. He treated me like I was his property – merely a possession that he could do whatever he wanted with and to.

I stopped challenging him. His reactions to my non-compliance grew more serious.

What love was left within our toxic relationship withered away.

On my nineteenth birthday, we got into an argument about what we were going to drink that night. He wanted beer. I didn't like beer. It was his money. It was my birthday.

The altercation resulted in him grabbing my face and headbutting me as hard as he could, causing me to bite through my tongue and break one of my teeth.

He apologized a few days later.

I forgave him.

I'll say it again: God tends to give us the same trials over and over until we pass them. I was so hard headed that I never learned my lesson, and therefore He continued giving me the same test over and over, more extreme each time so that I might actually learn from it.

I chose to stay in such a mentally, verbally and physically abusive relationship even though it annihilated my very soul. The fire that once burned so passionately within me faded into ashes. Once upbeat and outgoing; now sluggish and introverted. Once excited to take on each new day; now wanting to sleep my days away. Once wanting to be surrounded by multitudes of people I loved, now preferring isolation.

The most disturbing part of it all was that I was so dangerously emotionally codependent on D that when he would try to leave me, I would beg him to stay. My greatest fear was being left alone. I'd block the door, telling him he was not going anywhere. There was no way he was getting the upper hand of leaving me after all I endured because of him. If I belonged to him, then he belonged to me.

Finally, he decided that I was going to be the one who left. He threw all of my belongings out of the window and door, as I cried and begged for him to stop and reconsider.

"Please, D! I'm sorry! Stop! I love you! Don't do this!"

"Get the fuck out cunt! I'm fucking done with you!"

He pushed me out of his way, slamming me into the wall so that I could not stop him from throwing more of my things out.

When all of my possessions were piled into the hallway, he grabbed me by my hair and dragged me out of the apartment, locking the door behind him. I banged on the door crying hysterically for him to let me back in. I had no place to go, and surely no place to bring all of my belongings.

Everyone in the building heard the commotion, and a gentleman from two floors down ran up to see what was going on.

"Are you okay?!" He asked in a panic.

"No!" I sobbed, laying on the pile of all of my things, "What the fuck did I do to deserve this?"

"Honey, I called the cops. This is not okay. You need to get away from that kid. We hear you guys fighting all the time, and the way he treats you is disgusting."

I'd heard those words so many times that they meant nothing to me.

I didn't care that I had a bloody nose or that my body ached from him throwing me around. What killed me inside was that he tossed me away like I was trash, just like everyone else in my life had done. Being consumed in that worthlessness trumped any physical damage I endured.

The police showed up and upon one look at me, immediately arrested D. I told them I did not want to press charges, because I didn't want to see him go back to jail – that it was just a stupid fight that got out of hand. I tried to take the blame for it, but they explained to me that in domestic occurrences when it was obvious that abuse was a factor, they no longer gave the option of pressing charges. So often women were dependent on the abuser and were so psychologically damaged, as I was, that they would defend the abuser and suffer worse abuse – sometimes even death – in the future.

They insisted that I head to the station to provide a video statement of what happened. To my dismay, I had to provide that statement. Still remaining loyal to D, I tried to take the fault but they saw right through me. This time he would be shown no lenience. A no contact order was put into place, and extra time would be added to his sentence if we were caught communicating either directly or indirectly.

When he made no attempt to contact me after his arrest, I knew it was over.

Back into my lonesome state of depression I slipped, as life as I knew it was taken from me once more. I was left to reside in the home we shared together, with nothing but the painful memories of what had happened. I numbed each passing day with a multitude of drugs and alcohol, wanting to forget the pain and escape from such reality. I surrounded myself with attractive men, sleeping around with them, seeking their attention and approval in order to regain my false sense of self worth. It was an endless cycle.

With D out of the picture, Sly spent a lot of his time with me, trying to support me emotionally and make sure I was okay. I saw the hopefulness he had that we would end up together, and it destroyed him to know that I would never be true to him. I hooked up with other guys right in front of him, not thinking twice about how it affected him. I was caught up in my own little destructive world. Even with that, his undying love for me still conquered through his heartache. He knew how weak and vulnerable I was, and made it his mission to protect me.

Dan (the creepy stalker from Chad's house) was walking by one summer day, as my friends and I were partying in the parking lot outside of our building. He asked me if I wanted some kush. Ignorant to his intentions and use to men always giving me what I wanted, I was flattered! Who turns down free weed?!

He told me he would scale it up inside the house so there wasn't heat on him. We went into the building, up the stairs and into my apartment, now far away from where everyone else was. We entered my room and he weighed me up some weed. I thanked him and turned to walk back outside. He stood in front of my doorway and inched toward me.

As I backed away, I stumbled backward onto my bed. He took it upon himself to get on top of me. I was high as a kite, so my instincts weren't exactly functioning properly. I tried to laugh it off, telling him to please let me up. He ignored my request and started kissing me, telling me how bad he wanted me. He was a pretty big and muscular guy, so my attempt to push him away was not very effective.

After multiple attempts, anger built within me.

"Get the fuck off of me," I said sternly.

Still he did not listen. Instead, he started to feel me up.

"You're a fucking little tease." He was turned on by my resistance.

Sly must have sensed something was wrong because in he burst, a wrath of vengeance written all over him.

"She said get the fuck off! Are you fucking deaf?"

He grabbed Dan and threw him off of me like the guy was weightless.

"Get the fuck out before I knock you the fuck out! And stay the fuck away from her!"

Then he turned to me, "Are you okay?"

"Yes, Sly. I'm fine. Relax."

I brushed it off like it was nothing, but I knew that if he hadn't shown up, I'd have been powerless. Who knows what would have happened?

God kept throwing it right in my face: *THIS IS WHAT LOVE LOOKS LIKE!* and I disregarded his message every time, caught up in my disillusioned paradigms.

I continued on with my destructive patterns, trying to fill the void within. It must have really torn Sly apart, because he broke down to Kayne (who he had once fought over a girl in the past and was not very fond of) about how much he loved me but couldn't take it anymore. It hit me how badly I was toying with his emotions, and I began to detach myself of my emotional reliance on him for the sake of his sanity.

The drugs kept coming and the days all blurred together.

At some point in the midst of my little binge, I received a letter in the mail that was addressed to a woman's name I did not recognize, but I immediately recognized D's hand writing.

I tore the envelope open, and inside were pages and pages of letters he had written me, apologizing and exclaiming how much he loved me and needed me. There were endless drawings, poems and plans for our entire future. He begged me to be there when he was released, and he promised no more bullshit; that we were going to run away together and start a new life.

He still loves me.

My cousin Bo and his girlfriend Tysha were very supportive through my dilemmas. They listened for hours to my ranting, and always knew just what to say to make me feel a little lighter. They also hooked me up with a lot of drugs.

I found comfort in their presence and began spending a lot of my time at their house. Bo and D had been friends since they were kids, so Bo knew the real him behind the drugs and the masks. They supported our being together and believed entirely that we would work through everything. They were probably the only people in the entire world who still supported our relationship.

"D called here for you this morning," Bo announced hesitantly one afternoon when I showed up.

So many emotions overwhelmed me.

What did he want? Is he ok? Will I have another chance to talk to him? Is he getting out? How long is he in there?

"He said he would call back tomorrow morning at 9am when he has phone privileges and he hopes you can find it in your heart to talk to him. If not, he understands and will try again soon."

I wasn't sure I was ready to talk to him, but I felt obligated since he was risking his freedom just to speak to me. How could I deny him of that? He was alone in there, with no one to turn to, and that saddened me to the very core.

A tormenting battle between my brain and my soul - I didn't even know what I wanted or how to feel about anything anymore. Logically, I completely understood what was happening and recognized that I needed to let go of him to find happiness, and more importantly – sanity! I needed to break the cycle once and for all. But I just could not find it in my heart to give up on him. Maybe it was because I knew how it felt to have the people I love and trust give up on me when I needed them most. How could I do that to someone who loved me?

I felt insane!

And I suppose by definition, I was.

I was slowly but surely beginning to realize the patterns of our behaviors. I had even grown to accept a life without him, and was afraid to go backwards and give him another chance to destroy me again. I was getting just as sick of it as everyone else was.

Never trusting my judgment, and being so brainwashed by his passionate words, I spent the night at Bo and Tysha's to make sure I wouldn't miss his call.

I set my alarm for 8:00 a.m., tossing and turning all night in anticipation of the outcome of our call.

Would he even call? Would he come to his senses and change his mind?

I was still awake when the alarm went off. I sat up in bed with the phone beside me, anxiously waiting for it to ring. Shortly after nine, it did.

PRIVATE CALLER popped up on the display.

"Hello?" I asked nervously.

"Hello. You have a collect call from ..." Before the automated machine had a chance to finish, I pressed one to accept the charges.

"Baby? Is that you?" He sounded relieved to hear my voice. And it was great to hear his.

"Yeah ... it's me."

"I didn't think you would want to talk to me. Thank you. How are you? Are you okay?"

"Yeah, I'm good," I lied.

"It's so good to hear your voice. I miss you so much ... I'm so sorry baby, for everything. I don't know why I keep doing this shit ... But I know I need help. I've already set up anger management for when I get out and I've been getting counseling here. I'm even completing my GED. I'm serious this time babe. I'm clean off drugs and I feel great. I just want a fresh start with you and give you everything you deserve."

The weight of the world slowly lifted off my shoulders.

"That's amazing D. I'm so proud of you ..."

I heard the sincerity of his intentions. I trusted his words and believed that he was trying to prove himself. Him actively trying to change his path was all I needed from him.

"I need you to do something ... if you're ready for it that is ..."

"What's that?" I asked with uncertainty.

"You need to write a letter to the courts asking for the no contact order to be lifted, and bring it to my lawyer. I don't want to sneak around to talk to you and risk getting more time. I want to get out and be with you without worrying. Can you do that?"

"Yeah, I can do that," I responded warily.

He always worded his requests as demands, making me far more likely to give in to what he wanted of me. I was very easily swayed by him, and he used it to his advantage, always getting what he wanted from me. He didn't ask me if I wanted to give him another chance, he told me that we were going to be together, and that was how it would be. He had full control over me and he knew it.

"I need to ask you one more thing … This isn't how I wanted to do this, but I need to know …"

"Uhm … okay … whatsup?"

"Will you marry me?"

"Are you serious?"

I couldn't help but to laugh, not to mock him, but because I was so taken aback and didn't know how to respond.

"I know this isn't the way you pictured it, and I promise I'll get you a ring as soon as I get out. But I want to marry you. I know we'll be together forever, so let's make it official! We don't need to have a big wedding or anything. Let's just go sign papers and make it legal."

I went silent. So many thoughts raced through my mind. My heart told me yes and my gut told me not to be a fool.

"Will you be my wife?" He asked again impatiently, hoping for a response.

I couldn't believe it! Maybe he really was changing in there!

With no consideration, the word escaped my lips, "Yes."

We both cried and laughed in sync.

"So that's it? We're getting married?" he asked one more time to confirm.

"I guess so," I responded.

Every bad day was washed away. I was hopeful for the future and what new beginnings it would hold in store for us.

"My time is up Mrs. Manson!" he stated enthusiastically. "I don't get the phone again until Friday, but I'll call you then! Please write me back! And get that order lifted! I love you so much!"

I hung up the phone, asking myself what the hell just happened. Less than twenty-four hours ago, I was adamant about starting a new life, and now I was engaged to the very same person I was trying to escape.

Before I had a chance to speak to D again, Jaxon called me from the same prison.

"How's your pussy boyfriend?" He asked me without wasting any time, laughing like he knew something I didn't.

Jaxon hated D for everything he put me through and wanted nothing more than to demolish him. I knew they were both in the same jail, but as far as I knew they were on two completely different ranges.

"What do you mean?" I didn't even want to know the answer. Jaxon was top dog in there which meant anyone would do anything for him to remain in his good graces.

"Let's just say the little punk has been getting his karma in here."

"What are you talking about Jax?"

As much as D had hurt me, I wished no pain upon him.

"I put out the word that he's been beating on my little cousin and different man's been banging him out every day."

He was sadistic. There was no crossing him or the people he cared for.

"Jaxon! Are you kidding me right now?" I appreciated that he was protective of me, but sometimes he took it way too far.

"Maybe he'll think twice the next time he wants to beat on you."

"Leave him alone. We're good ok?"

"Nah gangsta. He'll be getting his karma every day he's in here, sorry. You don't wanna look out for yourself then I have to."

"Jaxon, I love you. I really do. But I'm sure he learned his lesson, let it go please."

"You might wanna ask him about the pictures he sold of you around here too, eh? Dude's fucked. You need to give up on his sorry ass."

"What the hell are you talking about?"

Pictures he sold of me?

I had no clue what he was talking about.

"Did you send him pictures of yourself last time he was in?"

"Yeah ... a few..."

"He probably used them to make some quick cash for his drugs. Even sold some for chocolate bars. Ask him about it."

I didn't know what to say. Jax had never lied to me before.

"Time's up," he said. "I gotta go. Make an appointment to come visit, will you?"

"Yeah ... Okay ... See you soon."

The next time I talked to D, I confronted him about the photos. He told me that someone robbed them and he didn't want to tell me because he didn't want me to freak out that there were half-nude photos being passed around the jail for a bunch of criminals to beat off to.

I took his word. There was no way he would ever stoop that low for some drugs, was there?

Eventually Kayne, Macy, and I decided to part ways. They went off to get a place of their own and I moved in with Bo and Tysha for a while. We lived in an old basement unit in a well-known crack house – ironically enough, a building that I lived in for a few years growing up.

They had been addicts for a number of years – mostly oxies and cocaine. But the people that they hung around with were on another level from what I was even used to. It was a revolving door for users, addicts, gang bangers and prostitutes. Still, it didn't bother me whatsoever. I was now comfortably a part of that world.

As you could probably predict, with such a lifestyle came many dangers. Visiting from time to time was much different than living life with them day in and day out. Things went downhill fast, escalating to new extremes. People started ripping each other off and fighting over drugs. So many threats were made upon that house that I couldn't sleep at night without wondering whether we'd be ambushed by angry junkies trying to rob or jump us, or in the alternative, if we'd be raided by the police.

When they started smoking crack in the house and allowing people to shoot up there, I knew I had to go. Crack, meth, and heroine were on a level I knew I never wanted to be.

I called my grandfather, the only person in my family who made sure to check up on me since I'd been on my own. He would buy me groceries now and again, lend me money despite his better judgement, and even give me rides when I couldn't afford to pay for cabs.

He and his amazing wife Nancy agreed to let me move into their basement. They provided a better space for me where I could fall asleep without fear at night, where I was well nourished, and where I had genuine love and support around me. I respected them and didn't want to do anything to jeopardize my relationship with them. They gave me good advice, made me feel welcome, and checked up on me every day to make sure I was doing okay. They really cared.

I did my best to stay away from the drugs because I didn't want them to see like that. I respected them far too much. We really bonded in the time that I stayed there, and for once I had the motivation to make someone proud. It was good for me.

When it was time for D to be released, my grandfather agreed to come to court and sign off as his guarantor, meaning that D would be coming to live with us and if he violated his terms of probation, it could come back to bite my grandparents. Grandfather didn't like the idea of it, but he just wanted to make me happy. He would always do anything for me.

Having D around caused tension in the house. I knew they did not want him there – he was very clearly from the wrong side of the tracks, and they realized first hand just how bad an influence he was on me. They heard us fighting all the time. I can only imagine what stress that must have caused them. Still, they were supportive of me making my own decisions.

Normally, I reverted back to my happy and loving self as soon as D would get out of jail. And after accepting his proposal for marriage, I should have been smitten to have him back. But I really wasn't. I didn't realize it, but the only things keeping me attached to him were my pride in him not leaving me, and my fear of the unknown life without him.

The love I once shared with him was gone. I tried everything to get those feelings back, even resorting to going through couple's counseling together. Nothing worked. He just wasn't the same anymore.

The night before Halloween, D and I were laying in bed watching television when a dark look crossed his face.

"Hey … isn't tonight Devil's night?" He asked in a very unnerving and unfamiliar tonality.

"Yeah …" I wasn't sure where this was going.

"You've never spent Devil's night with me … have you?"

It was as if something evil came over him in that moment. His energy scared the shit out of me.

He forcefully got on top of me, pinning down my arms, and kissed me aggressively and emotionlessly. We had a lot of rough, wild sex, but this was different. I tried to push him back in a way that expressed I wasn't into whatever he was trying to do, but he overpowered me, ripping off my pants and having sex with me as I lay motionless on my back, tears running down my face.

In my twisted head, he did nothing wrong. I mean, we'd been having sex for like three years … as violated as I felt, it couldn't be classified as rape …

Big surprise, it wasn't long before D landed himself back in jail again. I don't even remember what for anymore – probably a breach or robbery or something of that sort. Maybe it was for beating on me. Everything became a blur. Luckily my grandfather was not penalized in any way. As usual, I spent every day writing him letters and waiting for him. I sat around the house waiting on his unexpected calls. It was a sick routine I could not break free of.

His sentence was short. With a record like he had, you'd think he would be slammed with a harsher penalty. For one, the jails were already crowded and they needed the space for violent and high-risk offenders, and for two, D was very manipulative and had no problem convincing the courts every single time that he had really learned his lesson.

The day he was released, I was devotedly waiting for him in the courtroom. As soon as we exited the courthouse, he informed me that we were running away.

"My mom bought us a house way up north. She has jobs lined up for both of us and a car we can use until we save for one. We can get married while we're up there and start over." It sounded like everything we wanted! "But we're leaving today."

"What? I can't do that D. I need time to say goodbye to everyone, especially to my grandfather. I can't just up and leave on him after everything he's done for me … for us …"

"Okay baby," he agreed, like he was actually giving me some control over my life. "Go say your goodbyes. We will leave tomorrow. I have some things to take care of and I'll be home later tonight."

I wasn't sure I even wanted to move away with him. What if something happened so far away, and I end up stranded with nowhere to go, in a foreign place with no one to help me?

The fear of being without him outweighed my fear of what might happen if I went with him. We'd made it this far together, maybe this was our big break.

Can we just take a moment right here to acknowledge how much of a broken record I was? From the outside looking in, it's so obvious to point out everything that was wrong with me. How naïve I was, how ignorant I was, how dependent I was, and how desperate for love I was. But back then, I did not see any of those things. I was so confused and misinformed, trying to adapt to a cruel world being trapped in a cycle of manipulation and victimization. I believed I was powerless, worthless, and that no one else would ever want me or love me. That is what abuse does to the soul.

I made my rounds to all of my friends and said my goodbyes. It was the first time in my life I left my small town, and I had no idea when I would be back. It was terrifying and exhilarating all at once.

My grandfather and Nancy tried to talk me out of going. They could already predict the turnout. But I was adamant about my decision and thanked them for everything they'd done for me.

D's mom picked us up the next morning.

We drove for hours and hours until we reached a small little cabin deep in a forest – literally in the middle of nowhere.

"Home sweet home," his mother announced.

I looked at D in utter confusion.

"The house isn't ready," he told me when his mom wasn't around. "We're going to stay here until it's done."

I was a little disappointed, but figured it was still a new adventure for us to embark on. We were finally away from all of the drama, the drugs, and the bad memories.

It was the smallest cabin I'd ever seen. It was built to lodge maybe two people, and there were five of us: D, myself, his mom, his mom's new husband, and his little sister … and three dogs.

It was extremely overcrowded.

But that wasn't the worst part.

There was no shower, no hot water, and no source of heat. We had to walk an hour to a community centre any time we needed a shower, cut down trees and burn logs for heat, and boil water to sterilize it just to do dishes. I felt like a damn pioneer. (First world problems, right?) I did NOT sign up for any of it!

He admitted that he lied just to get me out there because he knew I wouldn't go with him under such conditions. I could not believe how manipulative he was being! I was stranded in the middle of nowhere!

As the weeks passed, I noticed him going a little stir crazy. He was on the cusp of a mental breakdown, like he was slowly going insane. He was clean from drugs for the first time in a long time, and the withdrawals consumed him completely. He broke down and told me that I needed to leave him. He believed he was a dark entity, and that he deserved to die.

I'm not going to lie, it began to scare me. I wanted to leave. I could feel the evil taking over him.

Every time he came back from jail, he became more lost in himself, and drifted further and further from the person I knew him to be.

Being stuck in an overcrowded cabin with a bunch of lunatics caused a lot of tension, and D's mother kicked him out after a huge fight broke out between them. She dropped us off at the bus station, bought us two one-way tickets and told us to leave.

We took the bus to a city a few hours away (a little closer to where we were from) and stayed with his uncle for a couple of months.

It was during that time I found God.

I hadn't spoken to my mom in quite some time. We didn't communicate much at all. I carried so much resentment toward her for all of the grief I blamed her for causing me. When she called me one evening, I had very mixed emotions about whether or not to answer.

Something within me needed to talk to her.

I could tell that something was different about her. Over the past few years, every time we spoke there was hostility between us. This time, there was a softness in her voice. After a few minutes of small talk – The *hey, how's it going? How's life? What's new?* she broke the news about why she was calling

"You know how I'm prone to bad migraines and I could never figure out why?"

"Yeah …" I replied. My pulse increased.

"Well the doctor sent me to do some tests and they're fairly certain that they detected an aneurysm …"

I had no idea what an aneurysm was, but it did not sound good.

"What do you mean … What's an aneurysm?"

"It's basically a growth in the brain filled with blood that can burst at any time for no reason in particular. And if it bursts, you bleed out into your brain and can die immediately."

The world stopped spinning. The noise around me was silenced.

I held myself together the best I could and assured her that I was certain everything would be okay. For the first time in forever, I told her how much I loved her, and told her I would talk to her again soon.

I hung up the phone and raced outside into the black night. The rain poured upon me, soaking me from head to toe as I fell to my knees in the middle of the wet street. Something took over me as I looked to the sky with my hands pressed together in prayer, crying uncontrollably.

"God, please!" I prayed aloud. "I need you! Please don't do this to me! Please! I'm so sorry! I can do better! Please spare my mother! I promise I will change my ways! I swear I will turn my life around! I love her so much and I'm so sorry for everything! I need her God, do not take her from me!"

I meant every word I said.

CHAPTER TWENTY

The Limit

*"One of the most courageous decisions you'll ever make is to
finally let go of what is hurting your heart and soul."*
– Brigitte Nicole

Living with D's uncle didn't last very long. D had a tendency of burning every bridge he was given.

Next stop was his cousin's house, only about forty-five minutes away from our home town. This transition would mark the final days of our relationship once and for all.

Finally, right?

D's cousin Jay was a drug addict (at this point, I didn't know anyone who *wasn't*), and everyone that hung around were addicts as well. He and D bonded right away, and put their skills together to form a partnership moving drugs together – mostly to highschool kids, which was a pretty big market in that area.

I watched him rapidly decline. It was the cycle of an evolving addict that I knew and couldn't deny – constantly lying and manipulating me, coming home from "work" unable to function from being so messed up, showing no emotion or remorse for his actions, and running the streets all hours of the night. He even started ripping off dealers and sabotaging his partnerships – resulting in my watching helplessly as one of them smashed his face in with a hammer.

I lost all the respect I had left for him, and finally realized that there was nothing I could possibly do to save him. The D I fell in love with more than three years before was long gone, taking my very soul with him. It was time to accept it.

He stopped making time for me and made it crystal clear that he didn't give a damn whether I stayed with him or not. He brushed me off every time I tried to talk to him, not wanting to give me the time of day – no matter how much I pleaded with him to recognize what was happening. He was too busy hanging out with high school kids and making money off getting them fucked up.

I finally had enough.

He didn't think I'd ever leave.

I found out that Stephanie and Sage were both living in the same city that I was. With D always gone, I started spending most of my time with them.

We were all in similar situations. Stephanie and her boyfriend had a very toxic relationship that revolved around drug abuse and violence. Sage's boyfriend was a woman-beating junkie.

It was like God brought us together to help us heal each other. They rebuilt my backbone, and I regained more and more of my power each day I spent with them, finally understanding that I deserved better than the life I was accepting for myself .

With their ongoing support, I finally gathered enough courage to leave D for good, hoping they would follow my lead and do the same.

I contemplated my next move for weeks, trying to figure out where to go from where I was. I knew D sensed that I was actually thinking about leaving because he attempted multiple times to reinforce his power over me.

If he wasn't going to have me, then no one was. I belonged to him.

Just after New Years of 2011, I was in the shower one afternoon, numb from all of the abuse. I stood motionless as the scorching hot water scalded my body, going over every possible scenario and turnout in my head, figuring out my best option. I was running on autopilot for months in a dark depression, feeling lower than scum and having no hope that anything better existed for me. I remember turning the heat up so high that it was burning my skin, just so that I could feel something other than my internal despair. It was the lesser of two evils.

I was snapped out of my trance when I heard D come through the basement door.

Maybe he'll see my bags packed and snap back into reality ...

Being the victim that I was – that is, being beat down for so long that I genuinely believed my life held no value – I still hoped that he would come to his senses. To me, love was forever. It killed me to think about what would happen to him if I left. But what would happen to me if I stayed?

The bathroom door swung open.

Before I had a chance to prepare, he slammed open the shower door and grabbed me by my hair, yanking me out of the shower and dragging me across the floor soaking wet.

He tossed me into the middle of the living room hardwood floor, towering over me as I layed curled up in a fetal position butt naked.

"You wanna leave me do you? Here! Let me help!"

I was terrified. I'd never seen him get to this point of rage before. When I looked into his eyes, there was no trace of his soul left.

He dragged me toward the stairs as I begged for him to stop. I felt helpless – more vulnerable than I can ever begin to explain. I couldn't find the strength to defend myself.

"I'm gunna toss your ass out into the street myself you little cunt! How do you like me now? This is what you want, right?"

I tried to block out his tormenting voice as he continued to taunt me.

Fear pulsated through my body like never before. Every inch of my body was on fire.

"Please! Stop! I'm sorry! I won't leave! I love you!" I screamed and cried, trying to tell him what I thought he wanted to hear, in fear that he would actually throw me out butt naked into the snow.

"That's what I thought, bitch."

He tossed me aside like trash knowing he had defeated me, and walked back up the stairs, leaving me exposed in the middle of the cold, hard floor.

Instinct took over. Moving faster than ever before, I got dressed, gathered all of the belongings I could carry, and raced out of the house.

Crying uncontrollably and struggling to breathe through the immense inner pain, I walked three hours to Stephanie's apartment through a snowstorm with no money and no plan.

Cinder blocks crushed my chest. My throat clenched so tightly that air could barely make it to my lungs. My eyes throbbed from the swelling. Adrenaline and anxiety surged through my veins. Dark thoughts took over. I wanted to die.

I just kept moving – there was no looking back this time.

Steph and James took me in with open arms and insisted I stay with them. James would keep me safe if D tried to come after me.

My phone did not stop ringing for days.

I tried ignoring the calls, but he would just call back again. I tried turning off my phone, and the minute I turned it back on it was ringing again. I had a man pretend to be my new boyfriend hoping he would give up. Nothing worked. He left voicemail after voicemail threatening me, then begging for me to come home; demeaning me, then crying and apologizing.

I was serious this time.

It killed me, but I knew it was the right thing.

After hundreds and hundreds of calls and voicemails from D, I finally spoke with him and agreed to return about a week later to try and find closure, and pick up the rest of my belongings. When I showed up, he wasn't there. He had left his computer open and I noticed strange messages open – obviously done purposefully. He had been messaging dozens of females, including my friends, trying to hook up with them.

Even though I knew it was probably a ploy to make me jealous and fight for him, all of the anger I had built up boiled vigorously to the surface. He had betrayed me in every way imaginable! He had finally tipped me over the edge.

I grabbed his computer and smashed it to pieces.

In fact, I demolished the entire apartment, destroying every last thing he owned.

It was nothing short of a mental breakdown.

Once one of the most compassionate people you could ever meet – living with gratitude, loving deeply and passionately, and finding beauty in a cruel world – I now shut off my emotions completely and hated everyone and everything. I saw nothing but evil and corruption around me.

You see, when someone does us wrong, it's easy to see them as being deceitful or untrustworthy, forgetting the good qualities they possess. The more we are done wrong by others, the more we focus on the bad traits in mankind. Everyone seems corrupted and selfish, operating with ill intent.

But here's what I've come to learn: everyone fucks up. We're human. We're not supposed to be perfect. Sometimes people don't understand the extent of their effect on others lives or emotions, and sometimes they don't intend to hurt us. Sometimes they do – out of a need for revenge or validation, or a number of other justifications. Those reasonings come from their own internal conflict – it's not personal to us.

With this understanding, we need to remember that at the end of the day, we have no control over anyone other than ourselves. We will be treated the ways we allow ourselves to be treated. If someone is not capable of showing up in our lives respectfully and lovingly, it is not our job to fix them, it is our responsibility to hold higher standards in our lives and move on.

When I reflect on my own life, I have hurt so many people unintentionally; people who would probably say I did it deliberately, and their perceptions of me would likely be very negative. But my choices and actions were never personal to them. I was dealing with my own shit, and didn't realize that I was affecting other people. I thought I was worthless so how could I possibly have had an impact on anyone?

When we see humans for the bad within them instead of the good, we begin to see evil all around us, and view the world as an evil place. We create negative beliefs, and in turn we form negative views, thoughts, and emotions. As a result, we become absorbed into a cycle of negative patterns and habits.

When you operate from a space of constant negativity, you attract and connect with other negative people who share in that like-mindedness for viewing the world as an evil place, which in turn attracts even more negativity. Eventually, everything that surrounds us is negative. See the pattern?

Being abused in any manner – whether you're a man or woman, child or adult – is something that can cause a lifetime of anguish if it is not properly dealt with. It causes a person to view themselves and the world entirely differently – from a lens of distrust, anger, or sadness. Abuse can affect someone for the rest of their life, on so many levels, in so many ways. It changes us in ways we don't often recognize. Most times, the extent of the psychological impact isn't evident until months or even years later. Different people are affected in different ways.

As for myself, I was reborn as a heartless bitch.

I reverted to the glimpse of my man-hating self I had briefly met the summer I stayed at Chad's. Believing I was completely unworthy of love, I told myself no man would ever love me. Love was all a hoax. It wasn't real. All men wanted was sex, to live life in a selfish little bubble, and I did not beleive they were capable of real loyalty or devotion.

In all of the madness, all of the struggle, and all of the terror I endured, my standard of happiness became more and more diluted. I began to latch onto anything that made me feel even remotely good in any way.

In all of the betrayals, all of the broken promises, and all of the abuses, my trust in people – men more specifically – completely evaporated.

I started to see the negative side of every man I looked at. I watched men check me out when their girlfriends weren't paying attention. I saw the way men looked at me, and at women in general, like they were stripping them down in their minds, visualizing the things they wanted to do to them. All they wanted to do was fuck. I saw men cheat. I saw them lie. I saw them manipulate, and I saw that they had hidden agendas.

I even started seeing Kayne through a negative light in his relationship with Macy. I think that's where I lost all faith in men entirely. Kayne was always a fine example of what a boyfriend should be – respectful, loving, loyal, empathetic, and romantic. If I couldn't see him through eyes of love and understanding, there was no hope left.

No longer seeking emotional attachment, the only thing I selfishly wanted from men was for my own personal satisfaction - sex. On my terms.

Being the small world that it is, Stephanie's boyfriend James was the brother of my first boyfriend JT (the one who dumped me on Valentines day and broke my heart for the first time).

JT lived with us as well, and so inevitably we started sleeping together soon after I left D. We spent a lot of time together since we both lived in the same house, and shortly after our romantic involvement began, he developed feelings for me. Only, I wasn't the innocent little girl he once knew. I was into him, but I still resented him for hurting me the way he did.

I started sniffing coke on a regular basis and going out with Steph and Sage to clubs every weekend. We made quite a name for ourselves, being the life of the party everywhere we went. Everyone knew us as bar stars, and we sure built the reputation to go with the label.

Clubbing was an incredible new experience for me. It was a great release of all the tension I'd been carrying for so long. It was somewhere I could go and let loose, and forget about everything. I could get as drunk as I wanted, as high as I wanted, and do whatever I wanted to do – no repercussions. The loud intoxicating music, the beautiful people dancing freely and carelessly – it was the best escape there was. I felt confident and sexy, and my only concern in the world was finding sexy guys to buy me drinks and dance with me – which wasn't hard to do. I never hooked up with any of them, probably out of respect for Steph and James. I wasn't going to bring random guys back to their house, especially when I was sleeping with James' brother.

I still had some morals …

JT hated watching me go out night after night totally obliterated, knowing I was out being promiscuous with different men. But I was single and loving my new found freedom! There was no way I was going to be tied down to another person and I made that very clear! He knew I didn't want that so if he chose to keep sleeping with me, that was his problem.

The girls and I always got in free, and I don't think we ever paid for our own drinks or drugs. It was the good life! Sage got a job as a bartender at one of the clubs, and I became a promoter. Clubbing became our way of life. Any night the clubs were open – you'd find us there. We knew the owners and the bouncers, the DJ's and the bartenders. We knew all the regulars, and became very well known ourselves. We strutted through the strip like we owned it. And at the end of every night, JT would be up waiting for me to get home.

I had the best of both worlds.

What started as a good time rapidly turned into a shit show.

We were always stirring up drama as most teenage girls do – starting fights, leading guys on for drinks then ditching them, and even getting ourselves kicked out of the strip club for fighting with the DJ over the loud speaker.

We became entitled bitches who thought we ran every club we were in. If someone so much as looked at us the wrong way, they'd better watch out.

Night after night we'd go out on the town, then go back to James' and joke about all the stupid shit we did.

With my rapidly diminishing morals, I pushed my boundaries even further, and against my better judgement I decided to go home with a stranger one night.

We met toward the end of the night and had a great time dancing together. He was pretty cute – tall, blond hair, blue eyes, and was dressed nicely. He asked me if I wanted to come back to his place, smoke some weed, and hang out. The night was still young, so I agreed. He didn't seem to be a threat of any sort.

Who on cocaine ever has good judgement?

We jumped in a cab and drove through the snowy night. I was a little more incapacitated than I thought I was, and lost track of what route we took to get to his house. Being new to the city, I had no clue where the hell I was when we finally reached the destination.

The first red flag when we arrived was him telling me to be very quiet when we entered the house, after he had already told me it was his "own house." He led me through a dark garage and down a set of stairs into the basement of the house.

We tiptoed through the basement until we reached a closed door. When he opened the door and turned on the light, the appearance of his room was like any typical 20-year-old, single male's room. There were posters on all the walls, video games laying around, a sitting area set up for blazing, and the room was not unusually cluttered. Nothing screamed WEIRDO.

But his demeanor sure did.

As soon as we arrived, he began explaining every single thing he had in his room: where it came from, how much it cost, what it meant to him – you name it. He must have been able to tell I was annoyed so he changed the topic by apologizing and informing me that he was just nervous to have "such a beautiful girl" in his room.

That was a little strange to me since all the guys I knew were totally comfortable around any female, no matter how "beautiful" they were. He didn't seem at all uneasy at the club, so what was so different all of a sudden?

I took my shoes off and sat down on his bed. The room started spinning.

I was way more drunk than I thought I was.

"Do you want to smoke a bong?" he asked to end the awkward tension.

"Actually, I'm just gunna wait a few minutes, I just got the spins all of a sudden. I think I need to lay down."

"Come on, come smoke one with me," He insisted, speaking as more of a demand than a request.

"Not right now man, straight up. I need to lay down for a minute."

He paused for a moment.

"Come. Here," he demanded sternly, hitting the seat of the couch beside him in sync with his words to gesture for me to come over.

What the hell is wrong with this guy?

He persisted.

"I said … Come. Here."

The tone of his voice deepened.

He sounded angry that I was not obeying what he was demanding of me. I wondered if he might have a couple of screws loose in his head.

When I still didn't budge, he grabbed my ankles and pulled me across the mattress toward where he was sitting on the couch at the foot of the bed.

As I mentioned before, I was pretty aware of how psychologically damaged people function and what makes them tick, so I decided to just play along. I really didn't have any other choice.

"Fiiiiinee," I said jokingly, "You win! I'll smoke one."

I packed a popper and smoked it. It sobered me up a little.

I blew out my cloud of smoke, and turned to face him. It seemed that he was struggling with uncontrollable thoughts. He was hunched over in his seat with his hands on his head and was twitching a little. I tried making small talk, but he was obviously not hearing anything I was saying.

"Why are you here?" he asked suddenly, lifting his head and staring at me blankly. He had a very odd look on his face.

"Uhm ... to come hang out and smoke a show with you ...?"

It was a weird question considering he was the one who asked me to come in the first place ...

"You shouldn't be here," he stated firmly with a cold, dangerous energy. "I'm not a good person."

His voice sent chills up my spine.

Saying I was terrified would be an understatement. I honestly thought he was going to murder me in that moment.

As an uncontrolled reaction, tears flowed rapidly from my eyes.

This is it. I thought to myself. *I'm dead! No one knows where I am. Hell, I don't even know where I am!*

Tears started to build up in my eyes.

"Why are you crying?" he asked anxiously, sounding genuinely concerned.

Maybe he's bipolar or something ...

"Because you're scaring me," I said honestly.

All of a sudden, he looked ashamed and worried.

He picked me up and cradled me like a baby, rocking me back and forth, and rubbing my hair.

"Shhhhhh," he said almost fatherly. "Don't cry, I'm so sorry! I didn't mean to scare you!"

What. The. Fuck. This guy is delusional!

I knew I had nowhere to run. It was the middle of the winter, three o'clock in the morning, and I had no idea where I even was. Not to mention I was still wearing a little dress and high heeled shoes. My best bet at escaping safely was to play at his level until 6 a.m. when the buses started running and use the bit of change I had left to take it ... anywhere. I knew that there were bus stops all over the city, so it was very likely I could walk a few minutes and find one.

"Idiot! Idiot! Idiot!" he exclaimed in frustration as he hit himself in the head like he was punishing himself for what he said.

"It's okay. Don't worry," I told him reassuringly, playing along with his delusion.

I placed my hand on his cheek as if to comfort him and assured him that he didn't hurt me. It seemed to really be tearing him apart that he made me cry.

"But you know," I started, "I'm really feeling like shit. I'd like to lay down if that's okay?"

"Of course!" he agreed.

I got up from the couch and layed on his bed, trying to stay as far away as possible from him.

He was staring at me, observing me so intensely. I was uncomfortable that I didn't know what was going through his mind. I had to get him to a different mind state.

"Why don't you come cuddle with me? I'd really like to snuggle," I suggested.

I hoped that my "interest" would ward off any negative thoughts that were consuming him.

I was right.

He snuggled up with me and fell asleep. But not before nuzzling his face under my head multiple times and making noises like a growling dog.

Psychopath ...

I set my alarm for 5:45 a.m. and passed out as well.

When I woke up to my alarm a couple of hours later, he offered to walk me to the bus stop. I said that would be fine. Being out in public with him seemed a lot safer than setting him off now.

He got on the bus behind me. I sat at the very front, and he proceeded to sit closer to the back. Five minutes into the ride he walked to the front of the bus, handed me his apple juice without saying a word, then returned to his seat.

Finally, it came to a stop I recognized. I got off the bus, he stayed on.

I let out a sigh of relief. That was the end of it.

That was the first and very last time I ever went home from the club with a stranger – one of the very few lessons I actually learned the first time.

Another reminder of why men could not be trusted.

Being on the brink of yet another potentially disastrous situation put an abrupt, but temporary, end to my recklessness.

CHAPTER TWENTY ONE

Playing with Fire

"Most of our mistakes, the big ones at least, are the result of allowing emotion to overrule logic. We knew the right choice, but didn't obey."

– Unknown

With all of the harnessed emotions finally out of my system, I felt a temporary sense of relief and fulfillment. I was ready to get my life on track.

Somewhere through the grapevine I heard about a program called Youth Quest. Their mission at Youth Quest was to help delinquent youth who lacked guidance and support to develop the skills needed to be a productive member of society. They educated their students about proper work etiquette and helped them to overcome personal barriers to attain work and be self-sufficient. They paid their students to sit in a classroom five days a week from 9 a.m. to 4 p.m. (similar to being in school – but getting paid) and then transitioned them into a job in the community that they helped the students to acquire.

Due to limited funding, the program would only accept a certain number of people. Their choice was dependent on who they felt sincerely needed the help and who would take it seriously.

I attended a first and second interview, just as you would for a regular job, and soon after got the call that I was accepted.

Yes! I remember thinking. *Some easy money!*

I didn't take it too seriously at the time; I didn't think anyone could help me.

I was wrong.

The class consisted of a small group of youth between the ages of about seventeen and twenty-two. On the very first day we were required to participate in ice-breaker activities to get to know each other, one of which required sharing our stories. Listening to everyone speak was confirmation that I was not alone in my struggles. We connected right away, opening up to each other about matters that felt impossible to share with anyone else. Hearing the others put their stories into words helped me to find the voice in me to express my turmoil and anguish.

I felt heard. Understood.

We spent all of our days together in the classroom, and within only days began spending most of our free time together as well. We formed incredible bonds, which was beneficial in some ways and destructive in others. We understood each other in ways nobody else understood us, and thus were able to shed insight into each other's lives and work through situational dilemmas as a team. We drew strength from each other and united as a family. But we were also all broken, and struggled with addictions of different sorts – mostly alcohol and drugs, so in our spare time, take a few guesses at what our pastime included …

Lunch breaks meant outdoor sessions getting high in various places: parks, underground parking lots, sometimes other people's houses …

whatever was close enough to make it back to class on time. Evenings typically meant drinking and smoking up ... maybe a few lines of this or that – nothing too crazy because none of us could afford to miss a day on our paychecks. It was easy money.

Weekends meant reeking havoc - clubbing, strip clubs, house parties ... it didn't matter as long as we were getting absolutely trashed – it was our celebratory congratulations to ourselves for getting through another week doing something productive.

I'm not entirely sure why, but the instructor of our program, Jessica, took an immediate and obvious liking to me. When I spoke, she became very emotional. She listened. She understood. And she saw something in me that I didn't see in myself. She made that very clear to me. For the very first time, I felt hope that there was something better in store for my life than what I knew; that I was worthy and capable of more. So naturally, when Jessica suggested that I speak with one of the on-site counselors, Gregory, I took her advice.

Speaking with Gregory was exactly what I needed. Though we only spoke a few times, he made me feel comfortable enough to open up to him. To my absolute surprise, I trusted him. A man.

Gregory was an older fellow, heavy-set with a short white beard and spectacle glasses. Right away his genuine smile put me at ease. I opened up to him about some of the past traumas I'd encountered. When he shed tears listening to my story, I regained an ounce of faith in men.

Maybe they aren't all insensitive and manipulative assholes ...

It's truly incredible how deeply a small act of empathy can impact someone.

Unfortunately, my case was one that he was not able to properly advise due to lack of relative understanding. I ended the sessions with him, feeling that I was not getting much out of it. Still, he did his best to help me in the only way he knew how. He expressed that it was apparent to him that I was very unhealthy – weighing less than 90lbs from the drugs and lack of proper nutrition over the years. He was concerned about my deteriorating health, so each week he provided me with meal replacement drinks to give me some form of nutrients.

Throughout the course, I bonded with everyone in different ways, but there were three individuals who I connected with the most. Their names were Aneesa, Mark, and Nathan.

Aneesa and her younger brother were placed in adoption agencies as young children, and by God's wonderful grace, they were adopted into a family together. As a teenager, Aneesa struggled with identity issues and eventually gave birth to a child who suffered from severe fetal alcohol syndrome due to her struggle with alcoholism. The guilt consumed her to the very core, causing her to fall even more deeply into the world of addiction.

Mark and Nathan were best friends and more or less just needed proper guidance and support. They were both extremely intelligent individuals, but both dealt with multiple issues ranging from ADHD to anxiety and depression, and of course addiction.

A few weeks into the course, Aneesa expressed to me that she had a younger brother Jake (who was a year older than me) who was coming out of a relationship similar to the one I had just come out of, and she wanted us to meet. She told me that he had been with his ex-girlfriend, Candy, for a few years, and that she was very manipulative, controlling and abusive to him. That was a weird dynamic to me. She thought we might be able to help each other through the grieving process and lean on each other for support.

While waiting for Aneesa's bus with her one day after class, I noticed a very handsome guy across the street who appeared to be walking directly toward us. We locked eyes immediately. My heart began to pound as he walked directly toward us, and I started to feel nervous.

Aneesa turned around to see what had my attention.

"Jake!" She yelled excitedly.

Holy shit!

It was her brother. I did not expect him to be so ... hot! I was at a loss for words.

My face felt like it was on fire! I told Aneesa I had to use the washroom, and quickly turned around and walked away. I stayed inside of the bus terminal to collect myself. I was acting like a complete fool!

A few minutes went by when I heard an alert on my phone. It was Aneesa:

Hey girl. Jake thinks you're really cute. Can I give him your digits?

I responded:

Uhm ... hell yes.

I spied on them through the window of the terminal, analyzing his every move.

To most, he probably wouldn't stand out much in a crowd, seeming as timid as he projected himself to be. But to me he was a work of art. He was built like a brick house, very muscular and brawny, but so subtle in his movements. He had dark eyes and tanned skin, and a smile that could illuminate darkness. I admired that smile as Aneesa read him my reply. He then went on his way, glancing around to see if he could spot me before departing.

There were those butterflies I hadn't felt in so long!

Less than an hour later, I received a text message from an unfamiliar number:

Hey cutie

It was him! I had to play it off. I couldn't let him know I'd been anticipating his text!

Me: Hey? Who is this …

Jake: It's Aneesa's brother, Jake

Me: Oh, hey :)

Jake: What's up :)

Me: Not much, just kickin it. You?

Jake: Not much

This is always the awkward part in the conversation where both people are trying to decide if they should be the one to break the ice and how to do it … Well, he definitely did it …

Jake: So why did you run away from me earlier?

Shit! Was it that obvious?!

Me: I didn't … I had to use the washroom lol

Jake: Yeah … right lol

Me: Don't flatter yourself

Jake: Hahahah Aneesa warned me you were feisty

Me: Oh, did she now?

Jake: She was right.

Me: Yes, she was

Jake: So, tell me about yourself

Me: What do you want to know lol

Jake: I don't know, anything. Do you smoke weed?

Me: Yeah, you?

Jake: Yeah lol let me know if you ever need any, I can hook you up

Me: Actually, I'm looking right now if you're around

Jake: Sure. Where are you?

I totally lied. James sold weed and I got it for free from Stephanie. I just wanted an excuse to see him. I told him where I was staying and he said he could be there in twenty minutes. When the time came, I ran outside to meet him.

I was so nervous that I didn't even try to converse with him. I thanked him and ran back across the street. Out of my peripheral I saw that he hadn't moved. He stood still, observing me presumptuously.

"Hey!" he called after me.

I turned around to face him. He was smiling that infectious smile.

"What are you doing tonight?"

"Not sure yet," I yelled back, smiling from the contagiousness of his.

"Wanna hang out?"

I tried my best to conceal my excitement.

"Sure," I replied, without seeming too thrilled.

"Alright. Cool. I'll text you." He smiled and continued on his way.

We made arrangements to go to a local pub that evening with Aneesa, Mark, Nathan, and a couple other friends from my program. I wasn't looking for anything and didn't want to give him the idea that I wanted a boyfriend, so I thought it'd be best that we hang out casually in a group of people.

We didn't talk much out of mutual nervousness, but we could hardly keep our eyes off each other.

In the middle of a game of pool, I noticed that Jake was sitting alone in the booth, so I sat down next to him. After some small talk and a lot of built up tension, we were making out without a care in the world as to who was watching.

From that night on, we spent much of our time together.

Jake would meet me on my lunch breaks and pick me up after class. We did everything together – it didn't matter what, we enjoyed each other's company. As much as I liked him, I was very open about not wanting to jump into anything. I explained what I had been through and that my heart needed time to heal, and he felt the exact same way being in the similar situation Aneesa said he was. He didn't talk much about his issues, so I didn't pry. I figured he would talk if and when he was ready.

We were both more than happy being *friends with benefits*. We had fun together and the sex was great, what could go wrong?

The closer we got, I recognized that Aneesa became a little uneasy. I felt like there was something she was not telling me. As usual, I ignored that little voice in the back of my head.

Jake explained that he had just moved into a small apartment by himself after leaving his ex, not far from where I was staying with James and Stephanie.

After a long night of clubbing, we ventured there so that he could put on some comfortable clothes before coming back to my place for the night.

There wasn't much furniture in the apartment, and the walls were bare. He told me it was because his ex took everything, and this was all he had left for the moment.

We sat down to smoke a bong on the couch, and before I knew it we were in his bed having sex. When he got up to get me a glass of water, I noticed a pink robe on the back of his door, and a pair of women's slippers on the floor. I thought it was odd and wondered why any of Candy's stuff would be at his place if he moved there to get away from her, but I decided it was none of my business. Who was I to talk? I was openly sleeping with both him and JT without any intention of committing to either of them.

While waiting for him to return with my water, I noticed what appeared to be a magazine clipping on the floor. Being the nosey person I am, I picked it up to see what it was. It was a picture of an ultrasound. I thought nothing of it.

Just then, Jake entered the room.

"Something you wanna tell me?" I teased, waving the ultrasound photo at him.

He looked at me wide-eyed and put his head down.

"I was joking," I assured him.

He sat down on the bed.

"Well … actually … yeah. I should have told you. I just found out I'm having a baby. Candy is pregnant."

"Oh …" I responded, not really knowing what to say. Unsure of what the reasoning was for it, I felt sick to my stomach.

"I'm sorry. I should have told you." He was ashamed and embarrassed.

"No, Jake. You don't owe me anything. We're having sex, were not dating."

He looked up at me in instant relief: "You're so amazing."

"*This* is so amazing! Congratulations! You're going to be such an amazing father."

He attacked me with kisses and tackled me onto the bed, getting in another quickie before we made our way back to James and Steph's.

JT didn't like Jake, for obvious reasons. Everyone could tell that JT grew very attached to me since we'd started sleeping together, and even told me he loved me. It didn't phase me. I had zero emotional connection. My walls were way too high. I told myself it was his karma for what he did to me back in high school, and that gave me a sense of power.

As I grew closer to Jake, I veered away from JT.

As much as we both tried to fight it, Jake and I began to fall for each other as time went on. We pretended there were no feelings involved, but the chemistry we shared was undeniable.

Like every other time in my life, when things started to look up, someone had to interfere. I received a Facebook message from Candy:

I have no idea who the hell you are but why the fuck is there a photo on the internet of you with my boyfriend? Do you know he has a girlfriend who is pregnant with his child? We're trying to work things out between us so back the fuck off bitch.

Either she was even crazier than Aneesa made her out to be, or Jake had some serious explaining to do. I showed him the message and waited for his response. The guilt he displayed should have determined my conclusion. Verbally he confirmed what I suspected, but by now we all know I was a sucker for seeing the best in people, even when it wasn't there.

He assured me that she was a lunatic who would not give him up easily, and did not want him moving on when they would be having a child together. He went on to explain that she was addicted to opiates, and working at a rub-n-tug even though she was pregnant. He wanted nothing to do with any of it. I took his word and left it at that.

Observing what was happening between us – the stars in our eyes and the constant public displays of affection – Aneesa finally bluntly broke the news to me not long after I received the message.

"Jake and Candy are still together."

"What?" I could hardly believe what I was hearing. "Are you kidding me?"

"Their relationship is fucked. Neither of them are happy and they haven't been for a long time, so I don't know why they think they can make it work. They break up every other day. I thought when he met you he would leave her for good, but he doesn't have any balls apparently. Clearly you and my brother are falling for each other and I don't want you getting hurt so I needed to tell you. I'm sure he told you they're having a baby together, so maybe you should take a step back and let them see if they can work things out one last time. I hate the girl with a passion, but I grew up not knowing my family and I want that baby to have a shot at his family being together."

Everything started to make sense.

Part of me felt used for a brief moment in time, but I brushed it off and reminded myself that I was sleeping with someone else too, and that we agreed there were no strings attached. Still, I couldn't help but feel betrayed. I was open and honest about everything, and he was living a big lie …yet, I wasn't sure I was ready to let him go so easily …

I confronted Jake and he admitted everything Aneesa told me. Hearing the truth from his mouth cut me deeper than I expected. Maybe I did still have feelings...

We stood outside in the dark, busy street, arguing back and forth as the rain fell steadily upon us. I finally had enough as my anger and frustration built up, and told him I didn't want anything to do with him from that point on. I proceeded to walk away from him when he yelled after me.

"Stop!"

I ignored him and continued walking.

"Can you fucking stop?!" He pleaded.

Drenched from head to toe, I reluctantly stopped and turned to face him, now almost halfway up the block.

"What do you want from me?!" I screamed back, angry and annoyed.

He paused for a second.

"I just want ... you!"

We both stood frozen in that moment in time, staring at each other and pondering what *this* really was. Like magnets drawing us together, we started toward each other, meeting in a passionate embrace.

He was just as confused as I was.

Behind my denial, I was more attached than I was willing to admit to myself. After giving up on the possibility of ever feeling whole again, there was something about him that gave me hope and helped me to forget about everything that happened with D. He made my heart feel a little lighter - a ray of sunlight in some of my darkest and loneliest hours. We were the same.

Another part of me, the logical side that I never listened to, told me to let go of whatever was going on with us – that it was not worth all the drama that would surely be in store. We'd barely been seeing each other a few months ... it wouldn't have been devastating if I never saw him again.

After contemplating my thoughts, my feelings and my options, I reminded myself that I didn't care for any kind of commitment. Whatever Jake chose to do with Candy was none of my business. I liked what we shared and how he made me feel, and the selfish piece of who I'd become was okay with that. If he needed time to figure his shit out with her, then so be it. All it meant to me was that I could hook up with other guys in the meantime – there were no strings between us.

Being emotionally driven as most women – actually, most people really – are, I allowed my most prominent emotion to rule me: fear.

Fear of being alone again; fear of being the last choice; fear of not being good enough.

The intensity of my emotions was my greatest asset and yet my greatest hindrance. My charisma could spread happiness and joy everywhere I went. But the lack of control over my insecurities and weaknesses easily overtook me. I pretended I had no feelings, and even convinced myself that that was true, because I didn't understand how or why I was feeling the emotions that coursed through me, and had no idea how to manage them. The drug induced amplification only made things that much worse.

CHAPTER TWENTY TWO

A Shadow of Myself

"I am just another Alice who's trying to find her way out of her head and into a wonderland."

– VaZaki Nada

Having a new circle of friends, coming to terms that I was not alone in my struggles, and acquiring insight into my self-induced and externally programmed limitations, the in-class portion of Youth Quest came to an end, and it was time to get out in the real world of work.

Aneesa, Nathan, Mark and I were all placed into a job together. We would be helping an entrepreneur whose name was Drew to build his business from the ground up.

Drew was in his early thirties. He was kind hearted, outgoing and downright entertaining. His mission was to help build the community in whatever ways we could brainstorm and put into effect. He took us on, as well as a few other students from another sector of our program, knowing full well that we were working through many types of internal struggles. He was patient with us, and devoted himself to teaching us how to be productive, independent, and goal-oriented. He taught us the importance of being punctual, working independently and as a team, and of being able to be relied on. He gave us each specific positions in the company that entailed a fairly significant amount of responsibility. He even gave up his own home to rent out to Nathan, Mark and two other employees from our program: Shaw and Easton. We called it our "work house." Though I still lived with Stephanie, I spent most of my time there. It became a home to me ... to all of us. We were a little family – all pieces of a broken puzzle that fit perfectly together.

In the beginning, I took pride in the faith Drew had in me, and I strove to do my best to help his business thrive. When the novelty of my new form of independence wore off, I grew bored and easily frustrated. Anxiety grew prominently within me from all of the sudden changes and the pressure to be a better version of myself. I wasn't sure I could live up to it. For a very short time, I believed I could change my life, but it wasn't long before that deep-rooted sense of unworthiness consumed me once more.

It doesn't matter how many realizations a person has if they do not have ongoing mentorship, support, and discipline to work through the necessary changes. A realization does not spark a new mentality or a total transformation, it's merely a gateway opening to those possibilities. Sure, I knew that my habits and lifestyle were catastrophic, and I wanted better for myself, but I had no idea how to get there, so I didn't really believe it to be possible.

I had no faith.

I was totally lost and trying to figure out how to live my life avoiding anymore pain – a term I later identified as survival mode.

In survival mode, we are limited to an awareness of only the things we need to keep ourselves alive – shelter, protection, water, and food. Every day is a struggle trying to ensure that those things are provided. We wake up each morning wondering how to acquire the basic necessities for survival and trying to manage the fear that we know all too well. Only when we succeed in acquiring those basic needs each day do we feel a sense of ease. It's a daily cycle that requires full focus and attention. There is no mental capacity to long for anything more. Accepting this as a way of life, we numb ourselves by escaping the only reality we know through whatever means necessary. If we have not seen a better life for ourselves, how do we even know it exists?

I had found God, but I did not know him yet.

I was trapped in survival mode from the time I was a small child. To me, nothing greater than what I knew life to be was attainable as much as I wished it to be possible. I was brought up to believe that money would never be in the picture for me; that no matter how smart I was or how well I did in school, I would never be truly successful. Even a concept as miniscule as traveling would never be an option for me.

Showing up for work every day became a challenge, not only because of my increasing dependence on drugs and alcohol, but because it was the first time in years that I was focusing on my personal development instead of being the rock for someone else. Helping others was never an issue for me, because I love people and thrive off of helping anyone in any way I can. Helping myself was my barrier, because I never loved myself enough to care what happened to me. It was extremely confronting.

I stuck it out through the overwhelming emotions because I knew I needed the money, but because of the lack of motivation, I went into work not wanting to actually work – like I was entitled to a paycheck just for being there ...

By lunch time each day I was ready to call it quits and go home, just for the temporary relief of a quick fix. I would try to justify the excuses in my head, telling myself that I couldn't handle the stress, or that I would only be losing a small portion of money on my check if I only missed half a day. Sometimes I did give in to that urge. Sometimes I would sniff a little something to get me through the day.

I made a habit of sleeping in and showing up late, and I challenged everything Drew said, creating a significant power struggle between the two of us. It made his job as a leader extremely difficult, because I was a leader in my own way, and a very powerful one at that. Some of the other employees fed off of my energy.

Drew remained patient and understanding.

He never once treated me with the same disrespect that I continuously showed him. When I refused to complete a certain task, he allowed me to ponder through my issues and keep me on the clock – still paying me out of empathy for my situation. When I lashed out at him, he silently took it.

After weeks of my continuous drama, he finally cracked. He broke into tears when he explained that he was at his wits end with me, and did not know how else he could help me; that if I couldn't get my shit together, he would have to let me go.

His acknowledgement and understanding of what I was going through snapped me into reality momentarily. I regained another increment of compassion and respect for men. I didn't realize that my selfishness and poor decisions could impact a grown man so immensely. There I was making myself a victim in every way possible. I tossed blame around on everyone for anything that happened to me, while Drew broke his neck for me and tolerated me. I treated him like dirt in order for me to still support myself financially. I didn't admit my wrong doing, but I was ashamed of my behavior and I made a conscious effort to do better.

My focus switched to work. I stopped worrying about the hardships of my personal life. I put serious thought into our brainstorming sessions, and brought innovative ideas to the table. When it came to physical labor, I would bust my ass until I had nothing left to give. It made me feel a part of something great.

I helped to build community gardens throughout the city, organize charity events, and had the opportunity to network with some very amazing people. It was a new sense of empowerment that foreshadowed what could be in store for my future.

I saw a shadow of myself.

Unfortunately, it was not yet my time to advance.

Mark and Nathan progressed through the same stages that I did. Together we took a few steps forward, enthusiastic about what the future could hold for us, then just as quickly we reverted to old habits, taking ten steps backward.

Our habitual behaviors are directed through our paradigms, or belief systems. Until we work on the root cause - that is, changing those belief systems, especially about ourselves, we will continue to fall into the same habitual patterns over and over again.

The work house became a trap house. The guys lost sight of the great act of kindness Drew had bestowed upon them by allowing them to reside in his home; when nobody else would approve them to rent anywhere based on their instabilities, rocky histories, and bad credit. They started pulling the whole "this is our house; we pay the rent; we know our rights as tenants" act and everything went to crap.

I stopped hanging around as much. What once was a beautiful and welcoming home was a dirty, smelly, and grungy trap house. All sorts of questionable people started hanging around, and the house was rapidly torn apart.

I went around from time to time to hang out and smoke up. Just before the guys were kicked out, I showed up randomly for a short visit. Upon entering the house, I was immediately drawn to a beautiful young girl who was sitting on the couch with her low-life, wannabe-thug-looking boyfriend.

She was the most gorgeous girl I had ever seen in real life. With a beautiful olive skin tone, long dark hair and bright blue eyes encompassed by long, thick eye lashes, she looked like she could be on the cover of a magazine.

She emitted such an attractive energy, but there was great sorrow in her expression.

I noticed right away that she had a faded black eye. Being beat on countless times by D in the past, it didn't take me long to put two and two together.

I smiled at her and introduced myself. She shyly notified me that her name was Aisha.

"What happened to your face?" I asked her bluntly.

I didn't give two shits what her loser boyfriend had to say about it. I had zero tolerance for domestic abuse. My wounds were still very fresh, and I had no filter.

She uncomfortably held firm eye contact with me, like she knew I could see right through her.

"I fell down the stairs."

Number one cover-up story of all time, right?

Projecting my knowledge of what really happened, I sarcastically replied, "Ah … yeah. I hate when that happens," and gave her a look so as to say *come on girl, really?*

She bowed her head and glanced to the floor, ashamed of herself for lying to protect the abuser who sat next to her.

I went on my way, carrying an unresolved attachment to Aisha. It would not be the last time I'd see her. In fact, she would become the best female friend I'd ever have, and we would go through life carrying each other through hardships and pushing each other to greatness, helping each other to heal and chasing our dreams together.

Stephanie and James broke up a few months after I moved in due to the toxicity of the relationship – probably induced by all of the drugs and partying. When James ended up in jail, Steph and I started looking for a place together, ready to start a new life of independence.

We tried convincing Sage to leave her boyfriend, Toozie, and move in with us – our own bachelorette pad! Unfortunately, she was not yet strong enough to make the transition. She and Toozie had been together on and off since they were young kids, and she was also trying to save him from his battle with addiction. I couldn't judge her. I completely understood.

Needless to say, Steph and I found a beautiful two story, three-bedroom condo in a suburban neighborhood in our city, so we asked Macy if she wanted to room with us as well. She was all for it!

That was when the real fun began! You wanna talk about a non-stop party? We went hard every day, and even harder than when we went clubbing every weekend. The after parties were usually at our place. From morning to night, day in and day out, we lived life to the fullest! The days all merged together and life became an everlasting blur.

When my placement with Drew came to an end, I got a job at a daycare. I was always great with kids and loved working to educate them, but evidently my lifestyle was not a match for that type of commitment. I only stayed a month or so.

I wasn't worthy.

Falling into old habits, I started selling drugs – mostly weed, but sometimes other stuff if the numbers made sense – to make some money to support myself. After dealing various types of drugs alongside D for so long and becoming used to the fast money, I really didn't want to go work a nine to five job. I would have had to bust my ass making next to nothing with the lack of credentials and education I had.

We created our own trap house. There were so many people in and out of our house, I almost forgot who actually lived there. So often there were strangers passed out on the living room floor still messed up from the night before. We just assumed it was someone that one of the other girls must know. We never really questioned anyone's presence. Our door was always open to anyone.

Our little bachelorette pad quickly became known as the *REAL-LIFE JERSEY SHORE HOUSE*. Our lives revolved around sex, drugs and partying. We'd wake up every morning with no recollection of what happened the night before, finding humor in piecing the bits of information we had between us. I had no shame in bringing different men back to my house to hook up, since that was all I needed from them anymore. I'm not saying there were tons, but there were a select handful. It was my house and my life, and I didn't care what anyone had to say about it! I had nothing to prove to anyone.

Jake remained my constant, but without a desire for commitment, I still had my fun on the side. I grew to care very much about him, but my heart was cold, my soul was lost and my wounds were deep. I had no room for serious commitment. I'd have sex with a guy and never talk to him again. Hell, I'd allow men to fall in love with me and never talk to them again.

What's love anyways?

Over the duration of the time since I left D, he persistently tried to contact me. I discovered that he was dating one of the high-school girls who hung around our place while we were together, and it infuriated me. I wondered whether they had something going on before I was even out of the picture, and it made me even more bitter. Though I knew I didn't want to be with him, I'd call him up to have sex once in a while, just to know I could have him if I wanted him. After all the hell he put me through when I gave him every piece of me, there was no way I could accept him being happy and loyal to someone else.

He got away from the drugs temporarily, recognizing how bad he messed things up between us and hoping for another shot. I considered taking him back. He left his girlfriend in hopes that we had a chance, but I decided that I liked my freedom too much to ever go back to him.

I played with his emotions the way he did mine. I let him and Jake come around at the same time, just to watch them fight over my attention. Throw Shaw into the mix (he worked with me for Drew and stayed at the workhouse). He was a total sweetheart who brought me gifts to work on a regular basis, left flowers on my desk countless mornings, and made a point to tell me how beautiful and amazing I was every chance he got. He had a huge crush on me, and tried tirelessly to influence my return of sentiment.

For a little while, the three of them fought for my absent love, each knowing about my relations with the others. I didn't understand how they could all be so desperate. One would bring me flowers, so the next day another would bring me nicer flowers. Then the next day, the other would do something even more romantic or thoughtful. They did it all right in front of each other and remarked frequently about who would win me over! It went back and forth for weeks!

When the game got old and I was fully gratified, I cut ties with D and Shaw once and for all, deciding I was content being with Jake, my mirror.

I recognize how horrible a person this makes me sound, and to be honest, I'm not proud of my decisions. I was manipulative, insensitive, and cold. But I see now that abuse coupled with previous traumas can induce some serious mental instabilities. I covered up my lost sense of direction and place in the world by projecting my pain onto others. It made me feel better to see other people's lives fucked up and I felt unspeakable satisfaction from knowing I had power over men; or rather, that they no longer had power over me.

I never felt so in control, but ironically enough, I was completely *out* of control!

Before I knew what hit me, cocaine was all I thought about.

First thing in the morning, I would wake up and roll over to the end table beside my bed to sniff a line before my eyes were even completely open. I barely put food into my body. The coke was my fuel. The only substance my body craved was the drug. Until I had it in my system, I had no sense of motivation – no desire to go through the day.

Cocaine kept me sane. It helped me to speak openly about my life and my struggles, and eliminated all of the fears that resided within me. When I didn't have it, I felt like I was living in a nightmare. I felt the extremes of every bad emotion that exists. Tantalizing fear. Uncontrollable anxiety. Unspeakable guilt. Shame. Paranoia. Loneliness. Confusion. Vulnerability. On top of that was the physical impact – the sweats, the shakes, nausea, weakness.

But I think I hit my all-time low the night I sniffed a line in front of Chuck and Danielle.

Ever since I was separated from them as a child, I vowed to myself that I would get a place of my own where they could come stay any time they needed – a place where they would always be welcomed and safe.

Over the years I was with D, they did visit regularly, and I was as much a part of their lives as I could be. I did my best to teach them how to take control over their lives and to not be victims to circumstance. I was teaching them from a naïve standpoint – for I, myself, was a victim.

I displayed to them the wrong kind of control – the manipulative and destructive control I had learned. Control where I was powerful and people feared me, and where they would never have to worry about anyone crossing them, because I would always protect them. I truly thought that was what they needed, because it was what I myself had longed for – protection.

I held true to that vow the best way I knew how: always being there for support, spending time talking with them and trying to understand them, never missing a birthday or holiday, always bringing the family together for special occasions to give them a sense of belonging that I never had, buying them things that they needed and trying to break them out of their shells … and of course knocking Danielle's first boyfriend out after he cheated on her.

After crashing from my high the next morning and coming to terms with the fact that I used cocaine right in front of them, an unsettling feeling remained in me for years to come. It took me a very long time to forgive myself for such a selfish and brainless move. Still, there are times I catch myself really feeling that shame. My brother and sister looked up to me as a role model – and I let them down terribly.

Nevertheless, I understand fully that addiction overrides any sense of logic. The person who made that choice was not me.

Even after multiple scares with overdose, having an out of body experience where I believed I was dead, and waking up in temporary paralysis, I still did not stop. It would take nothing short of a miracle to get me off the path I was on.

Only an angel of God Himself would be able to save my soul.

CHAPTER TWENTY THREE

Tall, Dark and Handsome

"Maybe the journey isn't so much about becoming anything. Maybe it's about unbecoming everything that isn't you, so you can be who you were meant to be in the first place."

– Unknown

Months passed as quickly as the river flows. Absent to the changes that were happening all around me, life was passing me by before my very eyes. I lived very much in the moment, but was far from present with anything going on. I lived on the edge. Every day was a new adventure. But there was always something missing. I existed in an alternate reality, barely a figment of who I was destined to be.

People came in and out of my life faster than I had a chance to even know them. Most of the "friends" I once had were long gone – either incarcerated, having progressed to harder drugs, or given up on me. With very few exceptions, the only people who came around were people I did drugs with, sold drugs to, or partied at my house.

My house was always full, but my heart was very empty. Seeking validation through the acceptance of other people was clearly no way to find happiness.

Even as resistant as I'd become to the idea of love, deep within me was an innocent girl awaiting Romeo to waltz into her life and make all of the pain disappear. But my high walls would not allow me to admit that. I was independent. I didn't need a man.

Jake and I formed an open relationship with a very cracked foundation based upon drugs, partying, and sex. On some twisted level, we cared very much for each other, and shared hopes of one day building a solid foundation for a relationship – we were just too off track to find our way. I developed very strong feelings for him, which I perceived to possibly be love, and after nearly eight months of doing everything together and becoming very attached to one another, I considered that maybe we shared something real. He had broken things off with Candy for good, but she held a very dangerous card over his head. She threatened that if he didn't go back to her and raise their child as a family, she would keep him from ever knowing his son. I watched it torment him for months as he sniffed his fears away with me.

When his son Jason was finally born, Jake remained with me, doing drugs to avoid dealing with his responsibilities and issues with Candy. I encouraged him to do whatever he needed to do to be in that child's life. There was nothing more important than his son. He insisted that he wanted us to be together, creating a fantasy where we would raise his son together. I knew I was in no shape to be responsible for a child.

The whole situation was like something out of a soap opera, and I had no idea how to handle it. With my encouragement, Jake spent more time with Candy and the baby. A part of me wanted us to end up together, but I knew there was no way that was going to happen. I explained to him that I could never come in the way of his responsibility as a father, but the only way things would work between us was if he and Candy came to some kind of effective arrangement as co-parents. One where they weren't playing house together. He fought as hard as he could for his rights as a father, finally cleaning up from drugs and focusing on advancing himself, hoping that it would hold up in the courts if she tried to keep him from Jason.

I was patient with him, giving him time to figure out a solution while he continued going back and forth between Candy and I. Eventually, I got tired of hoping and pushed for him to work things out with her – maybe it would be for the best.

I started working at a nightclub called Vex. The job allowed me to be as high and drunk as I wanted to be, which was very convenient considering I had no intention of making changes to my lifestyle anytime soon. It was a perfect fit – I got paid to do what I loved.

Working in the club meant revolving doors of drunk men hitting on me and trying to pick me up. No longer flattered by this attention, I developed a tactic where I would have them store their numbers in my phone when they asked for mine so that they would have no way to contact me. It worked out marvellously. I could still play along and flirt to reap the benefits of good tips and free drinks, without having to be a bitch and ignore them when they blew up my phone the next day, or stalked me when I was not working (yes, I learned that the hard way). I had it all worked out.

The job had tons of perks. I got to drink for free, got paid to party, and my boss even let me use the back room of the club for personal events. It was a large area sectioned off from the rest of the club by a giant theatre curtain, and consisted of a dancefloor, some booths, and a stage with two stripper poles. I decided to use the space to celebrate Steph's birthday.

We put James in charge of security so that we could manage exactly who we wanted in. I told him to find a bunch of hot guys to balance things out since we already had a room full of all of our girlfriends.

It was surreal. I felt like an A-List Celebrity. I don't remember too much because I blacked out halfway into the night. I remember segments of time throughout the night: popping bottles and toasting to the birthday girl. Sniffing rails off the bathroom counter. Thanking my boss for being so amazing. Inviting random people from the club to join us for a VIP experience, and watching the faces of other people in the club trying to figure out who we were to have been so privileged. Dancing freely on the stage and grinding on the poles. Sitting on the stage trying to refrain from puking as the world danced in circles around me.

The last thing I remember was looking toward the entrance just in time to see James let in the most gorgeous human being I'd ever laid eyes on. He was over six feet tall, slender but built and very well defined, had dark skin, and was swagged out from head to toe, looking like he just stepped out of a rap video. Exactly my dream come true! Normally, I probably would have done whatever it took to get his attention, claiming him before anyone else got their hands on him. Only that night, I could barely even see straight and didn't want to bother embarrassing myself.

Screw it. I recall thinking to myself reluctantly. *He's way too fine. There are so many beautiful women here tonight, he probably wouldn't be into me anyways. It's not even worth the try.*

I sat on the edge of the stage with my eyes closed to lessen the spins, waiting for the night to end so I could go to bed. Suddenly, I heard a soft voice in front of me.

"Sup girl ... you aight?" I lifted my head and opened my eyes, gazing from beneath the pile of hair in front of my face. It was the gorgeous guy I just talked myself out of approaching!

Shit! Of course this happens when I'm this wasted!

"Yeah, I'm fine," I slurred, attempting to sound as casual as I could. I guess it didn't come out the way I hoped.

"You wanna go outside and get some air?"

"Got a smoke?" I blurted out impulsively.

A cigarette would do me wonders with the spins I had.

"Yeah," he chuckled in amusement. "I've got a smoke."

He helped me off the stage and assisted me outside. Everything after that is pretty foggy. I slightly recall standing outside wrapped up in his strong arms as I smoked a cigarette ... then he was gone. I remember looking around through blurred vision trying to figure out where he went.

Though his demeanor read "PLAYER," there was something so gentle and sweet about him ... He seemed ... genuinely kind. I was very intrigued – a fascination that was hard to shake.

Over a month passed after the night of Stephanie's birthday. Jake kept stringing me along telling me he was ready to jump in full force with me, but his actions stated otherwise. Done with the games once and for all, I made the decision to give up on all men and worry about myself for the first time in my life. I realized that I would never find fulfillment if I didn't work on myself. I was so serious, in fact, that I went through my entire phone and deleted every single man from my contact list. Dozens of numbers I saved from work popped up. I didn't recognize a single one.

Delete.

Delete.

Delete.

Suddenly, I stopped on a name that caught my attention.

JEREMIAH ANDREWS

Maybe it was the fact that it was the only person saved in my phone that contained a full name, but something compelled me to find out who he was.

I pondered for a few minutes, trying to recall who Jeremiah could be. I had no clue. I tried to let it go, but for some peculiar reason, I just couldn't. I took a shot in the dark and messaged the mysterious man in question:

Hey, this is totally random but do you have this number saved in your phone?

A few hours went by without a reply. I let the wonder subside, not expecting a response. Later that evening, an unexpected alert sounded on my phone.

Jeremiah: Hey, sorry just got off work. No, I don't ... Who is this?

Me: Never mind lol. I have your number saved in my phone and I have no clue who you are.

Jeremiah: What's your name?

Me: Sasha lol

Jeremiah: Blonde hair? Blue eyes? Tattoo on your lower back? Work at Vex?

Me: LOL yes ...

Jeremiah: I was hoping you would text me sometime

Who the hell was this guy? It was a little creepy that he remembered me so vividly when I told him my name, yet I had no idea who he was. I was curious to find out who the mysterious man could be ...

Not wanting to lead him on, but extremely curious to find out just who he was, I invited him over to smoke some weed and hang out.

I expected some unattractive weirdo to show up, but in the off chance that wasn't the case, I dressed up a little and made sure I was looking fly. When he texted that he was close, I went outside to wait for him.

A dark purple Dodge Stratus with tinted windows and loud bass pulled into the parking lot and drove past me. From it emerged the sexy, mysterious guy from Vex. Turns out I used my trick of the trade on him and had him enter his number into my phone the night we met.

He was more stunning than I even remembered.

Oh. My. God. He is SO fine!

He was dressed all in red: a red jersey, red hat and matching red shoes. He was light-skinned Jamaican/Caucasian mix, standing more than 6 feet tall, and a smile that radiated like I have never seen; the very definition of tall, dark, and handsome. I had to stop myself from drooling. One look of his piercing blue eyes and I could barely contain myself.

No one had ever had such an effect on me before. The butterflies were more like birds flapping around in my stomach. I couldn't remember the last time a man had made me nervous. My legs were shaking and my body started sweating in places I'd never sweat before. I could not believe my eyes. The confidence I had was suddenly gone – I could barely find words. I was not prepared to meet this perfect man who had evidently stepped out of my wildest dreams.

"Hey," he said politely as he strutted toward me. Even his voice was hot. I could barely look him in the eye.

Not sure I even had the capacity to speak from the nervousness, I replied shortly, trying not to smile so hard.

"Hey."

I led him into my condo, thinking to myself the entire time: *This has GOT to be a mistake. This guy is way too hot for me. He's gunna politely come in for a few minutes and get the hell out.*

Jeremiah seemed a little thrown off when he entered my room to see that it was occupied by dozens of people. We barely got two words in to each other in the short time he was there.

I offered him a line, assuming he did drugs because everyone I knew did. He declined my offer and told me he wasn't into that.

I couldn't wrap my head around it.

He sure looked like a bad boy to me …

In all honesty, it made him less appealing. There was no way we could vibe if he was opposed to drugs. That was the only life I grew to know. I didn't even know how to connect with people who weren't on my level.

Feeling uncomfortable, he politely said goodbye and went on his way.

I can't say I was completely disappointed … there was no way I stood a chance with him anyways. He must have had models falling all over him – he was THAT gorgeous.

To my surprise, he asked me to hang out again later that week.

He definitely just wants to fuck.

I didn't care. I wanted to fuck too.

This time before he showed up, I kicked everyone out of my room. I did a rail before he got there so that I could refrain from using while he was over, out of respect for him not being into it.

We sat on my bed taking turns smoking bongs and telling each other a little about ourselves. We seemed to have much more in common than I thought. I figured he was just being a typical guy, pretending to be interested in me so that I would sleep with him. But his kiss told me something quite the contrary.

His lips were so soft, so gentle, that I barely felt them press against mine. He was tender in the way he touched me, and stared so deeply into my soul that I could not look into his eyes longer than a few seconds. His gaze intimidated me – like he saw right through me.

As our clothing came off, I admired his magnificently sculpted body, with tattoos on his arms and every muscle so defined. He had a scar right above his belly button. I always thought scars were sexy. He was such a man in every way. And I mean *every* way.

No one ever turned me on the way he did. I was in awe of his perfection.

Before pulling out a condom, he asked my approval to have sex with me. No one had ever done that before. He was so … respectful. It felt so foreign.

We indulged in sensual, slow, soft sex. Even more foreign.

Slow and soft was not my forte. I enjoyed rough, wild sex. It was a release for me. I became a nympho, and sex was my therapy.

With Jeremiah, it was different … but satisfying in a way I didn't quite comprehend.

I was even more shocked when he asked me to hang out again after we already hooked up. I expected a guy like him to have a line up of girls to bang, why was he trying to see me again? Could the sex be THAT good?

We continued sleeping together for the next couple of weeks. Something about him was so intoxicating that I didn't even think about coke when he was with me. Mesmerized by his every move, I found fulfillment merely in his existence.

I was under the impression that we were having sex, no strings attached, and I was good with that. That was what I thought I wanted. Apparently, we weren't on the same page.

"Listen," Jeremiah announced unexpectedly one day, "I like you Sash. But I'm not gunna keep coming around if you're high on that shit all the time. Either you stop doing it or this is over."

Who the hell did he think he was? We were having sex, we weren't dating! As if he had the audacity to give me that sort of ultimatum.

Fuck it. I don't need you anyways.

Something in me shifted a few hours after he was gone.

Another pivotal moment for me.

I actually took what he said into consideration. Though my heart was cold and my walls were high, he was captivating and I couldn't help but to be curious. Maybe I just needed someone to recognize that I was worth more than what I saw in myself … maybe he was that person.

He told me every day how beautiful I was. How smart I was. How badass I was. How worthy and capable I was of making dreams for myself. He told me he knew there was more to life for me than what I knew. When he looked at me – he lit up like I had never seen before. His intention was pure, and it scared the shit out of me.

Just like that, with his constant reminder of my worthiness, and only a few slip ups, I quit using cocaine.

Jeremiah helped me the best he could to get through my withdrawals. He had never been into hard drugs, so he wasn't exactly sure how to help. Withdrawing from blow was like coming down off a great high, and the crash never ended. The physical side of it really wasn't that torturous to me. I was nearly immune to the physical pain from all of the abuse I endured throughout my life.

It was the mental aspect that was the hardest: not giving in to the insatiable desire for the drug. Going days without sleep because insomnia does not allow for it. Waking up in hysterics from horrible night terrors.

Reliving flashbacks of all the things I suppressed for so many years, and battling with different versions of myself within my own mind.

There was no more escaping.

However, there was distraction strong enough to give me temporary relief through the fight. It was him. Jeremiah.

God sent him to me when I was at the fork of a road that I might have been lost on forever. He saw that I had had enough and I was ready to thrive.

Jeremiah acknowledged that I was desperately trying to change my life just to keep him around. I think that was why he fell for me.

On the evening of September 26th, 2011, I packed us a picnic and we went down to the beach to watch the sun set. I wasn't sure what was happening to me. With his quirky sense of humor, and irresistible charm, I felt myself falling for him. Hard.

As we sat peacefully in the lifeguard tower overlooking the golden rays of sun sparkle amongst the dark blue waters, Jeremiah broke the silence.

"Can I ask you something?"

"Sure," I responded shyly. He still intimidated me after weeks of being around him.

"What would you say if I asked you to be my girl?"

I couldn't believe my ears!

I turned to face him, expecting to read deceit all over him. But there was not a trace of bad intention anywhere. He genuinely wanted to be with me. All this time I resisted the feelings I was developing for him, positive that I did not stand a chance with such a remarkable being.

My experiences told me it was dangerous.

My pride told me it was not possible.

My logic told me it was a waste of time.

But my heart told me to go for it.

I was scared shitless that he would hurt me like everyone else, but I couldn't give up without at least giving him a chance. Even if he wasn't my forever, I desperately wanted to experience him fully and be able to call him mine.

"Yes," I smiled from ear to ear, and we kissed passionately beneath the light of the moon and twinkling stars.

CHAPTER TWENTY FOUR

A Hard Road To A Better Me

"Every story has an end. But in life, every ending has a new beginning."

– Unknown

I was afraid from the very beginning that Jeremiah would find me unworthy and find someone better than me. It had nothing to do with him – it was derived from my own insecurities. So, I held on tight. Too tight.

Jeremiah and I moved very quickly – mostly at my demand. After only a few months, I convinced him to move in with me – against his better judgement. I told him it was because I didn't want a "juvenile relationship," but the reality that I could not bear to vulnerably express, was that I needed the security of having him under my radar so that I didn't live in fear of him abandoning me like everyone else. Selfish, I know. But I didn't see it like that at the time. It was a coping mechanism; a survival instinct that I acted on in order to protect myself, without any consideration for how he felt or what was best for him. I just wanted to love and be loved. And though my intentions were pure, I acted from a state of reaction because I had not healed my heart from my past experiences.

At the time, I didn't see that as control. But let's be real – that's exactly what it was.

I put down my guard and let him into my heart so quickly, and I couldn't bear another heartbreak.

He was not used to my kind of lifestyle. You know, living in a sort of trap house surrounded by drugs and constant partying. He worked upward of 40 hours a week doing hard labor in a factory and spent his free time recovering and preparing for the next day of work. He was focused on and committed to creating a better future for himself – a concept that had never even crossed my mind.

As much as he tried to adapt to my way of life, I tried to adapt to the way *he* thought things should be as well. I stopped partying every night so that he could sleep well for work. I began to eat regularly because I enjoyed cooking meals for him when he got home from work. I took better care of myself because I felt more confident being loved by him.

It all happened so organically and felt so right. But before long, I felt like a housewife. I really battled with whether or not that lifestyle was for me; desiring so deeply to continue on the only path I knew – self destruction.

Jeremiah and I had very different ideas of how to live our lives. But I wanted him more than I wanted to remain committed to my destructive ways. It became a very delicate balance. We challenged each other constantly.

It wasn't long before I realized that we both had a lot of baggage we were bringing to the table. We both came from a past of a lot of trauma, betrayal, and heartbreak. That's probably why we connected so deeply, so quickly. It was bizarre how parallel our lives had been.

We got each other. We were complete reflections of each other. Our enormous hearts, and our stubborn egos alike.

Unfortunately, being so young and naïve, neither of us fully realized that in order to not bring toxicity from the past into a new relationship, we should have taken the time and put in the necessary work to heal from it all first. With that lack of understanding, I see now that it was inevitable that we would project our pain, insecurities, and distrust onto each other. It was a recipe for disaster – doomed from the very start.

As much as Jeremiah acted like he had everything figured out, he was a lost soul and had no sense of identity. I saw through that because I was the exact same.

As intelligent and caring as he was, his emotional triggers controlled him. He lived in a constant state of reaction – that is, allowing fear and anger to take over and cause him to act impulsively, and make poor decisions out of spite.

It was easy to make him the bad guy, especially when I didn't look hard enough at myself to realize that I did the same thing.

As much as his heart felt so much love for me, he had no idea how to express love in a healthy way.

Then again, neither did I.

But it didn't stop us from trying. We fought for each other with everything we had. The problem was, we also fought *with* each other just as intensely.

As you can probably imagine, it wasn't long before my insecurities and abandonment issues took over and I decided I didn't need him. I was getting too attached and my heart was not ready for that type of commitment. I broke things off with him before he had the chance to leave me. I was in too deep and it scared the shit out of me.

But God had other plans. Our journey together was far from over.

The evening after I broke up with Jeremiah, I received a phone call from his mother.

"Sasha. You need to get to the hospital now. Jeremiah had a seizure." She was frantic.

Okay ...? I thought to myself. *A lot of people have seizures. What's the big deal?*

In my (lack of) experience, I believed that seizures were not that serious most times. My mom had them all the time, and she was fine ...

"I guess you didn't know," I responded compassionately, "but we broke up. I don't think I should be the one to go."

"Sash, he has no family up there. No one is able to get to him. You need to get there. NOW."

The urgency in her voice told me two things. One: if I didn't get to that hospital, this would not be the last time I would hear from her. And two: that it may be more serious than I had thought.

Panic set in. My ego shut off and my heart took over.

I hope he's okay ... please God, let him be okay...

It was nothing short of a blizzard outside: dark, snowy, and well below freezing temperatures. I threw on a coat and boots and ran as fast as I could to the hospital. My face was frozen as I ran with squinted eyes through the blowing snow. My heart pounded ferociously through my chest as I panted for breath in the dry, icy air. The ten-minute walk took me about three minutes with the surging adrenaline.

When I finally found where he was in emergency care, I told the nurse I was there to see him. She informed me that he had suffered from at least one grand mal seizure that could have been fatal. She went on to tell me that it was very severe, and that he was having a hard time remembering the last two years of his life. He believed that he was two years younger, and that he still lived miles away at a previous home.

I demanded to see him immediately.

"I'm very sorry, but only immediate family is able to visit," the nurse said empathetically.

"I'm his girlfriend," I insisted.

"We asked him if he had a girlfriend, and he said that he did not."

"Okay, if I'm being honest," I began, "we broke up last night. But his family lives miles away and I'm all he has. His mom called me and told me I needed to be here for him. Please let me see him."

She had immense compassion in her eyes: "Okay, here's what I'll do. I'll go in and ask him, if he did have a girlfriend, what would her name be. That way I can legally permit you to go in to see him."

She was very understanding and I could tell that she genuinely wanted to help.

She returned a few moments later, "What did you say your name was, hon?"

"Sasha."

"Oh ... I'm very sorry," she seemed terribly disappointed. "But when I asked him what his girlfriend's name would be to his recollection, he said 'Taya.'"

I broke down crying in devastation. Taya was his Jeremiah's ex-girlfriend from nearly two years ago. The only girl I had known him to love before me. He had no memory of me whatsoever.

The nurse must have been able to tell that I had no ill intention, or maybe she just felt bad for me when I fought with everything I had to hold back my tears. She agreed to let me enter the room to see if he remembered me to see my face, but if he had any negative reaction or became too stressed out, that I would have to leave.

I felt extremely grateful in that moment.

All too soon, the familiar feeling of abandonment and being forgotten set in. Part of me didn't want to see him, because I didn't think there was any way possible that he would remember who I was. I was setting myself up for more pain.

I walked into the room slowly, peering over to where he was laying in the bed. He was unrecognizable!

He had bitten through his lip so badly during the seizure that it appeared to be hanging off of his face! It was red, bloody and swollen. His eyes were puffy and swollen as well. Half of his face was drooping, as though he had had a stroke. My heart began racing. I could hardly catch my breath. In that moment, the only thing that mattered was that I loved him. It hurt me so much to see him in that state.

What if I had lost him for good?

As I entered into his peripheral vision, I caught his attention.

For a moment, he looked at me blankly.

All of a sudden, it was like he was struck with memory. He anxiously jolted up, eyes widening in such a way that it appeared he was having some kind of epiphany. He reached his arms out for me without hesitation.

I began to make my way toward him slowly, my eyes filled with tears and my heart filled with hope, as he began to speak.

"I don't know who you are. But I know that I love you." He had so much confusion, yet so much certainty in his voice, but his soul remembered mine.

In that exact moment, without question, I knew that what we had was real. I knew that the love we shared was something so rare. I knew I had no reason to let my insecurities intervene.

I collapsed into his arms and we cried wholeheartedly together.

I had never in my life felt so seen. So loved. So … certain.

My life began to shift after that moment. A burden that I had been carrying with me for many years had been lifted.

I felt safe.

Secure.

I wanted to do better. To be better. To love openly without barriers.

It would be a long journey, but I wanted to make it. I wanted my life to be different.

Jeremiah had a tough road to recovery, but I was there for him every step of the way. It took him days to stop waking up and asking me who I was, or asking me to explain how we had met. Helping him to heal helped me to heal in some ways too. Reflecting back on it now, I think that was what began our journey of growth together. We became bonded in a way that I never knew was possible.

After searching my entire life, I thought I had finally found my person.

Jeremiah pushed me.

He pushed me out of my comfort zones.

He pushed me to challenge myself.

He pushed me to confront myself transparently and own my insecurities.

He even pushed me to go to college – where I graduated top of my class.

Our love was very real. But so were our challenges.

You see, we both carried a lot of baggage. Our intentions were good, but we just did not have the understanding, tools or experience to navigate through our disputes or confrontations. For that reason, things between us grew very toxic at times.

Very, very toxic.

We did not know how to communicate our feelings with one another, so instead, we lashed out at one another, feeling attacked, misunderstood, and unheard.

We hurt each other intentionally out of spite and vengeance.

We were jealous and untrusting, and projected those insecurities onto each other as well as other people who got caught up in our mess.

We withheld ourselves from loving each other fully, in fear of betrayal, or heartbreak.

We fought, broke up, got back together, and repeated it all again. Over and over.

We were both good people with enormous hearts – people who would do anything for one another, but we were also very hurt people who did not know how to build a healthy foundation and relied on survival instincts to lead our decisions.

We gave it everything we had. But the hard truth is that love just isn't enough.

We don't always get what we want, but we always get what we need.

I learned some of the most valuable lessons of my life with Jeremiah, and for that I will always be grateful. In the years I spent with him, we grew immensely together. He instilled some very pivotal shifts into my mind, and for the first time in my life – I wanted more. We conceived dreams of a bright future free of pain and full of abundance. We dreamed of living in luxury, of having children, and of giving them a life we never had.

And for the first time in my entire life, I developed faith. I wanted more for myself, and I had hope that I could do it. In that awareness of such a life being possible, I would be set onto a whole new journey into the next version of myself, with its own set of challenges to overcome and lessons to learn.

You see, our lives don't just magically change overnight, and no one is going to come save us from our pain. It all starts with us – how we feel about ourselves, what our belief systems are, and what decisions we make. To transform our outer worlds, we must start by changing ourselves internally.

I wish I knew then what I know now - that my reality was merely a reflection of my inner chaos. I would have done things so differently. But God has a greater plan for my life than I can possibly conceive, and in understanding that, I must walk in faith.

That's the beautiful thing about life: when we ask God to grant something into our lives – He does not just hand it over. Where would the growth be in that? No, instead He will send us every lesson possible to get ourselves to that place we desire.

CHAPTER TWENTY FIVE

For What It's Worth

"No regrets in life. Just lessons learned."
– Unknown

Let's address the elephant in the room.

Most of my life, I was desperately chasing love.

For a while, I was really embarrassed to confront this truth. It made me feel weak, desperate and pathetic; the exact opposite of the persona I worked so many years to create. However, I have finally come to a beautiful place in my life where I have accepted the hard truths in my journey – faults, vulnerabilities and all. I no longer fear judgment nor live in shame for expressing the truth of my story, because I am human. I am not meant to be perfect. I was conditioned to think and behave the ways that I did. I didn't know any better. I was meant to experience the hardships that I did; I have become a very powerful woman because of the difficult road I have walked. I have insight into the truths of life that many people are blind to, and I have the ability to connect with and help people emerge from some of the darkest places - because I've been there.

Never forget that accepting vulnerability into your life and allowing yourself to express your real feelings is the only way to truly get to know yourself.

Life can fucking break you.

In fact, it almost inevitably breaks every single one of us, in one way or another.

When our hearts break, we build walls of protection – but those walls become barriers in expressing and receiving true, unconditional love.

I spent years dwelling in the pain and sorrow that were the product of my circumstances growing up. I hated the world, and blamed everyone for the mistakes I made and for all the bad things that happened to me. Hating and blaming were not serving me. In that place, there is no responsibility.

Taking responsibility for ourselves does not mean justifying anything anyone has done to bring us down or contribute to our pain, but it does mean that we take back our power and realize that our lack of awareness, lack of self love, lack of standards and boundaries, and poor choices all contribute to our life unfolding the way that it has.

When we know better, we can do better. But it doesn't always mean that we will. Not until, as Tony Robbins says, "the fear of staying the same outweighs the fear of change."

Through self awareness, and in confronting all of the suffering I've endured, I was left with two choices: I could feel sorry for myself and waste the rest of my precious time living a self-fulfilling prophecy of agony, thinking about all of the heartache and torment over and over on repeat, OR I could forgive those who have done me wrong, with the understanding that they too, are products of their own environments, and accept that only I have the power to make a change in my own life.

It is not my fault that I was used and abused. But my unhappiness will be my fault if I continue to live the life I was living with the knowledge I have now. And as much as it wasn't my fault, my lack of standards and willingness to learn and grow kept me in a state of being easily victimized.

Only YOU have the power to create yourself and produce the life that will bring happiness and peace to your soul. No one is going to waltz into your life and save you from your troubles, or give you a free ticket to a better life. Waiting for someone to save you puts you in a state of victimization. Let me be the first to tell you – making yourself a victim will lead you only down a path of further pain and victimization.

To view something in a way that doesn't serve you is a choice. Life is all about perspective. What perspective do you choose to view your life through?

I spent so many years believing that I was unworthy of love, that there was something wrong with me, and that I needed to be tough in order to survive. But those were beliefs that I took on as a result of the things that other people had said or done to me. They weren't Truth.

I also believed that I needed to control situations in order to protect myself from being hurt. I learned the hard way (big surprise, right?) that trying to control everything only causes you more pain, and pushes people away. It prevents you from being able to truly connect with other people, including yourself. I mean, I get it. It's incredibly scary to be vulnerable and really let people inside your heart when it has been broken, and your trust has been betrayed. But what other purpose is there in life if not to love and be loved? With that, how can you ever know who you are and what you truly want if you aren't real with yourself? How can you understand your needs, grow through your pain, and set standards for your life if you can't confront those things head on?

Remember that there are no toxic people – there are only people with toxic behaviors. That does not mean that we should accept substandard treatment by people who do not have emotional intelligence or self control. Nor does it mean that we should justify harmful acts against us. It does, however, mean that we cannot always point the finger outward. We need to look at ourselves and see what types of reactions, behaviors, and patterns we exhibit as well that may contribute to our pain.

I have been so many different versions of myself throughout my lifetime, each version completely different than the others. I have been shy and I have been confident, I have been a victim and been powerful, I have been submissive and been dominant. I have been loyal and unfaithful. Honest and told lies. Dependent, codependent, and independent. Immature and responsible. A follower and a leader.

If you use the reasoning "this is who I am" or "that's not me," you are limiting yourself. If you lean on excuses of circumstantial conditioning to justify behaviors, habits or mindsets – you need to expand your mind. If you do not take control of your own life, circumstances will continue to control you. You will never be happy, and you will never be free.

When you spend your life in survival mode, it can be hard to know who you are or what you want, because there is no room for thinking that big when you are focused on surviving. Sometimes it is just about deciding what you don't want, and making choices that will move you away from that place. The more we "un-become" the things we are not, the clearer we become on who we actually are.

If I could share only one thing to take with you from my story – it is the understanding that YOU are the creator of your own story. You cannot change the things that happened to you, but you alone are responsible for what you do going forward. If you asked me to share my story with you ten years ago, I would have told you something very different – because my perspective was very different. If you asked other people involved in my life story what their take was on each situation, their story would likely be completely different. That's the thing about life, it is literally what you make of it – as cliché as that sounds. Anything that happens in life is nothing more than the logical step-by-step sequence of the actions and events that occurred. The emotion that you attach to it is a matter of perspective. Your life is a composite of the stories you've created based on the experiences that molded your outlook.

With that infinite awareness, ask yourself: what stories have limited you? Have shaped you?

Can you pinpoint the root causes of your heartache and pain? Can you change your perspective on those occurrences to something more positive? Can you change your story and reshape the way you view the world?

Of course you can.

Everything written in the pages of your life until reaching that realization, was written by you without you ever knowing you were the one in control all along. When you start to recognize how your life is composed of a series of choices you have made, whether consciously or unconsciously, you begin to take grasp of that pen more firmly and intentionally.

Grasp control of that pen and start creating your Legacy.

This was only the beginning of mine.

CPSIA information can be obtained
at www.ICGtesting.com
Printed in the USA
BVHW052105250422
634897BV00003B/6